How Vision Works

How Vision Works

THE PHYSIOLOGICAL MECHANISMS BEHIND WHAT WE SEE

Nigel Daw
Yale University

Oxford University Press, Inc., publishes works that further
Oxford University's objective of excellence
in research, scholarship, and education.

Oxford   New York
Auckland   Cape Town   Dar es Salaam   Hong Kong   Karachi
Kuala Lumpur   Madrid   Melbourne   Mexico City   Nairobi
New Delhi   Shanghai   Taipei   Toronto

With offices in
Argentina   Austria   Brazil   Chile   Czech Republic   France   Greece
Guatemala   Hungary   Italy   Japan   Poland   Portugal   Singapore
South Korea   Switzerland   Thailand   Turkey   Ukraine   Vietnam

Published by Oxford University Press, Inc.
198 Madison Avenue, New York, New York 10016
www.oup.com

Oxford is a registered trademark of Oxford University Press, Inc.

ISBN 978-0-19-975161-7

Cataloging-in-Publication data is on file with the Library of Congress.

9 8 7 6 5 4 3 2 1

Printed in China

This book is dedicated to Edwin Land, Ted MacNichol, David Hubel, Torsten Wiesel,

and my wife Leila, all of whom nurtured and assisted my career

PREFACE

I have long wanted to write this book. I started off my career working on the psychology of color vision. That was followed, by a series of serendipitous events, with the physiology of color vision, effects of the environment on the development of vision, mechanisms of directional sensitivity, and mechanisms of the effects of visual deprivation on the visual cortex. An invitation from Colin Blakemore to write a book on visual development kept me distracted from the task for several years. Now, finally, I have the time to go back to the basic topic of how vision works.

There are many books that cover the psychology and physiology of a single aspect of vision, such as color vision or eye movements. There are some excellent books on the psychology of all aspects of vision, such as *Basic Vision* by Snowden, Thompson, and Troscianko, and the topic is summarized in any textbook on sensory perception, such as the one by Jeremy Wolfe and colleagues. The physiology of vision is dealt with in any textbook for medical and graduate students of neurobiology. There is an encyclopedic discussion of all aspects of vision—*The Visual Neurosciences*, edited by Chalupa and Werner—which was a great help in writing this book. However, there is no book that I know of covering the psychology, the anatomy, and the physiology of all aspects of the visual system in less than 300 pages. Just as, 50 years ago, scientists and teachers recognized that it did not make sense to study the anatomy and physiology of the nervous system in separate courses, pioneered by the formation of the Department of Neurobiology at Harvard, there is increasing understanding now that one needs to look at the psychology, anatomy, and physiology of vision together, with the lonely example of the Center for Visual Science at Rochester as a model.

What this book does is to take each aspect of vision, one by one, and describe the basic phenomena, where in the brain this aspect of vision is dealt with, the properties of the cells in those areas, and the deficits that result from a lesion in those areas. It is intended for graduate students in psychology who also want to know about the physiology, students in neurobiology, optometry, ophthalmology, or orthoptics who want to have their various courses brought together, and senior undergraduates or graduate students who take courses on vision. Hopefully experts in the field will also learn something in areas outside their area of expertise, and in some cases may be even experts within their area of expertise (one of my expert reviewers did!).

Needless to say, the preparation of the book has been a massive undertaking, involving the reading of many papers for each one that was quoted. I apologize to any friend or colleague who feels that his or her paper(s) should have been included. I have also tried to mention the classic papers in each area, for the benefit of those readers who do not look at anything that occurred before the Internet was invented.

I thank the experts who went over individual chapters and gave me comments: Jeremy Wolfe, Rich Krauzlis, Greg de Angelis, Bevil Conway, Stuart Anstis, Bob Wurtz, Jamie Mazer, Steve Luck, Joel Price, David Berson, Scott Johnson, Bruce Cumming, and Haidong Lu. Steve Holtje read the whole manuscript and provided many useful suggestions I also thank all those authors who provided high-resolution copies of their figures from low-resolution publications, particularly those who redrew their figures for the occasion, and Sverker Runeson, who arranged for Johansson's movies of biological motion to be put on the Uppsala University Web site.

CONTENTS

How Vision Works

1

Introduction

Animals have a large variety of eyes and visual systems, depending on their habits and the surroundings in which they live (Walls, 1942). We will be concerned with how vision works in the human. However, the mechanics of the system are often best illustrated by experiments in other vertebrate species with the same mechanisms. Many have contributed to our understanding of how photoreceptors and the retina work: the cat has illustrated the primary visual cortex, while the macaque monkey is a particularly useful model for mechanisms in all parts of the visual cortex and the eye movement system, as well as the retina. Unfortunately, even the macaque visual system is not a perfect model in all respects, particularly those relating to cognitive function (Passingham, 2009). Fortunately new techniques are becoming available for use in the human, such as imaging of the brain (functional magnetic resonance imaging [fMRI]), which enables us to fill in some of the unknowns. Between retinal mechanisms discovered in lower vertebrates, findings in the macaque and other mammals about the central visual system, and work in humans using fMRI, we now have a fairly complete picture of the whole system.

The human eye, like all vertebrate eyes, is an image-forming eye. That is, it has a lens, like a camera, that forms an image on the retina at the back of the eye. This feature enables inspection of the details of a scene, as well as an increase in the amount of light that can be detected, in contrast to most invertebrate eyes, which have photoreceptors in cells on the surface of the skin. Vertebrate eyes have also evolved with inverted retinas, in which the light passes through the cells of the retina on its way to the photoreceptors, to satisfy the large metabolic requirements of the photoreceptors. This arrangement means that the retinal fibers projecting to the central nervous system pass over the surface of the retina to the optic nerve head, which produces a blind spot where there are no photoreceptors. This might seem like a bad design, but it arises out of the way that the eye develops in the embryo, for reasons that make sense but are beyond the scope of this book.

Humans are carnivores, and carnivores in general depend on hunting prey for their food. Most hunting animals have developed a specialized part of the retina with high acuity to detect their prey. In the case of primates, this is accompanied by pushing aside the cells that would otherwise be on top of the photoreceptors (and would interfere with the optics) to form a pit, called the fovea. Within the fovea, the photoreceptors are narrower than elsewhere, and packed more tightly together, to aid further in high acuity. Other hunting animals, like the cat family, have a high density of photoreceptors in the area centralis, without the foveal pit. Some birds have two foveas, one arranged to look forward for objects ahead, and the other arranged to look down for prey below.

If we are to be able to direct our attention to an object of interest, then we also need a sophisticated eye movement system to turn the eyes toward the object and also a system to determine what is of interest. Thus, eye movement control and attention are very much a part of how human vision works. This contrasts with herbivores, who are hunted prey rather than hunters. For example, rabbits do not move their eyes very much, and they have a visual streak looking at the horizontal meridian rather than a fovea or area centralis. There is a high percentage of cells in the horizontal streak specialized to detect movement. Activation of these cells by a moving predator leads to immediate flight.

We are also diurnal animals. We have two classes of photoreceptors: the rods, used at nighttime (scotopic vision), and the cones used in daylight (photopic vision). A rod will respond to a single quantum of light, whereas a cone needs several. In addition, a single cone in the fovea is connected to a single fiber (ganglion cell axon) projecting to the central visual system, whereas ganglion cells connected to rods receive input from hundreds of photoreceptors spread out over a wide area. Threshold for both scotopic and photopic vision thus depends on the absorption of 5–7 quanta of light, but in the case of photopic vision the quanta can be spread out over a wide area, whereas in the case of scotopic vision they have to fall on a single photoreceptor, giving a difference of 1000 between the two thresholds.

Humans and old-world primates also have trichromatic color vision. This means that they can match any color with just three primary wavelengths (in some cases, when matching very saturated colors, one of the primary wavelengths may need to have a negative weight, meaning that the match is 2 made to 2, rather than 3 to 1). This is due to three kinds of cone photoreceptors: red absorbing (L cones), green absorbing (M cones), and blue absorbing (S cones). In the interests of high acuity, only M and L cones are found in the very center of the fovea, and no S cones or rods. The highest density of rods is found near the fovea, in the parafovea. For this reason, if a dim star is not visible, one may be able to see it by looking slightly to one side. As the image moves away from the fovea, the density of M and L cones drops off, and the number connected to each ganglion cell increases, to give lower acuity and higher sensitivity.

The differences between central vision near the fovea and peripheral vision in regions outside of this are reflected throughout the visual system. Essentially, peripheral vision is for noticing objects, and central vision is for inspecting them. Attention combines with the eye movement system to determine what gets placed on the fovea and inspected. The areas concerned with inspection lie along what has come to be known as the "what" pathway, and the areas concerned with noticing lie along the "where" pathway (Goodale & Milner, 1992; Ungerleider & Mishkin, 1982). Color vision, which is concentrated in the fovea and is concerned with identification of objects, is heavily represented in the "what" pathway. Movement, which helps to notice objects, is heavily represented in the "where" pathway. The fovea is heavily represented in areas along the "what" pathway in ventral visual cortex. The periphery is more heavily represented along the "where" pathway in dorsal visual cortex, and in eye movement areas such as parietal cortex, frontal cortex, and superior colliculus. Details will be given in the next chapter.

If we tried to analyze every detail in all parts of the field of view, we would be swamped with information. The division of the visual system into parts for noticing and parts for inspection avoids this, which increases the efficiency of the system considerably. Similarly, if we had to be able to respond to every situation from dim moonlight to bright sunlight, this would present an impossible task for the photoreceptors and the cells connected to them. In total, the visual system responds over a range of intensities of light of 11 log units. The bottom 3–4 log units comprise scotopic vision, the top 4–5 comprise photopic vision, and the middle 3–4—a range where both rods and cones are active—comprise mesopic vision. The pupil dilates and constricts to cover less than 2 log units of this range. To cope with the other 10 log units, the photoreceptors adapt and respond to just 2 log units of intensity of light around the level of adaptation.

All objects are seen in relation to their background. An object 1 log unit brighter than the average of the objects around it is white, and an object 1 log unit darker is seen as black. Similarly, the color of objects is determined by the wavelengths coming from them in relation to the average of the wavelengths from the surround, the movement by the velocity in relation to the velocity of the background, the orientation in relation to the orientation of objects around, the depth by the disparity in relation to the disparity of objects nearby, and so on. Essentially, nearly all vision is relative, not absolute. Where absolute intensities need to be assayed for specialized purposes, such as the pupillary reflex and circadian rhythms, this is dealt with by a pathway separate from the main pathways in the system.

A final point is that absence of a signal is interpreted by the visual system as continuity. For example, we do not notice the blind spot in our retinas (Ramachandran, 1992). If we close one eye and place a black spot where the blind spot is, the black spot will not be seen (Fig. 1–1, top). If we then look at a set of black lines, the lines will appear to be continuous (Fig. 1–1, bottom). In both cases, the surround (the white background in the first case, and the lines in the second) appears to fill in the area of the blind spot. This point will come up again in relation to neglect in lesions of the parietal cortex, and blindsight in relation to lesions of primary visual cortex. It is a general property of the nervous system, not just the visual system.

FIGURE 1–1. Demonstration of filling in at the blind spot. Close the left eye, fixate on the top left X, and approach the figure. At a distance of about 6 inches, the O to the right will disappear, when its image falls on the blind spot of the right eye. Now fixate on the lower left X. There is no apparent discontinuity in the set of lines to the right. The visual system fills in, with white in the top display, and with continuous lines in the bottom.

In summary, the visual system is specialized for the species, the surroundings, and the habitat. A large amount of data is discarded, and the essentials are retained. In many ways, the system is incredibly efficient. It may make mistakes, such as the visual illusions that we all know well (Howe & Purves, 2005). However, these illusions are simply a by-product of the operation of the system to produce the correct result in the majority of situations.

References

Goodale, M. A., & Milner, A. D. (1992). Separate visual pathways for perception and action. *Trends in Neuroscience, 15,* 20–25.

Howe, C. Q., & Purves, D. (2005). *Perceiving geometry.* New York: Springer.

Passingham, R. (2009). How good is the macaque monkey model of the human brain? *Current Opinion in Neurobiology, 19,* 6–11.

Ramachandran, V. S. (1992). Blind spots. *Scientific American, 266,* 86–91.

Ungerleider, L. G., & Mishkin, M. (1982). Two cortical systems. In M. Goodale & R. W. Mansfield (Eds.), *Analysis of visual behavior* (pp. 549–586). Cambridge, MA: MIT Press.

Walls, G. L. (1942). *The vertebrate eye.* New York: Hafner.

2

ORGANIZATION OF THE VISUAL SYSTEM

The retinas are the initial organs for all effects of light on the human visual system. They project to the lateral geniculate body, the superior colliculus, and the suprachiasmatic nucleus (Fig. 2–1). The primary pathway for seeing goes from the lateral geniculate nucleus to primary visual cortex (called striate in the human, because there is a stripe in it that can be seen without a microscope), then to other areas of visual cortex. The superior colliculus is concerned with eye movements and attention. There is also a projection from the superior colliculus to areas of visual cortex outside striate cortex, going through the pulvinar, which is known as the extrastriate pathway. In accordance with the division of function discussed in the introduction, there is a heavy representation of the fovea in the striate pathway and a heavy representation of peripheral retina in the extrastriate pathway. The suprachiasmatic nucleus is concerned with circadian rhythms.

Both "what" and "where" pathways are represented in primary visual cortex (V1) and in secondary visual cortex (V2). (See Table 2–1 for a list of abbreviations.) After that they diverge (Fig. 2–2). The "what" pathway projects to V4 and lateral occipital cortex, and temporal cortex. The "where" pathway projects to MT, MST, parietal cortex, frontal cortex, down to the superior colliculus, and on to cerebellum and brainstem. There are numerous feedback projections and also numerous interconnections between the "what" and "where" pathways, so these generalizations are simplifications, but useful ones nevertheless.

Retina

Considerable processing of information takes place in the retina before signals are sent on to other parts of the visual system. The retina contains three layers of cells; two layers of connections underlie this processing (Fig. 2–3). The photoreceptors are on the outer surface, since the retina is inverted. They feed in to the bipolar cells in the inner nuclear layer, with a layer of interconnections in the outer plexiform layer. The lateral interconnections are carried by horizontal cells, with cell bodies in the inner nuclear layer. The bipolar cells then connect to the ganglion cells in the inner plexiform layer. More lateral interconnections in the inner plexiform layer, from processes of amacrine cells (also with cell bodies in

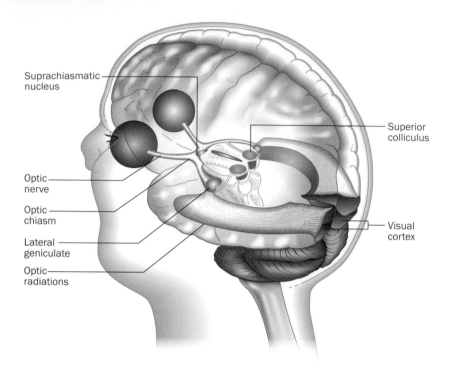

Suprachiasmatic nucleus

Superior colliculus

Optic nerve

Optic chiasm

Lateral geniculate

Optic radiations

Visual cortex

FIGURE 2–1. Projections from the eyes to lateral geniculate nucleus, superior colliculus, and suprachiasmatic nucleus, and on from lateral geniculate nucleus to visual cortex.

the inner nuclear layer), provide further processing. The axons of the ganglion cells provide the fibers of the optic nerve.

The photoreceptors are the three types of cone (L, M, and S), providing daylight and color vision, and the rods, providing vision in dim light (Carroll, 2008). Photoreceptors respond to intensity of light, whereas nearly all ganglion cells respond to contrast. This is due to the lateral connections in the plexiform layers, primarily the horizontal cells in the outer plexiform layer. Each ganglion cell has a receptive field, consisting of direct input from photoreceptors near the ganglion cell through bipolar cells to form the center of the receptive field, indirect input through the horizontal cells to the bipolar cell to the ganglion cell, and more indirect input from bipolar cells further away through amacrine cells to form the surround of the receptive field. The direct input tends to excite the ganglion cells, whereas the indirect input tends to inhibit them. As a result, ganglion cells respond to contrast rather than intensity of light. Light falling on the surround of the receptive field inhibits the response from light falling on the center, to provide a response when light falls on the center but not the surround, and much less response when the whole of the receptive field is uniformly illuminated.

The bipolar cells connected to cones can be divided into two basic classes, those that depolarize in response to light, and those that hyperpolarize. In other

TABLE 2–1

Abbreviations

DMO	Dorsomedial occipital
DP	Dorsal prelunate
FEF	Frontal eye fields
FST	Floor of superior temporal area
HC	Hippocampus
IP	Intraparietal
IT	Inferotemporal
K	Koniocellular, for cells intercalated between the layers in the LGN, with cells responding to blue/yellow
LGN	Lateral geniculate nucleus
M	Magnocellular, for layers in the LGN with large cells, dealing with motion, and for the pathways from the retina, and on through V1, V2, MT, MST, and parietal cortex going through the M layers
MST	Middle superior temporal cortex, also dealing with motion
MT	Middle temporal cortex, originally named for an area in the owl monkey with cells responding to motion, also known as V5 in macaque and human
P	Parvocellular, for layers in the LGN with small cells, dealing with color and form, and for the pathways from the retina, and on through V1, V2, V4, and inferotemporal cortex going through the P layers
PULV	Pulvinar
SC	Superior colliculus
STP	Superior temporal polysensory area
TE and TEO	Inferotemporal areas
TF/TG/TH	Temporal areas F, G, and H
V1	Primary visual cortex, which is striate in human and macaque, and area 17 in human
V2	Secondary visual cortex
V3	An area around V2
V4	An area dealing with color and form
V5	An area dealing with motion, also known as MT
VP	Ventral posterior
VST	Ventral superior temporal

Notes: Prefixes are as follows: A, anterior; C, central; D, dorsal; L, for lateral; M, medial; V, ventral. Areas: F, frontal; O, occipital; P, parietal; T, temporal.

words, some bipolar cells respond to an increase in illumination, and some respond to a decrease. This distinction is maintained in ganglion cells, which fire action potentials (Fig. 2–4). The depolarizing bipolar cells excite ganglion cells that increase their firing rate in response to light, and these are known as ON ganglion cells. The hyperpolarizing bipolar cells excite ganglion cells that decrease their firing rate while the light is on and increase it in a rebound phenomenon after the light is turned off; these are known as OFF ganglion cells. This arrangement occurs because there are sublaminae in the inner plexiform

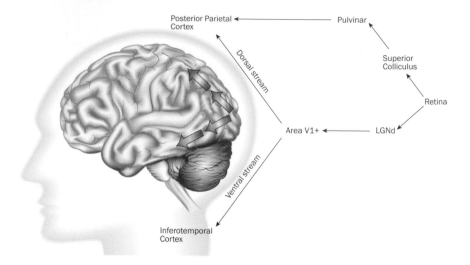

FIGURE 2–2. The "where" pathway, going to parietal cortex in the dorsal stream, and the "what" pathway, going to temporal cortex in the ventral stream.

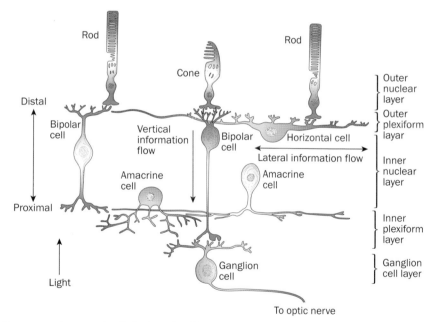

FIGURE 2–3. Layers and cells in the retina. Light comes in through the ganglion cells (bottom) and other cells of the retina to the photoreceptors (top), which consist of rods for dim light vision and cones for daylight vision. Rods and cones connect to bipolar cells in the outer plexiform layer, with lateral connections through horizontal cells. Bipolar cells connect to ganglion cells in the inner plexiform layer, with lateral connections through amacrine cells. The outer nuclear layer contains the cell bodies of the photoreceptors, the inner nuclear layer the cells bodies of bipolar, horizontal, and amacrine cells, and the ganglion cell layer the cell bodies of the ganglion cells. The axons of the ganglion cells form the fibers of the optic nerve going to the brain.

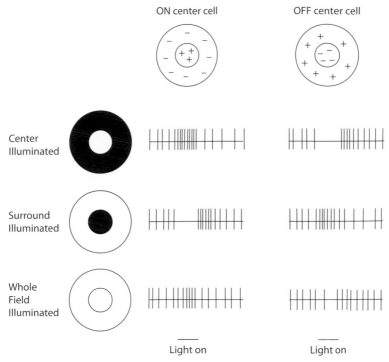

FIGURE 2–4. Receptive fields of ganglion cells in the retina. An on-center cell is excited by light in the center of the receptive field, and inhibited by light in the surround, so that diffuse illumination gives very little response. An off-center cell is inhibited by light in the center and excited by light in the surround so that again, diffuse light gives little response. The inhibition is accompanied by an increase in firing when the light is turned off.

layer—hyperpolarizing bipolar cells and OFF ganglion cells connect in the *a* sublamina, and depolarizing bipolar cells and ON ganglion cells connect in the *b* sublamina (Fig. 2–5).

The ganglion cells can be subdivided into more than 20 types (Dacey & Packer, 2003). In addition to the ON/OFF subdivision, there are ganglion cells concerned with color processing and those concerned with luminance processing. The color-coded cells may have excitatory input from L cones in the center of their receptive fields, and inhibitory input from M cones in the surround (red ON center), or vice versa (red OFF center). Alternatively, the center input may come from M cones, and the surround input from L cones (green ON center and green OFF center). There may also be input from S cones to the center, antagonized by input from L and M cones: the majority of such cells are blue ON center. Cells concerned with luminance processing may have sustained responses, or transient responses; cells concerned with color tend to have more sustained responses. Those cells giving transient responses have a particularly strong response to movement of the stimulus. A minority of cells respond to overall brightness rather than contrast, with a very sustained response. We will discuss

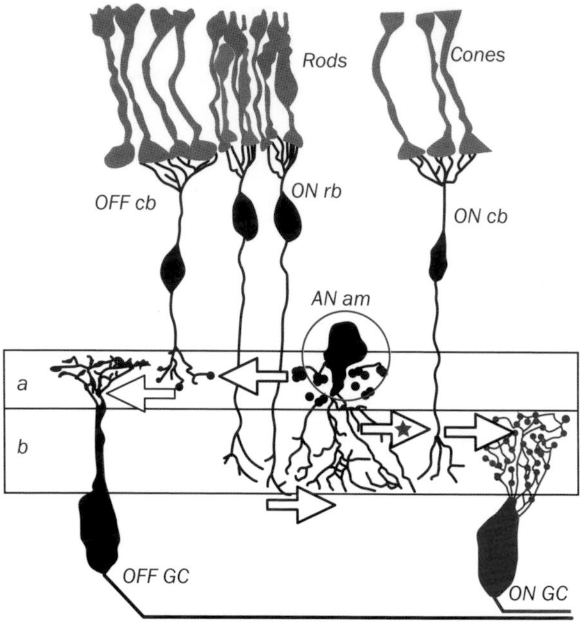

FIGURE 2–5. Connections in the inner plexiform layer of the retina. Hyperpolarizing cone bipolar cells (OFF cb) connect to OFF ganglion cells in sublamina a. Depolarizing cone bipolar cells (ON cb) connect to ON ganglion cells in sublamina b. Rod bipolar cells connect to the AII amacrine cell, which provides a depolarizing input to the ON ganglion cells through a chemical synapse to the ON cb in sublamina b, and a hyperpolarizing input to the OFF ganglion cell through an electrical synapse in sublamina a. (Figure courtesy of Ralph Nelson.)

these further when we get to circadian rhythms and the pupillary reflex, which are the two visual functions that require knowledge of the absolute level of illumination. It is the combination of all these properties (ON/OFF, luminance vs. color, sustained vs. transient, red/green vs. blue/yellow) that leads to the more than 20 types.

The 20 types can be distinguished by their anatomy, as well as their physiological properties (Fig. 2–6). The prime distinction here is between P cells, which project to one set of layers (the parvocellular layers) in the lateral geniculate nucleus, and M cells, which project to another set of layers (the magnocellular layers). P cells have smaller cell bodies and small dendritic arborizations, thus small receptive fields and high acuity (Fig. 2–7). Color-coded cells near the fovea are all P cells. The M cells have larger cell bodies and larger dendritic arborizations, and thus larger receptive fields. Their responses are more transient than those of the P cells, leading to a faster temporal response, and thus a better response to movement.

Most ganglion cells respond to rod input as well as cone input, and thus are activated in both daytime and nighttime conditions. This is due to a rather unusual arrangement. There are separate rod bipolar cells and cone bipolar cells,

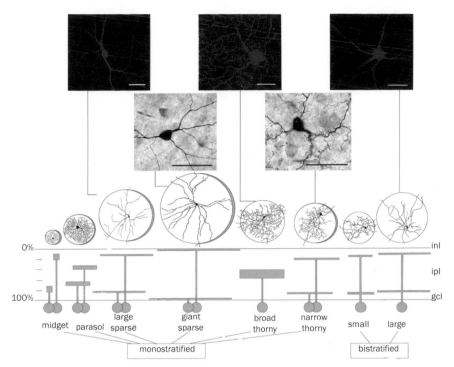

FIGURE 2–6. Various ganglion cells from the macaque retina, showing their arborizations in the inner plexiform layer. The monosratified cells arborize in one sublamina and give either ON or OFF responses. The bistratified cells give ON-OFF responses. Midget cells project to the P layers of the LGN, and parasol cells to the M layers, and are the majority of the cells. Small bistratified, large bistratified, and large sparse monostratified all contribute to the blue/yellow pathway. (Reprinted from Dacey & Packer, 2003, with kind permission of Elsevier.)

and the rod bipolar cells are all of one type—hyperpolarizing in response to light. In the inner plexiform layer, the rod bipolar cells synapse onto an amacrine cell called the AII, which has a small receptive field (Fig. 2–5). This cell in turn synapses onto the terminals of the cone bipolar cells, providing excitatory input in dim light to the depolarizing cone bipolar cells, and inhibitory input to the cone hyperpolarizing bipolar cells (Fig. 2–5). Thus, the sign of the input from rods and cones to the ganglion cells is the same in both photopic and scotopic conditions. This unusual arrangement probably arose because the cones developed first, and after the rods developed, they simply fed into the cone connections that were already established, thus avoiding duplication (Masland, 2001).

In summary, the retina takes signals from the photoreceptors and converts them into signals about contrast between an object and its surround, movement of a stimulus, the wavelength properties of the stimulus, and, in a small minority of cells, the absolute brightness of the stimulus. This is an oversimplification of the complete picture (Masland, 2001) and excludes a discussion of the various

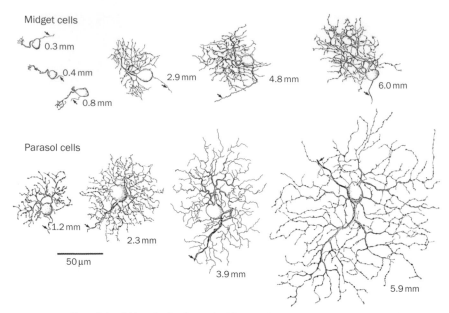

Midget cells

0.3 mm

0.4 mm

0.8 mm

2.9 mm

4.8 mm

6.0 mm

Parasol cells

1.2 mm

2.3 mm

50 µm

3.9 mm

5.9 mm

FIGURE 2–7. Size of dendritic arborizations of midget and parasol ganglion cells at different distances from the fovea, measured in millimeters. At every distance, the midget cells are smaller, giving higher acuity. The size of the arborization increases with distance from the fovea; thus, acuity decreases with distance from the fovea. (Reprinted from Ghosh et al., 1996, with kind permission of Wiley & Sons.)

types of cone bipolar cell, and the numerous types of amacrine cell, but it is a useful summary of what gets fed to higher levels in the primate.

Lateral Geniculate Nucleus

The lateral geniculate nucleus in the primate has six layers. The four dorsal layers have small cells and are called parvocellular (P cells). The two ventral layers have large cells and are called magnocellular (M cells). In addition, there are cells between the layers called K cells (Hendry & Yoshioka, 1994). The parvocellular layers get input from the small P cells in the retina, which includes the color-coded midget ganglion cells. The magnocellular layers get input from the large M cells in the retina, which includes the ganglion cells with diffuse dendritic arborizations, called parasol cells. The koniocellular (K) layers get input from the blue ON cells in the retina (Fig. 2–8).

This anatomy agrees with the physiology (Wiesel & Hubel, 1966). There are red/green color-coded cells (red ON center, red OFF center, green ON center, and green OFF center) and luminance cells (ON center and OFF center) in the P layers. There are blue/yellow color-coded cells, which are found less frequently than the red/green cells. Most of the cells in the M layers are not color-coded.

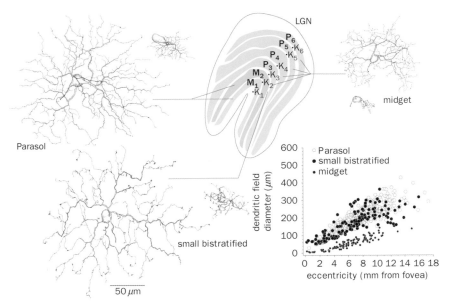

FIGURE 2–8. Projections of ganglion cells to the LGN. Midget ganglion cells project to the P layers, small bistratified ganglion cells to the K layers, and parasol cells to the M layers. For the various other cell types, see Figure 2-6. (Reprinted from Dacey, 2000, with kind permission of Annual Reviews.)

Red/green color-coded cells in the P layers may receive a contribution from a single cone to the center of their receptive fields (Sincich, Zhang, Tiruveedhula, Horton, & Roorda, 2009), coming from the midget ganglion cells in the retina. Thus, the receptive fields of the lateral geniculate cells are very similar to the receptive fields of the ganglion cells in the retina. Differences have to do with mechanisms of attention and whether the response is a burst response or a tonic response (Sherman & Guillery, 2004).

Primary Visual Cortex

The layering structure of the primary visual cortex is more complicated than most other areas of cortex. In general, input to the cerebral cortex comes in to layer IV and projects to layers II, III, V, and VI. Output from layers II and III projects to other cortical areas; output from layer VI is a feedback projection to the thalamus, which is the lateral geniculate nucleus in the case of the visual system; and output from layer V goes to nonthalamic structures outside the cortex, such as the spinal cord in the case of motor cortex, and the superior colliculus and an area called the claustrum in the case of the visual system. What is unusual in the case of primary visual cortex arises from the complexities of the input (Fig. 2–9). First, there are three layers of input—from the P layers of the LGN to IVA and IVCβ, and from

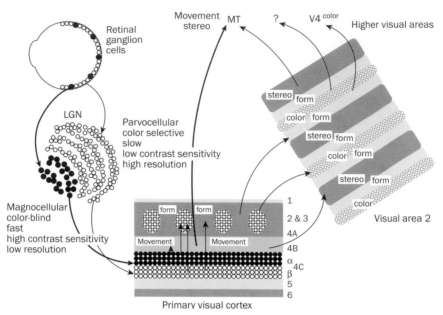

FIGURE 2–9. Projections from retina to LGN to V1 to V2. M layers of LGN go to layer IVCα then to IVB, then to MT and the thick stripes in V2. P layers go to IVCβ, then to the blobs and interblob regions in layers II and III. The blobs project primarily to the thin stripes in V2, and the interblob regions primarily to the pale stripes in V2, with some overlap. (Reprinted from Livingstone & Hubel, 1988, with kind permission of AAAS.)

the M layers of the LGN to layer IVCα. Second, there is a layer of fibers within layer IV, which is layer IVB, which carries output for the M pathway. Third, there is input from the K layers of the LGN direct to layers III and II, carrying blue/yellow signals. Thus, there are parallel and largely separate pathways all the way from retina to primary visual cortex—the P pathway from midget ganglion cells in the retina, to parvocellular layers in the LGN to layer IVCβ in cortex; the M pathway from parasol ganglion cells to magnocellular layers in the LGN to layer IVCα in cortex; and the K pathway from multistratified ganglion cells in the retina to the intercalated layers in the LGN to layers III and II in cortex.

Understanding of the organization of visual cortex has been helped considerably by the discovery that cytochrome oxidase staining shows patterns, particularly in the upper layers of the cortex (Wong-Riley & Carroll, 1984). If one flattens the cortex before staining it, then makes horizontal sections, these patterns become very evident (Fig. 2–10). There is a clear boundary between striate cortex (called V1 for primary visual cortex, and area 17 in Brodmann's classification for the human) and secondary visual cortex (V2, part of area 18). Within V1 there is an arrangement of dark spots, called blobs, and the area between is called the interblob area. Within V2, there is a series of stripes running perpendicular to the V1/V2 border. The dark stripes can be divided into wider ones, called the thick

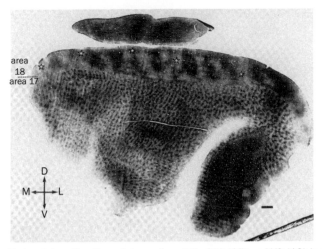

FIGURE 2–10. Horizontal section through layers II and III of V1 (17) and V2 (18) in macaque. In V1, the blobs are seen. In V2 there are thick (wide) stripes, thin (narrow) stripes, and pale stripes in between, running perpendicular to the 17/18 boundary. (Reprinted from Livingstone & Hubel, 1984, with kind permission of the Society for Neuroscience.)

stripes, and narrower ones, called the thin stripes (Hubel & Livingstone, 1987). The pale stripes can be divided into those medial to a thick stripe and those lateral to a thick stripe (Federer et al., 2009). The cytochrome oxidase staining reflects activity in the cells in the area stained, depending on how far they are excited or inhibited. Thus, it is not surprising that cells in the various areas have physiological differences that become apparent when the staining is combined with recordings from single cells (Livingstone & Hubel, 1984).

Moreover, there are distinct connections between the subdivisions of V1 and those of V2 (Figs. 2–9 and 2–11). The part of the P pathway from the lateral geniculate nucleus projects from layer IVCβ to the blobs in V1, then to the thin stripes in V2 (Hubel & Livingstone, 1987). The K pathway projects directly to the blobs, then to the thin stripes. The physiological properties of cells along these pathways will be dealt with in Chapter 4. The M pathway from the lateral geniculate nucleus projects from layer IVB to the thick stripes (Livingstone & Hubel, 1987a), and so do some cells from the interblob area (Federer et al., 2009). The physiological properties of cells along this pathway will be dealt with in Chapters 5 and 6. Another part of the P pathway projects to layer IVCβ, the interblob areas, and the pale stripes, with distinctions between the two types of pale stripes that need to be clarified (Federer et al., 2009). This pathway is believed to deal with contours and outlines of objects, and it will be dealt with in Chapter 7.

The separation of pathways continues beyond V2. Two of the main areas involved are V4 and MT, also known as V5. V4 was originally identified as an area with a high concentration of color-coded cells (Zeki, 1973). Numerous

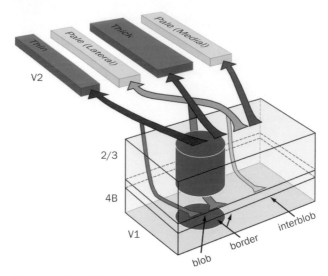

FIGURE 2–11. Projections from V1 to V2 in the macaque. The blobs project to the thin stripes. Layer IVB and an area next to the blobs project to the thick stripes. There are two sets of pale stripes, which receive input from different areas of the interblob region. (Reprinted from Federer et al., 2009, with kind permission of the Society for Neuroscience.)

papers since then have shown that many cells are specific for contours and shapes rather than color, but all authors agree that the percentage of color-coded cells is high. V5 was originally identified as an area with a high percentage of cells that respond to movement, and to direction of movement, but not to color (Zeki, 1974a). Some also respond to movement in depth, which may require movement in opposite directions in the two eyes (Zeki, 1974b). Subsequent work has shown responses to stereoscopic stimuli, so this is an area for both movement and depth.

The projections from V2 to these two areas can be assayed by putting tracers into the two areas and looking at the transport back to V2 (Shipp & Zeki, 1985). Indeed, if the tracer injected into V4 is yellow, and that into V5 is blue, the two projections can be seen side by side (DeYoe & van Essen, 1985). The results show that the thick stripes in V2 project to V5, and the thin stripes and pale stripe project to V4 (Fig. 2–12). V5 also receives a projection direct from layer IVB in V1 (Maunsell & Van Essen, 1983).

Columns in the Visual Cortex

This brief review shows that there are numerous properties of vision dealt with side by side in both V1 and V2, and also in the higher areas that we will deal with later. How is this organized? The answer is that the cerebral cortex in general is

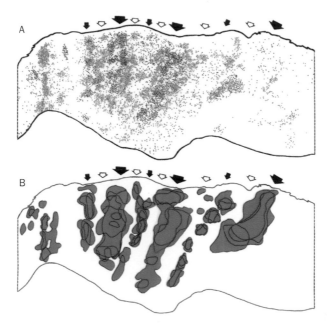

FIGURE 2–12. Separate stripes in V2 project to MT and V4. (*A*) Bisbenzimide, which is blue, is injected into MT and carried back to the thick stripes. Nuclear yellow is injected into V4 and carried back to the thin stripes. (*B*) Cytochrome oxidase stains the stripes. (Reprinted from DeYoe & van Essen, 1985, with kind permission of MacMillan Publishers.)

arranged in a columnar system. That is, if one records from a cell near the surface of the cortex and characterizes its properties, then other cells underneath will tend to have the same properties. On the other hand, if one makes a tangential penetration, the properties will change in a systematic way as one moves the electrode forward.

Three properties dealt with in V1 are ocular dominance, orientation selectivity, and color. The visual cortex is the first place along the visual pathway where the signals from the two eyes come together. Out of the six layers of the LGN, three get input from the contralateral eye and three from the ipsilateral eye; there is very little mixture between the two. Cells in V1 get input from both eyes, but the input from one eye still dominates the response. Thus, there are stripes dominated by the left eye, and stripes dominated by the right eye, with the blobs centered on the stripes (Fig. 2–13).

Orientation selectivity means that the cell responds to an edge of a particular orientation, and much less to edges with the perpendicular orientation. When a tangential penetration is made, the cells go through a regular progression of preferred orientations, all the way around the clock (Fig. 2–14). This sequence may be interrupted by cells with no orientation selectivity; these are the cells in the blobs, many of which are color-coded. The pattern of orientation selectivity

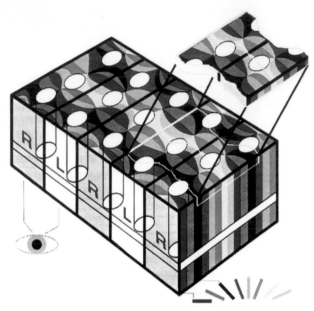

FIGURE 2–13. Schematic of columnar organization of macaque V1. Blobs are centered on the ocular dominance columns (R for right eye columns and L for left) and are missing from layer IV. Areas responding to horizontal orientations are marked in red, vertical orientations in light green, and other orientations with colors shown underneath the figure. These meet in pinwheels, which are usually not centered on the blobs. Orientation columns cross the ocular dominance columns and are interrupted by the blobs. (Reprinted from Grinvald et al., 2000, with kind permission of Cold Spring Harbor Press.)

may also be seen by viewing the surface of the cortex (using a dye that marks the level of activation), stimulating with successively different orientations, and marking which area is activated by each orientation (Blasdel & Salama, 1986). Using different colors for the different orientations, one can get a false color map of the orientation selectivity (Fig. 2–13). This picture shows that the various orientations are arranged around the blobs in a pinwheel fashion, which can be seen in the human with recent improvements in technique (Yacoub, Harel, & Ugurbil, 2008).

We have already dealt with the differences between the thin stripes, thick stripes, and pale stripes in V2. There are also columns within each stripe, although it is not clear whether one should talk about columns, or instead clusters of cells with similar properties. Within the thin stripes, one finds clusters for different colors, for objects brighter than the background, and for objects darker than the background (Xiao, Wang, & Felleman, 2003; see Fig. 3–14). Within the thick stripes, there are clusters of cells preferring objects nearer than the fixation point, and clusters of cells preferring objects further away than the fixation point, with a gradual progression from one to the other (Chen, Lu, & Roe, 2008).

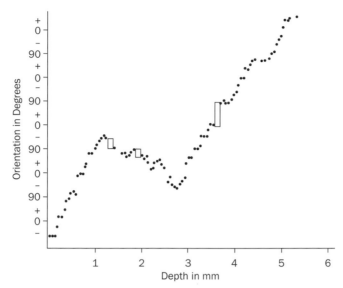

FIGURE 2–14. A long penetration with a microelectrode slantwise into V1 of macaque cortex. Most cells were selective for the orientation of the stimulus, with the orientation marked on the vertical axis. There is a regular progression of orientations around the clock as the electrode is moved forward, with areas where there was no orientation selectivity, marked with rectangles, which corresponds to the passage of the electrode through a blob. (Reprinted from Livingstone & Hubel, 1984, with kind permission of the Society for Neuroscience.)

Within the pale stripes, there is a pinwheel distribution of preferred orientations, very similar to that seen in the interblob areas of V1 (Ramsden, Hung & Roe, 2001).

This system of columns is seen all over the cerebral cortex, with the properties dealt with by columns depending on the area involved. V5, also known as MT, has columns for direction of movement (Albright, Desimone, & Gross, 1984; Zeki, 1974a) and columns for disparity (DeAngelis & Newsome, 1999), which will be dealt with in more detail on Chapters 5 and 6. V4 has clusters dealing with orientation separate from those dealing with color and form (Tanigawa, Lu, & Roe, 2010), and there may be columns for specific colors such as red, green, and blue (Zeki, 1973). When the responses of cells become more specific for particular objects, as they do in the occipitotemporal cortex, then there are columns for this specificity, which will be dealt with in Chapter 7.

In general, the columnar system seems to be designed to allow elaboration of the response to a particular feature. The input comes in to layer IV, with projections to layer II and III, and to V and VI, before projecting to other areas. The responses in layer IV tend to be simpler than those in II, III, V, and VI. The columnar system allows the complexity to be generated for each eye orientation, direction of motion, color, etc., without interference from the other eye, and other orientations, directions of motion, and colors.

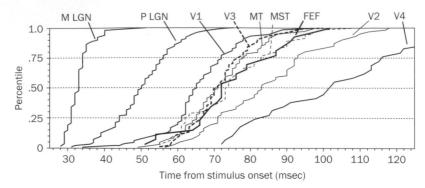

FIGURE 2–15. Latencies at various stages of the visual pathways. Note that the latencies on the M pathway (mLGN, MT, MST, and FEF) are all shorter than those at the same stage of the P pathway (pLGN, V1, V2, and V4). (Reprinted from Schmolesky et al., 1998, with kind permission of the American Physiological Society.)

Hierarchy of Areas

The stimuli that cells respond to become more complex within each column in an area and also as one area projects to another. In other words, one can arrange the various visual areas in the cortex in a hierarchy. One aspect of the response that changes in the hierarchy is the latency. Cells in higher areas have a longer latency of response simply because it takes the signal longer to reach them (Yoshor, Bosking, Ghose, & Maunsell, 2007). This is true within the "what" and "where" pathways (Fig. 2–15); because of the need for faster action for eye movements than for object recognition, signals are faster in the "where" pathway than the "what" pathway at each level (Schmolesky et al., 1998). Another aspect that changes is the size of the receptive field of the cell. Cells in lower areas converge onto cells in higher areas, so that the cells in higher areas are collecting information over a wider area of the retina (Fig. 2–16). In conjunction with this, there is coarser topographical organization at higher areas. In theory, while a ganglion cell in the retina may respond to a small spot of light localized to a particular place in the retina, after many stages of processing and much convergence, one might get to a cell in temporal cortex that responds to a gray rabbit placed anywhere in the visual field. In practice, it does not work quite like this, as we will see in Chapter 7, but the stimuli needed to activate a cell certainly get more complicated at higher levels of the hierarchy, and the localization of the stimulus in the visual field becomes less important.

The hierarchy at lower levels is pretty clear. The retina projects to the LGN, which projects to V1, which projects to V2. At higher levels, it is not so clear, because many visual areas are connected reciprocally. Fortunately there is an anatomical criterion for the connections between areas that distinguishes feedforward connections from feedback connections. The feedforward connections project from layers II and III (supragranular) in the lower area to layer IV in the higher area. The

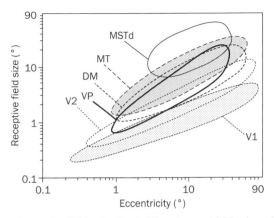

FIGURE 2–16. Sizes of receptive fields of cells at different eccentricities in various areas. In all areas, the receptive fields are larger at larger eccentricities. Also the receptive fields get larger as one moves up the hierarchy from V1 to V2, VP, DM, MT, and MSTd. For abbreviations, see Table 2–1. (Reprinted from Rosa, 1997, with kind permission of Plenum Press.)

feedback connections project from layers V and VI (infragranular) in the higher area to all layers except IV in the lower area (Fig. 2–17). The two sets of connections are both approximately point to point, with a little divergence in the feedforward connections and a little convergence in the feedback connections.

Higher Areas

Using this anatomical criterion, the various visual areas can be arranged according to their level in the hierarchy (Maunsell & Van Essen, 1983). This has been established in the macaque, where anatomical experiments have been done that are forbidden in humans. There are numerous areas associated with vision—in the macaque they comprise approximately half of the cerebral cortex—and one can unfold the cortex and arrange them in a map (Fig. 2–18). The number depends on the criteria used to distinguish them and whether the author is a "lumper" or a "splitter." It can range up to three dozen, with over 300 connections between them. Also, where to put an area in the hierarchy can sometimes be ambiguous. We give here two schemes, one of which emphasizes the number of areas, the hierarchy, the pathways all the way from the retina, and the large number of interconnections (van Essen, 2004; Fig. 2–19A), the other of which emphasizes the division into "what" and "where" pathways (Ungerleider, 1995; Fig. 2–19B).

The "where" pathway includes parts of V3, MT projecting to MST, then to several areas in parietal cortex (LIP, VIP, 7a and others), then to various areas in frontal cortex. Parietal cortex is an area that evaluates the salience of an object, whether it is worth turning the eyes to look at it (see Chapters 8

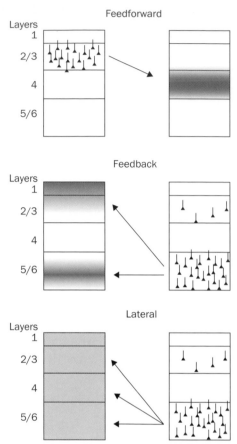

FIGURE 2-17. Feedforward and feedback connections. Feedforward goes from all layers except IV in area A to layer IV in area B. Feedback goes from layers V and VI (infragranular) in area B to layers II and III (supragranular) in area A. Lateral goes from layers V and VI in area B to all layers in area A. (Reprinted from Bullier et al., 2003, with kind permission of Oxford University Press.)

and 10). This decision is affected by both bottom-up information, such as whether the object is moving or particularly noticeable in other ways, and top-down information about whether the system is expecting something to happen in a particular part of the field of view. This evaluation is then sent to various areas in frontal cortex, such as the frontal eye fields and supplementary eye fields, which affect eye movements (see Chapter 8). The "what" pathway includes several areas in occipitotemporal and temporal cortices, such as inferotemporal cortex, divided into anterior and posterior portions, and various other names given by various other authors. These areas deal with recognition of objects and faces in several subdivisions that do not always correspond to the anatomical names (Chapter 7).

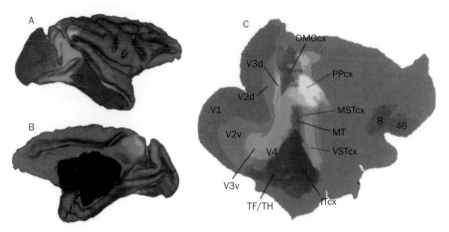

FIGURE 2–18. The cerebral cortex of the macaque, both lateral surface (*A*) and medial surface (*B*), can be unfolded and made into a flat map (*C*). Almost 50% of the cortex is visual. For abbreviations, see Table 2–1. (Reprinted from Van Essen, 2004, with kind permission of MIT Press.)

As already pointed out, the separation of functions into separate areas and separate pathways is not absolute. First, there are the cross-connections between pathways illustrated in both Figures 2–19A and 2–19B. Even V4 and MT, where the separation into motion and disparity in the latter and color and form in the former is one of the clearest, have interconnections with a pattern of terminations that is intermediate between feedforward and feedback (Maunsell & Van Essen, 1983). Second, there are connections between columns with different properties in each area, even though the majority of connections are between columns with similar properties (Lamme, Super, & Spekreijse, 1998). Finally, in a number of cases, there are projections that skip a level in the hierarchy. For example, MT receives a K pathway input direct from the lateral geniculate nucleus, as well as inputs direct from V1, V2, and V3 (Sincich, Park, Wohlgemuth, & Horton, 2004). These projections that bypass levels in the hierarchy, and connect areas at the same level in the hierarchy but on different stream of processing, can explain why lesions do not always abolish a function completely. The nervous system is wired in this way so that damage is not always incapacitating.

The human visual system occupies a smaller percentage of the cortex (30%) than in the macaque, because of the elaboration of cognitive areas, language, and emotion in the human, but it is no smaller in absolute extent. Using functional magnetic resonance imaging (fMRI) in conjunction with psychophysical tests has shown considerable correspondence between human and macaque in terms of topography, connections, and function (Tootell, Tsao, & Vanduffel, 2003). The correspondence is closest in V1 and V2. V3 has an extra division in the human, and the part that deals with motion is different. There is a human homolog of MT

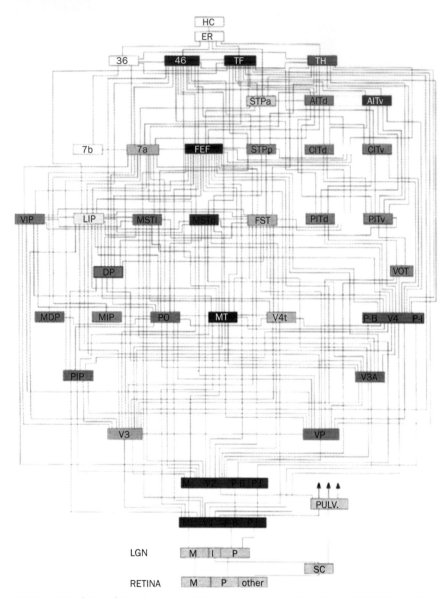

FIGURE 2–19A. Areas of visual cortex and their connections from Van Essen (1995). Since then, more areas have been found. For abbreviations, see Table 2-1. (Reprinted with kind permission of AAAS.)

and MST, dealing with motion and disparity. There is a human homolog of V4, and more careful analysis of both human and macaque shows that lesions of V4 do not abolish color vision, but lesions located nearby do. The largest differences occur in occipitotemporal cortex, in which the areas for faces, places, and body parts are not defined as well in the macaque (Chapter 7). A comparison of maps

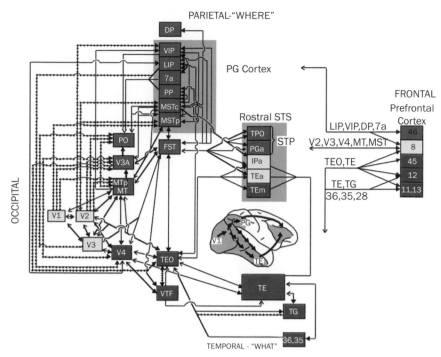

FIGURE 2–19B. Areas in macaque visual cortex, emphasizing the dorsal "where" and ventral "what" pathways. (Reprinted from Ungerleider et al., 2004, with kind permission of MIT Press.)

for macaque and human is shown in Figure 2–20. This is a comparison drawn in 2003; it most likely will be modified considerably over the next few years.

Function of the Feedback Connections

The function of the feedback connections has not been elaborated in detail for the individual pathways. Indeed, the function of the feedback connections is not at all clear in any specific pathway. So we will just make a few general comments here.

First, the feedback can be surprisingly specific. The M, P, and K pathways project to V1, and to cells in layer VI that have M, P, and K characteristics. These cells project back to the LGN, where they connect to cells in the M, P, and K layers that gave rise to the feedforward connections (Briggs & Usrey, 2009). Similar specificity of feedback from the compartments of V2 to the compartments of V1 is found where it has been investigated.

Second, the feedback affects the overall responsiveness of a cell, rather than the specificity of the stimulus that the cell responds to. For example, there are cells

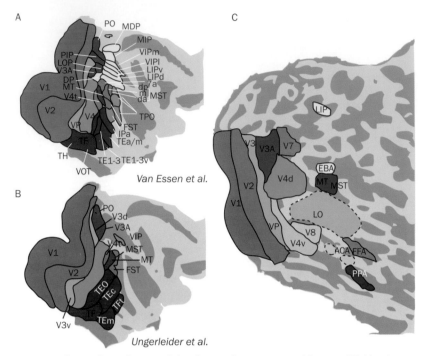

FIGURE 2–20. Comparison of maps of visual cortex in macaque and human. (*A*) Map in macaque from Van Essen et al. (2001). (*B*) Map in macaque from Ungerleider et al. (2004). (*C*) Map in human from Tootell et al. (2003). For abbreviations see Table 2–1. (Reprinted from Tootell, 2003, with kind permission of the Society for Neuroscience.)

in V1 that respond to the orientation of a line; cooling V2 to abolish the feedback may make the response larger or smaller, but it does not affect the orientation specificity (Sandell & Schiller, 1982).

Third, the feedback comes from a wider area of the field of view than the feedforward input. In general, the feedback acts to accentuate the distinction of an object from its background. It may enlarge the inhibitory effect of the surround (Bullier, 2003; Sillito & Jones, 2004), or it may accentuate the figure/ground border (Lamme et al., 1998), or it may enhance the response of a cell to an object that is moving in relation to the background (Sillito & Jones, 2004). A recent paper suggests that objects in the periphery of the field of view can affect the response in V1 to objects in the fovea, which has to be due to feedback (Williams et al., 2008).

Fourth, feedback modulates the feedforward influence, but it cannot drive the response by itself. For example, V2 gets feedback from MT, and MT can be driven by afferents that go through the LGN or SC but bypass V1. However, cooling of V1 totally abolishes the response in V2 (Schiller & Malpeli, 1977). The feedback from MT by itself is not enough.

Finally, feedback can act to accentuate the response of a cell when attention is focused on the object, with the attention being determined by higher areas such as parietal cortex. This, together with the other factors, can be illustrated by recording in V1. The cell responds after 48 milliseconds to the basic features of the response; after 57 milliseconds to segregation of the figure from the background, presumably due to feedback from V2, and after 137 milliseconds to the selection of the relevant figure in the task performed from irrelevant ones, presumably due to feedback from parietal cortex (Roelfsema, Tolboom, & Khayat, 2007).

Input From Other Senses

This book is about vision. However, input from other senses often is combined with visual input to govern a behavioral response (Beauchamp, 2005). This may come from the vestibular system for orientation in space, from the auditory and somatosensory systems for eye movements, and from all other senses to put together a complete experience. Moreover, other senses may trigger visual memories where all aspects of a complete experience have been stored together. Vestibular input to the "where" pathway at the level of MT and higher serves location in space; auditory and somatosensory input to the superior colliculus serves eye movements (Stein & Meredith, 1993); all the senses come together in the parietal cortex; and memories with visual, auditory, taste, smell, and other aspects are stored in temporal cortex.

Psychophysical Evidence for Parallel Pathways

The question of whether color differences contribute to depth, motion, and form perception has fascinated psychologists for many years. This is usually tested by observing depth, motion, and form in equiluminant displays (displays of stimuli that have the same luminance, but different colors). It is a difficult question to answer for technical reasons: color vision varies across the retina, so what is equiluminant in the fovea is not equiluminant in the parafovea or the periphery of the retina, and what is equiluminant also varies from person to person. Nevertheless, although form, motion, and depth may not disappear totally at equiluminance, there seems to be no doubt that they are reduced.

Livingstone and Hubel (1987b, 1988) accumulated a number of examples from the literature and added a few of their own. The sensation of depth can be reduced considerably, depending on the stimulus used (Lu & Fender, 1972). The sensation of movement from dots jumping from place to place may be lost (Ramachandran & Anstis, 1985). The perception of form from shading is lost (Livingstone & Hubel, 1987b; Fig. 2–21). The sensation of a sphere or cylinder rotating in depth becomes a sensation of a moving pattern of dots (see cylinders on http://hubel.med.

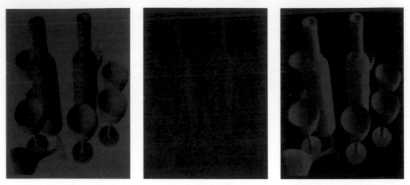

FIGURE 2–21. A figure that appears in depth with blue and black (left), and also with green and black (right) has no depth when presented in blue and green at equiluminance (middle). (Reprinted from Livingstone & Hubel, 1988, with kind permission of AAAS.)

harvard.edu/ilusion.htm and equilu at http://viperlib.york.ac.uk/). Moreover, a pattern of lines that appears to be solid shapes in black and white becomes just a jumble of lines in color without luminance differences (Fig. 2–22). These examples are just a few of the dozens that have been studied over the years. They support the results from anatomy showing that there are some connections between the color pathway and the other pathways, but there is also a significant degree of separation.

One difference between the P and M pathways, alluded to earlier, is that the spatial and temporal properties are different: the P pathway has a higher spatial resolution than the M pathway, the M pathway has a higher temporal resolution, and the M pathway responds more strongly to contrast (Shapley, Kapley, & Soodak, 1981). The P pathway does not respond to stimuli changing at more than 5 cycles/sec, whereas the M pathway responds up to 30 cycles/sec. Consequently, in the range of 7–15 cycles/sec, apparent movement and depth perception occur, but shape and orientation discrimination do not (Livingstone & Hubel, 1987b). Moreover, there are fine stimuli of 10–30 cycles/degree that can be seen but that do not activate a sensation of depth or movement. Finally, a rotating disc

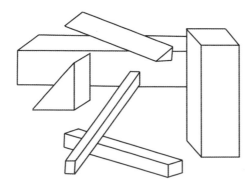

FIGURE 2–22. This collection of lines appears to be a collection of solid objects in black and white, but it becomes a jumbled set of lines in equiluminant colors.

of low contrast appears to rotate more slowly than one of high contrast, and it may even appear to be stationary (Campbell & Maffei, 1981). A different demonstration of the same phenomenon, that contrast affects speed of movement, may be seen at footsteps at http://psy2.ucsd.edu/~sanstis/SASlides.html. The temporal differences include the faster latencies seen at all levels of the M pathways, leading to fascinating visual phenomena such as the flash-lag effect (summarized by Bedell, Patel, Chung, & Ogmen, 2006). These spatial, temporal, and contrast properties emanate from the parasol and midget ganglion cells in the retina. The point that the differences can be seen in psychological phenomena shows that the differences are reflected all the way up the pathways to the level of perception.

Lesions

There are various lesions that affect the visual system. Many of them are specific for a particular aspect of vision (examples include lesions that affect primarily color perception, and lesions that affect primarily motion perception), and these are used as evidence that separate pathways deal with separate aspects of vision. There are lesions of parietal cortex that lead to neglect, and these will be dealt with in Chapter 10. There are also fascinating studies of people with lesions of occipital cortex, affecting primarily V1. If this is restricted to a small area, it leads to blindness in a small part of the field of view, called a scotoma. If it is extensive over a large part of the occipital lobe on one side, it leads to blindness in one half of the field of view, called hemianopia. Extreme cases with ablation of the occipital cortex on both sides result in total blindness.

Several neurologists during World War I noticed that soldiers with gunshot wounds of occipital cortex could not see objects in part of their field of view, but they could perceive motion (Riddoch, 1917). In other words, the scotoma for object perception was always larger than the scotoma for motion perception. Many years later, some of these patients that were hemianopic were studied in much more detail. They can point with their finger at a target, even though they do not see the target (Poppel, Held, & Frost, 1973). They may be able to avoid objects that they are not aware of (Striemer, Chapman, & Goodale, 2009; see Helen3 at http://viperlib.york.ac.uk/ and TN blindsight movie—last clip under In the Media at http://www.beatricedegelder.com/books.html). They may be able to discriminate wavelengths, if forced to guess, but cannot say what the colors are (Weiskrantz, Warrington, Sanders, & Marshall, 1974). They may be able to discriminate orientations without seeing the lines. They may be able to distinguish an X from an O without knowing that there are letters there. Some of them are totally unaware that they are seeing anything while performing these tasks; others are aware that something is happening, perhaps because they are aware of their eye movements, but they cannot describe what it is that is happening (Cowey, 2004; Weiskrantz, 2009).

These capabilities are known as blindsight (Weiskrantz, Warrington, Sanders, & Marshall, 1974).

What is happening here is that actions are being taken on the basis of signals that bypass V1 and go straight from lateral geniculate nucleus to area MT (Schmid et al., 2010), from the retina to superior colliculus to extrastriate cortex (Sahraie et al., 1997), or from retina to the nuclei of the optic tract. Thus, in hemianopic subjects (but not in normal subjects), global motion detection is disrupted by transcranial magnetic stimulation of human MT that interferes with the operation of the cortex underneath (Alexander & Cowey, 2009). The conclusions are supported by experiments in macaque, where the lesions can be much more clearly defined; careful tests show that the macaques do not perceive what the stimuli are (Cowey & Stoerig, 1995). The phenomenon thus supports the anatomy described earlier. It also shows that awareness of a visual stimulus is considerably reduced (Zeki & Ffytche, 1998) or totally abolished in the absence of activation of V1 and its projections to the "what" pathway. Activation of the "where" pathway alone does not seem to produce awareness.

References

Albright, T. D., Desimone, R., & Gross, CG. (1984). Columnar organization of directionally selective cells in visual area MT of the macaque. *Journal of Neurophysiology, 51,* 16–31.

Alexander, I., & Cowey, A. (2009). The cortical basis of global motion detection in blindsight. *Experimental Brain Research, 192,* 407–411.

Beauchamp, M. S. (2005). See me, hear me, touch me: Multisensory integration in lateral occipital-temporal cortex. *Current Opinion in Neurobiology, 15,* 145–153.

Bedell, H. E., Patel, S. S., Chung, S. T. L., & Ogmen, H. (2006). Perceptual consequences of timing differences within parallel-processing systems in human vision. In H. Ogmen & B. G. Breitmeyer (Eds.), *The first half second* (pp. 245–258). Cambridge, MA: MIT Press.

Blasdel, G. G., & Salama, G. (1986). Voltage-sensitive dyes reveal a modular organisation in monkey striate cortex. *Nature, 321,* 579–585.

Briggs, F., & Usrey, W. M. (2009). Parallel processing in the corticogeniculate pathway of the macaque monkey. *Neuron, 62,* 135–146.

Bullier, J., Fahle, M., & Greenlee, M. W. (2003). Cortical connections and functional interactions between visual cortical areas. In M. Fahle & M. Greenlee (Eds.), *The neuropsychology of vision* (pp. 23–63). New York: Oxford University Press.

Campbell, F. W., & Maffei, L. (1981). The influence of spatial frequency and contrast on the perception of moving patterns. *Vision Research, 21,* 713–721.

Carroll, J. (2008). Focus on molecules: The cone opsins. *Experimental Eye Research, 86,* 865–866.

Chen, G., Lu, H. D., & Roe, A. W. (2008). A map for horizontal disparity in monkey V2. *Neuron, 58,* 442–450.

Cowey, A. (2004). The 30th Sir Frederick Bartlett Lecture. Fact, artefact, and myth about blindsight. *Quarterly Journal of Experimental Psychology A, 57,* 577–609.

Cowey, A., & Stoerig, P. (1995). Blindsight in monkeys. *Nature, 373*, 247–249.

Dacey, D. M. (2000). Parallel pathways for spectral coding in primate retina. *Annual Review of Neuroscience, 23*, 743–775.

Dacey, D. M., & Packer, O. S. (2003). Colour coding in the primate retina: Diverse cell types and cone-specific circuitry. *Current Opinion in Neurobiology, 13*, 421–427.

DeAngelis, G. C., & Newsome, W. T. (1999). Organization of disparity-selective neurons in macaque area MT. *Journal of Neuroscience, 19*, 1398–1415.

DeYoe, E. A., & Van Essen, D. C. (1985). Segregation of efferent connections and receptive field properties in visual area V2 of the macaque. *Nature, 317*, 58–61.

Federer, F., Ichida, J. M., Jeffs, J., Schiessl, I., McLoughlin, N., & Angelucci, A. (2009). Four projection streams from primate V1 to the cytochrome oxidase stripes of V2. *Journal of Neuroscience, 29*, 15455–15471.

Ghosh, K. K., Goodchild, A. K., Sefton, A. E., & Martin, P. R. (1996). Morphology of retinal ganglion cells in a new world monkey, the marmoset Callithrix jacchus. *Journal of Comparative Neurology, 366*, 76–92.

Grinvald, A., Shmuel, A., Vanzetta, I., Shtoyerman, E., Shoham, D., & Arieli, A. (2000). Intrinsic signal imaging in the neocortex. In R. Yuste, F. Lanni, & A. Konnerth (Eds.), *Imaging neurons* (pp. 45.41–45.17). Cold Spring Harbor, NY: Cold Spring Harbor Laboratory Press.

Hendry, S. H., & Yoshioka, T. (1994). A neurochemically distinct third channel in the macaque dorsal lateral geniculate nucleus. *Science, 264*, 575–577.

Hubel, D. H., & Livingstone, M. S. (1987). Segregation of form, color, and stereopsis in primate area 18. *Journal of Neuroscience, 7*, 3378–3415.

Lamme, V. A., Super, H., & Spekreijse, H. (1998). Feedforward, horizontal, and feedback processing in the visual cortex. *Current Opinion in Neurobiology, 8*, 529–535.

Livingstone, M. S., & Hubel, D. H. (1984). Anatomy and physiology of a color system in the primate visual cortex. *Journal of Neuroscience, 4*, 309–356.

Livingstone, M. S., & Hubel, D. H. (1987a). Connections between layer 4B of area 17 and the thick cytochrome oxidase stripes of area 18 in the squirrel monkey. *Journal of Neuroscience, 7*, 3371–3377.

Livingstone, M. S., & Hubel, D. H. (1987b). Psychophysical evidence for separate channels for the perception of form, color, movement, and depth. *Journal of Neuroscience, 7*, 3416–3468.

Livingstone, M. S., & Hubel, D. H. (1988). Segregation of form, color, movement and depth: Anatomy, physiology and perception. *Science, 240*, 740–750.

Lu, C., & Fender, D. H. (1972). The interaction of color and luminance in stereoscopic vision. *Investigative Ophthalmology and Visual Science, 11*, 482–490.

Masland, R. H. (2001). The fundamental plan of the retina. *Nature Neuroscience, 4*, 877–886.

Maunsell, J. H., van Essen, D. C. (1983). The connections of the middle temporal visual area (MT) and their relationship to a cortical hierarchy in the macaque monkey. *Journal of Neuroscience, 3*, 2563–2586.

Poppel, E., Held, R., & Frost, D. (1973). Letter: Residual visual function after brain wounds involving the central visual pathways in man. *Nature, 243*, 295–296.

Ramachandran, V. S., & Anstis, S. M. (1985). Perceptual organization in multistable apparent motion. *Perception, 14*, 135–143.

Ramsden, B. M., Hung, C. P., & Roe, A. W. (2001). Real and illusory contour processing in area V1 of the primate: A cortical balancing act. *Cerebral Cortex, 11,* 648–665.

Riddoch, G. (1917). On the relative perceptions of movement and a stationary object in certain visual disturbances due to occipital injuries. *Proceedings of the Royal Society of Medicine, 10,* 13–34.

Roelfsema, P. R., Tolboom, M., & Khayat, P. S. (2007). Different processing phases for features, figures, and selective attention in the primary visual cortex. *Neuron, 56,* 785–792.

Rosa, M. (1997). Visuotopic organization of primate extrtastriate cortex. In K. S. Rockland, J. H. Kaas, & A. Peters (Eds.), *Cerebral cortex: Extrastriate cortex in primates* (pp. 127–203). New York: Plenum Press.

Sahraie, A., Weiskrantz, L., Barbur, J. L., Simmons, A., Williams, S. C., & Brammer, M. J. (1997). Pattern of neuronal activity associated with conscious and unconscious processing of visual signals. *Proceedings of the National Academy of Sciences USA, 94,* 9406–9411.

Sandell, J. H., & Schiller, P. H. (1982). Effect of cooling area 18 on striate cortex cells in the squirrel monkey. *Journal of Neurophysiology, 48,* 38–48.

Schiller, P. H., & Malpeli, J. G. (1977). The effect of striate cortex cooling on area 18 cells in the monkey. *Brain Research, 126,* 366–369.

Schmid, M. C., Mrowka, S. W., Turchi, J., Saunders, R. C., Wilke, M., Peters, A. J., Frank, Q. Y., Leopold, D. A. (2010). Blindsight depends on the lateral geniculate nucleus. *Nature, 466,* 373–377.

Schmolesky, M. T., Wang, Y., Hanes, D. P., Thompson, K. G., Leutgeb, S., Schall, J. D., Leventhal, A. G. (1998). Signal timing across the macaque visual system. *Journal of Neurophysiology, 79,* 3272–3278.

Shapley, R., Kaplan, E., & Soodak, R. (1981). Spatial summation and contrast sensitivity of X and Y cells in the lateral geniculate nucleus of the macaque. *Nature, 292,* 543–545.

Sherman, S. M., & Guillery, R. W. (2004). The visual relays in the thalamus. In L. M. Chalupa & J. S. Werner (Eds.), *The visual neurosciences* (pp. 565–591). Cambridge, MA: MIT Press.

Shipp, S., & Zeki, S. (1985). Segregation of pathways leading from area V2 to areas V4 and V5 of macaque monkey visual cortex. *Nature, 315,* 322–325.

Sillito, A. M., & Jones, H. E. (2004). Feedback systems in visual processing. In L. M. Chalupa & J. S. Werner (Eds.), *The visual neurosciences* (pp. 609–624). Cambridge, MA: MIT Press.

Sincich, L. C., Park, K. F., Wohlgemuth, M. J., & Horton, J. C. (2004). Bypassing V1: A direct geniculate input to area MT. *Nature Neuroscience, 7,* 1123–1128.

Sincich, L. C., Zhang, Y., Tiruveedhula, P., Horton, J. C., & Roorda, A. (2009). Resolving single cone inputs to visual receptive fields. *Nature Neuroscience, 12,* 967–969.

Stein, B. E., & Meredith, M. A. (1993). *The merging of the senses.* Cambridge, MA: MIT Press.

Striemer, C. L., Chapman, C. S., & Goodale, M. A. (2009). "Real-time" obstacle avoidance in the absence of primary visual cortex. *Proceedings of the National Academy of Sciences USA, 106,* 15996–16001.

Tanigawa, H., Lu, H. D., & Roe, A. W. (2010). Functional organization for color and orientation in macaque V4. *Nature Neuroscience, 13,* 1542–1548.

Tootell, R. H., Tsao, D., & Vanduffel, W. (2003). Neuroimaging weighs in: Humans meet macaques in "primate" visual cortex. *Journal of Neuroscience, 23*, 3981–3989.

Ungerleider, L. G. (1995). Functional brain imaging studies of cortical mechanisms for memory. *Science, 270*, 769–775.

Ungerleider, L. G., Pasternak, T., Chalupa, L. M., & Werner, J. S. (2004). Ventral and dorsal cortical processing streams. In L. M. Chalupa & J. S. Werner (Eds.), *The visual neurosciences* (pp. 541–562). Cambridge, MA: MIT Press.

Van Essen, D. C. (2004). Organization of visual areas in macaque and human cerebral cortex. In L. M. Chalupa & J. S. Werner (Eds.), *The visual neurosciences* (pp. 507–521). Cambridge, MA: MIT Press.

Weiskrantz, L. (2009). *Blindsight*. New York: Oxford University Press.

Weiskrantz, L., Warrington, E. K., Sanders, M. D., & Marshall, J. (1974). Visual capacity in the hemianopic field following a restricted occipital ablation. *Brain, 97*, 709–728.

Wiesel, T. N., & Hubel, D. H. (1966). Spatial and chromatic interactions in the lateral geniculate body of the rhesus monkey. *Journal of Neurophysiology, 29*, 1115–1156.

Williams, M. A., Baker, C. I., Op de Beeck, H. P., Shim, W. M., Dang, S., Triantafyllou, C., & Kanwisher, N. (2008). Feedback of visual object information to foveal retinotopic cortex. *Nature Neuroscience, 11*, 1439–1445.

Wong-Riley, M., & Carroll, E. W. (1984). Effect of impulse blockage on cytochrome oxidase activity in monkey visual system. *Nature, 307*, 262–264.

Xiao, Y. P., Wang, Y., & Felleman, D. J. (2003). A spatially organized representation of colour in macaque cortical area V2. *Nature, 421*, 535–539.

Yacoub, E., Harel, N., & Ugurbil, K. (2008). High-field fMRI unveils orientation columns in humans. *Proceedings of the National Academy of Sciences USA, 105*, 10607–10612.

Yoshor, D., Bosking, W. H., Ghose, G. M., & Maunsell, J. H. (2007). Receptive fields in human visual cortex mapped with surface electrodes. *Cerebral Cortex, 17*, 2293–2302.

Zeki, S., & Ffytche, D. H. (1998). The Riddoch syndrome: Insights into the neurobiology of conscious vision. *Brain, 121*(Pt 1), 25–45.

Zeki, S. M. (1973). Colour coding in rhesus monkey prestriate cortex. *Brain Research, 53*, 422–427.

Zeki, S. M. (1974a). Functional organization of a visual area in the posterior bank of the superior temporal sulcus of the rhesus monkey. *Journal of Physiology, 236*, 549–573.

Zeki, S. M. (1974b). Cells responding to changing image size and disparity in the cortex of the rhesus monkey. *Journal of Physiology, 242*, 827–841.

3

Brightness and Contrast

The amount of light that an object reflects is called its luminance. However, whether it appears black or white, light gray or dark gray, yellow or brown, depends on its surroundings, and is known as its lightness. Most people, in common parlance, would call this its brightness. To follow the definition of the field, I will use the term "lightness" here.

Lightness Constancy and Lightness Contrast

When the level of illumination is changed, the luminance (the physical amount of light coming from an object) is changed, but the lightness (our perception of the brightness of an object) is not. Light gray objects appear light gray on the beach, and also in the living room at night, where the level of illumination is lower by orders of magnitude. This is known as lightness constancy. Essentially, the visual system analyzes the reflectance of an object, a process that Helmholtz (1867/1925) described as "discounting the illuminant." The reflectance of an object, of course, is a property of the object independent both of the objects around it and type of illumination (daylight, tungsten light, moonlight, etc.). Hess and Pretori (1894) investigated lightness constancy by placing a square in a background at one level of illumination near another square at a different level of illumination and matching their lightness. The ratio of the luminance of the square to the luminance of the background was fairly constant over a wide range of levels of illumination. This process of lightness constancy helps us to recognize an object regardless of differing locations.

The first step in lightness constancy is that an object is seen in relation to its surround. This is called lightness contrast. The luminance of a black object on the beach is considerably greater than the luminance of a white object in room light, and the appearance of black and white occurs because of contrast with other objects in the scene. For a common illustration of lightness contrast, look at a gray spot in a white surround compared to a gray spot in a black surround. The spot in the white surround appears darker. This is a powerful phenomenon when the two spots are seen in isolation in a darkened room, but a feeble phenomenon when the two are near each other on the pages of a book, because the whole display affects the lightness of the spots, not just the immediate surround. A better illustration comes from a long horizontal rectangle of gray seen within a gradient from black to white (Fig. 3–1). Because of the surround, the right end of the rectangle appears darker than the left end. If the surround is blocked out, then the rectangle can be seen to actually be uniform in luminance.

Assimilation

However, an object is not always contrasted with its surround. Sometimes, its lightness moves toward that of the immediate surround, rather than moving away from it—a process known as spread (von Bezold, 1876) or assimilation (Helson, 1963). This is noticeable particularly in patterns of bars (White, 1979). The short gray bars on the right side of the figure appear darker than the short gray bars on the left, even though the immediate surround on the right is predominantly black

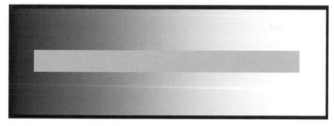

FIGURE 3.1 A horizontal rectangle of constant luminance is surrounded by a rectangle of low luminance at the left and high luminance at the right. The inner rectangle appears to be lighter on the left than the right from lightness contrast. If the outer rectangle is blotted out, the inner rectangle is seen to be actually uniform.

FIGURE 3.2 An example of spread or assimilation. The black stripes are interrupted by gray stripes on the left, and the white stripes by gray stripes on the right. The two sets of gray stripes are of equal luminance, but the right ones appear darker than the left ones by contrast with the gratings above and below, rather than by contrast with the stripes on each side of them. (Reprinted from White, 1979, with kind permission of Pion.)

and the immediate surround on the left is predominantly white (Fig. 3–2). The short bars are seen in contrast to the bars above and below, of which they are a component in the grating, rather than in contrast to the bars beside them, which are the predominant component of their immediate surround.

Helson (1963), who studied contrast and assimilation with gratings of variable line thickness and line separation, suggested that there is a continuum of results: a summative effect for short distances produces assimilation, and an inhibitory effect for longer distances produces contrast. However, the complete explanation is more complicated than this, because "White's effect" (as it is sometimes called) is seen at both high and low spatial frequencies. This will be discussed further later in this chapter. In any case, the predominant effect in nearly all situations is contrast rather than assimilation.

Sharp Boundaries and Gradients

Contrast occurs primarily at the edges of objects with sharp boundaries. Shallow gradients of illumination are much less noticeable and may even appear to be uniform (O'Brien, 1958; see Fig. 3–3). In some cases, the contrast created at a border, combined with the apparent uniformity of the object, makes regions appear to be different in lightness when they are in fact the same (Cornsweet, 1970; Fig. 3–3). In other cases, the contrast at a boundary makes an area appear not to be uniform when the luminance is in fact uniform—for example, the Mach bands seen in step wedges (Ratliff, 1965; see Fig. 3–4). Both these demonstrations show that steep gradients are important to the visual system, but slow variations are not.

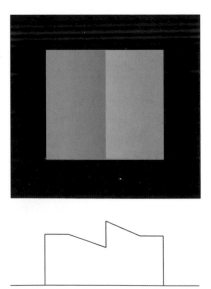

FIGURE 3.3 The gray square in the center is a 60% gray on the right side of the boundary in the center, with a gradient to 50% at the right edge, and a 40% gray on the left side of the boundary in the center, with a gradient to 50% at the left edge, as shown in the bottom graph. Look in the middle of the left half, and the left half appears uniform gray, darker than the right half. Look at the middle of the right half, and it also appears uniform, lighter than the left. The slow gradients are ignored, and the sharp boundary is noticed, with an effect that carries for some distance away.

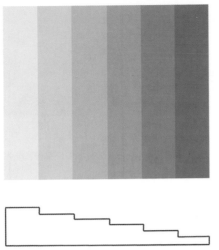

FIGURE 3.4 Mach step bands. The left side of each step appears darker than the right side, because of contrast with the next step. As shown in the lower diagram, the luminance across each step is in fact uniform.

Presumably the system analyzes the situation to detect objects, and it ignores changes in illumination across them.

Land and McCann (1971) suggested that lightness is computed by taking the ratios of luminances across the edges of objects while ignoring whatever slow variation of luminance there might be across the surface of the object. This predicted the lightness of objects within one of their Mondrian displays when the whole display was illuminated with a nonuniform gradient of illumination, and it is useful for O'Brien and Cornsweet illusions. However, it does not predict all displays, such as those investigated by Adelson (1993) (described later) and runs into problems with some Mach band illustrations. The concept is similar to the concept of filling in, where what is perceived in the blind spot, or in a scotoma, is determined by the edges around.

Remote Surrounds

An interesting illustration of the effect of more remote surrounds comes from an experiment by Shevell et al. (1992). They showed that the remote surround can have as much influence as the immediate surround (Fig. 3–5). In the top display, the left spot appears lighter than the right spot, which is the classical illustration of lightness contrast. In the bottom display, where both the annulus in the middle and the spot in the center have the same luminance, the spot in the center still appears dimmer, even though its immediate surround also appears dimmer than on the left (note that this perception, like that of the classical lightness contrast display, is much more dramatic when seen in a dark room than when seen on the

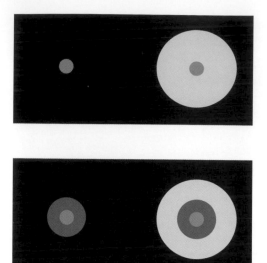

FIGURE 3.5 In the upper display, a gray spot is surrounded by black on the left, and white on the right. The right gray spot appears darker, by lightness contrast. In the lower display, both the central spot and the annulus next to it on the left have the same luminance as the spot and inner annulus on the right. The spot on the right still appears darker, by contrast with the outer annulus, even though the inner annulus on the right appears darker than the one on the left. (Reprinted from Shevell et al., 1992, with kind permission of Elsevier.)

pages of a book). The effect of the remote surround can be elicited by presenting the stimuli to different eyes, whereas the effect of the immediate surround cannot. Thus, there must be different mechanisms involved: a retinal mechanism for the immediate surround, and a cortical mechanism for the remote surround.

Perception of Shadows and Transparency, and Their Influence on Lightness

The perception that there is an illumination boundary in the scene (a shadow, for example), or that there is one transparent object in front of another, can affect the perception of lightness. Gilchrist (1977) produced an early example of this. He arranged two surfaces, one horizontal with a white area and a black tab, the other vertical with a black area and a white tab (Fig. 3–6). He then illuminated the horizontal surface brightly, and the vertical surface dimly, so that the luminance of the horizontal black tab was the same as the vertical white tab. When viewed monocularly, the display was seen as a set of four areas in a single plane, and the lower tab appeared lighter than the upper tab due to contrast with its predominant immediate surround. When viewed binocularly, the display was seen in its true configuration, with a horizontal plane and a vertical plane, and the upper tab appeared lighter than the lower tab, because each tab was seen in relation to its own plane.

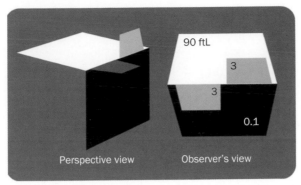

FIGURE 3.6 Horizontal surface with a white area and a black tab, lit brightly, and a vertical surface with a black area and white tab, lit dimly. When viewed monocularly (right), the upper tab looked darker than the lower tab. When viewed binocularly (left), so that the surfaces could be seen as horizontal and vertical, the upper tab looked lighter than the lower tab. (Reprinted from Gilchrist, 2006, with kind permission of Oxford University Press.)

Another series of examples were shown by Adelson (1993). In one of them, he arranged a pattern of triangles and squares so that two vertical shadows appeared to fall on them (Fig. 3–7). Square a_1 appears darker than square a_2 because a_2 is seen as being in a shadow (Fig. 3–7A). His observers had a hard time believing that the two squares actually have the same luminance! The perception of shadow can be reduced by rearranging the pattern, and the difference in lightness is reduced (Fig. 3–7B). A further rearrangement brings back the perception of shadow, and the difference in lightness comes back, even though one can now follow a path around the display and see that the luminances of c_1 and c_2 are the same (Fig. 3–7C).

Some of the most dramatic examples of how transparency affects lightness were shown by Anderson and Winawer (2005, 2008). The discs on the left of Figure 3–8A appear black behind white clouds, and the textured discs on the right appear white behind dark clouds, even though they have the same luminance, because they are seen as being beyond the clouds. The effect can be destroyed by rotating the surround 90°: the complete edges of the discs appear, and the perception of transparency is destroyed (Fig. 3–8B). The effect is even stronger when the disks are moving behind the clouds, which can be seen in the supplementary material to the papers.

Influence of Curvature

The curvature of an object also affects the perception of lightness (Knill & Kersten, 1991). This is illustrated in Figure 3–9. The display in Figure 3–9 top left shows a lighter rectangle on the right, and a darker rectangle on the left. The actual variation in luminance is shown in Figure 3–9 bottom. Each of the two rectangles appears uniform because of the slow gradient of luminance across them, with a

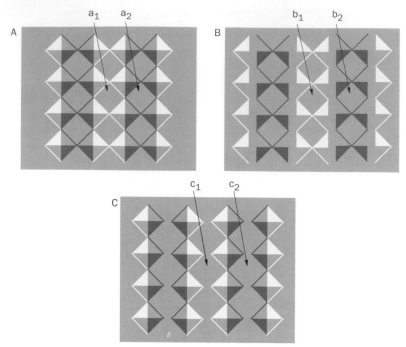

FIGURE 3.7 (A) Pattern of triangles and squares, where patches a_1 and a_2 have the same luminance, but a_2 appears to be in a shadow and appears lighter than a_1. (B) The same pattern as A, with the columns pulled apart to destroy the appearance of a shadow. b_1 and b_2 are much closer in lightness. (C) With a rearrangement of the inducing elements, the shadow returns, and the difference in lightness between c_1 and c_2 reappears. (Reprinted from Adelson, 1993, with kind permission of AAAS.)

difference in lightness produced by the sharp step of luminance at the boundary, as expected from the illustrations given earlier. When the appearance of curvature is introduced by making the top and bottom boundaries curved, the two halves of the display appear identical. The display is now interpreted as parts of two cylinders, with illumination coming from the side.

Contrast Adaptation

So far we have dealt with the perception of the lightness of an object, pointing out that an important component of this is the contrast at the boundaries of the object. The visual system adapts to the overall level of illumination to produce lightness constancy. It turns out that the visual system also adapts to contrast (Chubb et al., 1989). A pattern of dots of medium contrast seen against a background of high contrast appears to have less contrast than when seen against a gray background (Fig. 3–10). This is known as contrast adaptation.

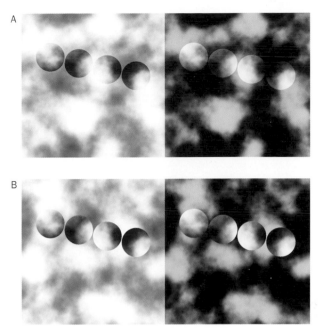

FIGURE 3.8 In the upper display, the discs on the left appear to be dark, with light transparent clouds in front of them, and the discs on the right appear to be light, with dark clouds obscuring them. In the lower display, the background has been rotated 90°, the complete edges of the discs appear, and the illusion disappears (the two sets of discs appear to be the same lightness). (Reprinted from Anderson & Winawer, 2005, with kind permission of MacMillan Publishers.)

Lightness as an Empirical Perception, Based on Previous Experience

It is clear from all these demonstrations that the perception of lightness is a complicated process. Contrast across edges and boundaries may be the first step in an analysis of lightness, but there are clearly a number of other influences coming in at higher levels of the system.

Purves and his colleagues have suggested that the overall perception of lightness is an empirical process, based on previous experience of situations encountered in viewing a variety of scenes (Purves & Lotto, 2003). In support of this they have conducted a number of experiments pointing out the similarities between the various phenomena or illusions described earlier (Mach, Cornsweet, Adelson, Anderson, Gilchrist, Chubb, White, etc.) and situations found in the real world. They have also pointed out how these illusions can accentuate each other (Fig. 3–11). Unfortunately their hypothesis does not state where in the brain this empirical process may take place, nor whether the learning occurs during development of an individual or evolution of the species. We will therefore have to proceed with a discussion of how and where lightness perception is dealt with

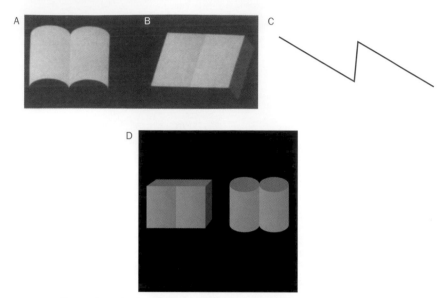

FIGURE 3.9 Two surfaces both with the luminance profile shown in the lower part of the figure.
The rectangles on the left appear different, with the left rectangle darker than the right.
The cylinders on the right appear the same and are seen as two cylinders with a gradient
of illumination across them. (Reprinted from Knill & Kersten, 1991, with kind permission of
MacMillan Publishers.)

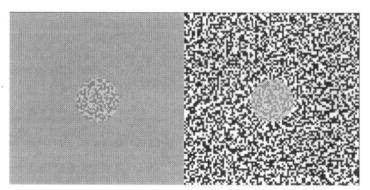

FIGURE 3.10 The two spots are identical—they have the same lightness and contrast. However,
the right spot appears to have less contrast, because it is embedded in a pattern of higher
contrast than the left one. (Reprinted from Chubb et al., 1989, with kind permission of the
authors.)

in the visual system by starting at the lowest level (the retina) and proceeding to
higher levels (lateral geniculate, V1, V2, and higher areas of visual cortex) and
describing correlations between responses in those areas and perception. There
is almost no literature on the development of lightness perception, so the whole

FIGURE 3.11 Enhancement of the Cornsweet illusion by a variety of cues (perspective, orientation, texture, additional gradients and objects, and a distinctive background) that all suggest that there are two surfaces with different levels of illumination on them. The average luminance in the upper background is the same that that in the lower background. (Reprinted from Purves & Lotto, 1999, with kind permission of the Society for Neuroscience.)

question of whether some aspects of lightness perception are learned rather than innate will be left aside.

Processing in the Retina

Mach, in his investigations of Mach bands, suggested that they are created because the visual system takes a second differential of the scene, and that this probably occurs because of lateral interactions in the retina (see Ratliff, 1965, for summary and translations). We now know that ganglion cells, which transmit the output of the retina, respond almost exclusively to contrast rather than luminance. In the ganglion cells of the mammalian retina there are two basic responses, one when the light is turned on in the center of the receptive field, inhibited by larger stimuli, and the other when the light is turned off, also inhibited by larger stimuli (Fig. 2–4; Kuffler, 1953). One type of cell essentially signals areas that are lighter than the background, and the other signals areas that are darker than the background. A few cells signal luminance, to control the pupillary response (see Appendix), but they are very much a minority.

Cells in the lateral geniculate nucleus have properties much like the ganglion cells, except that the lateral inhibition is stronger, so that the response to uniform illumination is reduced (Hubel, 1961). Thus, the signals reaching the visual cortex deal almost entirely with contrast. Other factors influencing the perception of lightness have to be superimposed on these incoming signals.

Processing in Primary Visual Cortex

Paradiso and colleagues investigated the modulation of responses by the remote surround as well as the immediate surround; they compared results in optic tract, lateral geniculate, and primary visual cortex (V1; Rossi & Paradiso, 1999). Their stimuli are illustrated in Figure 3–12 and were (1) a constant gray in the receptive field, with flanks modulated sinusoidally in time; (2) a black center with luminance-modulated flanks; (3) luminance-modulated flanks with drifting bars in the receptive field; or (4) luminance modulation in the center with static gray flanks. The flanks were outside the receptive field by at least 3° on each side. The responses were then correlated with the perception of lightness (physiological responses in cats, and perception in humans). Even in V1, only 10% of the cells correlated with perception in all these situations. In LGN it was fewer, and in the retina, none. Their conclusion is that the responses to contrast found in the retina are not enough to produce the correct perception of lightness. This is supported by functional magnetic resonance imaging (fMRI) experiments with humans

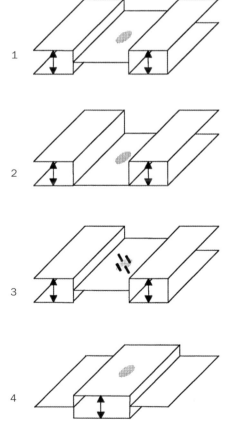

FIGURE 3.12 Stimuli used by Rossi et al. to investigate the effect of surrounds on lightness. Small oval in the middle represents the receptive field of the cell. Vertical level represents the luminance of the stimulus. (1) Central stimulus is kept constant at a mid-level, and flanks are modulated sinusoidally in luminance above and below it. (2) Central stimulus is a constant low level, with the flanks modulated. (3) The receptive field is stimulated with drifting gratings while the flanks are modulated. (4) The flanks are kept constant and the center is modulated. (Reprinted from Rossi et al., 1999, with kind permission of the Society for Neuroscience.)

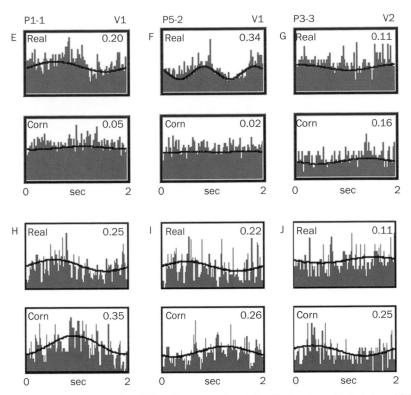

FIGURE 3.13 Responses in V1 and V2 to "Cornsweet" and "Real" stimuli modulated sinusoidally in time (see text). (*E*) A cell in V1 that responds more to the real stimulus than the Cornsweet. (*F*) A cell in a V2 pale stripe that also responds more to the Real stimulus than the Cornsweet stimulus. (*G–J*) Four cells in V2 thin stripes that respond as well or better to the Cornsweet stimulus than to the Real stimulus. (Reprinted from Roe et al., 2005, with kind permission of the National Academy of Sciences.)

(Pereverzeva & Murray, 2008). Further processing is required in the LGN and V1, and more after that.

Kinoshita and Komatsu (2001) came to the same conclusion when they recorded responses in V1 in awake macaques, finding that about 30% responded to changes in luminance and about 60% responded to changes in lightness. Thus, even with simple stimuli that do not take account of the effects of shadows, curvature, or transparency, few responses are related to lightness. More processing at higher levels is required.

Comparison of Responses in V2 with V1

Comparison of the responses of cells in V2 and V1 has primarily involved the O'Brien-Craik-Cornsweet demonstration (Fig. 3–3), where a sharp boundary with slow gradients of luminance on each side of it makes the two sides appear different in lightness but uniform across their extent (Roe et al., 2005). The two sides are sinusoidally modulated in time, and the response of a cell whose receptive field is away from the boundary is recorded (Cornsweet) compared to its response to a stimulus with the same boundary, but no slow gradient of luminance away from it (Real). Most cells in V1 and the V2 pale and thick stripes respond to the luminance changes seen in the Real stimulus, more than to the lightness changes without luminance changes seen in the Cornsweet stimulus (Fig. 3–13E and F). On the other hand, cells in the thin stripes of V2 respond to modulation of the Cornsweet stimulus as much as, or more than, the Real stimulus (Fig. 3–13G–J). As described in Chapter 2, the V2 thin stripes are also concerned with color. It seems that the color areas are segregated from the lightness areas (Wang et al., 2007). Moreover, there are two sets of lightness areas, one concerned with light objects, and the other concerned with dark objects, coming from the ON-center and OFF-center cells in the retina (Fig. 3–14). Experiments in humans confirm that primary visual cortex does not respond to the O'Brien-Craik-Cornsweet illusions, whereas areas in the caudal region of the intraparietal sulcus and the lateral occipital sulcus do (Perna et al., 2005). Unfortunately, techniques in humans cannot distinguish the various stripes within V2.

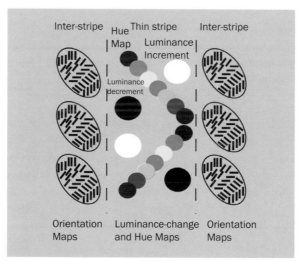

FIGURE 3–14. Schematic diagram suggesting a somewhat idealized arrangement of areas in the thin stripes of V2. The interstripes on each side respond to various orientations of the stimulus. Within the V2 thin stripes, there are areas responding to color, and areas responding to lightness. The areas responding to lightness can be divided into those responding to increases and those responding to decreases. (Reprinted from Wang et al., 2007, with kind permission of Oxford University Press.)

References

Adelson, E. H. (1993). Perceptual organization and the judgment of brightness. *Science,* *262,* 2042–2044.

Anderson, B. L., & Winawer, J. (2005). Image segmentation and lightness perception. *Nature, 434,* 79–83.

Anderson, B. L., & Winawer, J. (2008). Layered image representations and the computation of surface lightness. *Journal of Vision, 8*(18), 11–22.

Chubb, C., Sperling, G., & Solomon, J. A. (1989). Texture interactions determine perceived contrast. *Proceedings of the National Academy of Sciences USA, 86,* 9631–9635.

Cornsweet, T. N. (1970). *Visual perception.* New York: Academic Press.

Gilchrist, A. L. (1977). Perceived lightness depends on perceived spatial arrangement. *Science, 195,* 185–187.

Gilchrist, A. L. (2006). *Seeing black and white.* New York: Oxford University Press.

Helmholtz, H. (1875/1962). *Treatise on physiological optics.* New York: Dover.

Helson, H. (1963). Studies of anomalous contrast and assimilation. *Journal of the Optical Society of America - A, 53,* 179–184.

Hess, C., & Pretori, H. (1894). Messende Untersuchungen uber die Gesetzmassigkeit des simultanen Helligkeits-contrastes. *Archives of Ophthalmologie, 40,* 1–24.

Hubel, D. H. (1961). Integrative action in the cat's lateral geniculate body. *Journal of Physiology 155,* 385–398.

Kinoshita, M., & Komatsu, H. (2001). Neural representation of the luminance and brightness of a uniform surface in the macaque primary visual cortex. *Journal of Neurophysiology, 86,* 2559–2570.

Knill, D. C., & Kersten, D. (1991). Apparent surface curvature affects lightness perception. *Nature, 351,* 228–230.

Kuffler, S. W. (1953). Discharge patterns and functional organization of mammalian retina. *Journal of Neurophysiology, 16,* 37–68.

Land, E. H., & McCann, J. J. (1971). Lightness and retinex theory. *Journal of the Optical Society of America – A, 61,* 1–11.

O'Brien, V. (1958). Contour perception, illusion and reality. *Journal of the Optical Society of America – A, 48,* 112–119.

Pereverzeva, M., & Murray, S. O. (2008). Neural activity in human V1 correlates with dynamic lightness induction. *Journal of Vision, 8,* 1–10.

Perna, A., Tosetti, M., Montanaro, D., & Morrone, M. C. (2005). Neuronal mechanisms for illusory brightness perception in humans. *Neuron, 47,* 645–651.

Purves, D., & Lotto, R. B. (2003). *Why we see what we do.* Sunderland, MA: Sinauer Associates.

Ratliff, F. (1965). *Mach bands: Quantitative studies on neural networks in the retina.* San Francisco, CA: Holden-Day.

Roe, A. W., Lu, H. D., & Hung, C. P. (2005). Cortical processing of a brightness illusion. *Proceedings of the National Academy of Sciences USA, 102,* 3869–3874.

Rossi, A. F., & Paradiso, M. A. (1999). Neural correlates of perceived brightness in the retina, lateral geniculate nucleus, and striate cortex. *Journal of Neuroscience, 19,* 6145–6156.

Shevell, S. K., Holliday, I., & Whittle, P. (1992). Two separate neural mechanisms of brightness induction. *Vision Research*, 32, 2331–2340.

von Bezold, W. (1876). *The theory of color.* Boston, MA: Prang.

Wang, Y., Xiao, Y., & Felleman, D. J. (2007). V2 thin stripes contain spatially organized representations of achromatic luminance change. *Cerebral Cortex*, 17, 116–129.

White, M. (1979). A new effect of pattern on perceived lightness. *Perception, 8*, 413–416.

4

Color Vision

To see color, one needs at least two classes of photoreceptor, with different spectral sensitivities. A single class of photoreceptors with the same spectral sensitivity will just signal lightness. Humans have four classes—rods, and three classes of cone. One can see color using rods and the red-absorbing cones at the appropriate level of illumination (McCann, 1972), but in bright daylight the rods are saturated, so the three classes of cone are used. Our daylight vision is thus trichromatic—that is, one needs a three-dimensional space to describe colors, specified by the signals coming from the three classes of cone.

George Palmer (1777) suggested that color vision is trichromatic, and so did Thomas Young (1802). The idea was championed by Helmholtz (1875/1962). A number of experiments by Maxwell (1855), using spinning wheels with variable sectors of colored papers on them to produce additive mixtures of the three colors, showed that any color can be matched by a mixture of three others (sometimes the match has to be made by matching a mixture of two with a mixture of the other two, rather than a mixture of three matching the fourth). The photoreceptors have been identified, and their spectral sensitivities measured in individual cone cells (Brown & Wald 1964; Marks, Dobelle, & Macnichol, 1964). They are referred to as L (long-wavelength, or red-absorbing), M (medium wavelength, or green-absorbing), and S (short wavelength, or blue-absorbing) cones (Fig. 4–1).

Opponency in Color Vision

Ewald Hering (1878/1964) pointed out that some color combinations are not seen—there are red-yellows (orange), blue-greens (cyan), red-blues (magenta), and yellow-greens (chartreuse) but no red-greens or yellow-blues. He therefore suggested that colors consist of three opponent pairs, red against green, blue against yellow, and black against white. One can measure unique hues (Hurvich & Jameson, 1957), which may be on the yellow-blue axis (neither red nor green) or on the red-green axis (neither yellow nor blue). These tend to be about the same for different people.

In the nineteenth century the ideas of Helmholtz and Hering were regarded as disagreeing with each other, primarily because Hering thought of his opponent **49**

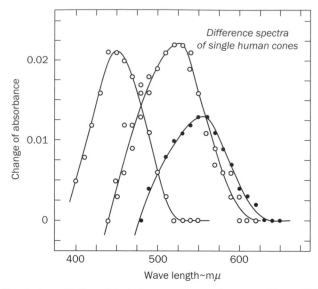

FIGURE 4–1. Spectral sensitivities of single human cones; an L cone peaking at 560 nm, an M cone peaking at 530 nm, and an S cone peaking at 460 nm. (Reprinted from Brown & Wald, 1964, with kind permission of AAAS.)

processes as being within photoreceptors. However, a number of people early in the twentieth century pointed out that the two concepts are compatible if one thinks of color vision as comprising two stages, or zones, with three classes of photoreceptor feeding into an opponent color stage (see Judd, 1966 for a summary). As we shall see, this is now known to be the case.

Simultaneous and Successive Color Contrast

The most saturated colors are seen by contrast with other colors. An object is most colored when placed in a multicolored scene illuminated by a variety of wavelengths. A monochromatic light seen in isolation appears comparatively colorless. The scene illuminated by a sodium street light, which is pure 589 nm (a yellow wavelength in the spectrum), is not a strong yellow. To see yellow, one needs a patch of sodium light surrounded by a variety of other wavelengths. Similarly, monochromatic light of 650 nm does not give the most saturated red, 540 nm the most saturated green, or 450 nm the most saturated blue. In all cases, contrast with other wavelengths is needed to produce strong colors.

Two examples of color contrast are successive and simultaneous color contrast, although the classical illustrations of these do not produce colors as saturated as those in a multicolored scene. A patch of gray seen after a patch of red will appear greenish, and a patch of gray seen after a patch of green will appear reddish (successive color contrast, or colored afterimages).

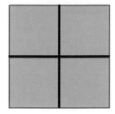

FIGURE 4–2. Successive color contrast, or colored afterimages. Fixate at the center of the upper display for several seconds, then look at the center of the lower display, where colors will appear—greenish top left, reddish bottom right, bluish top right, and yellowish bottom left. A stronger effect is seen with longer gaze at the upper display, and good fixation.

This can be seen in Figure 4–2: fixate at the center of the upper display for several seconds, then transfer your gaze to the center of the lower display. The lower display will appear to have colors switched diagonally from those in the upper display.

Similarly, a gray spot in a red surround appears greenish, and a gray spot in a green surround appears reddish (simultaneous color contrast). Like lightness contrast, this is not very dramatic when seen side by side on the pages of a book, because the whole scene, not just the immediate surround, affects the perception. However, it can be powerful when viewed in a dark room, and it has been used extensively by painters over several centuries, most recently by Josef Albers. One demonstration is in Figure 4–3, where the spot on the right appears warmish and the spot on the left appears coolish, even though they are in fact the same.

Color Assimilation

A line is sometimes seen in contrast to the continuation of the line, rather than in contrast to its immediate surround—the color version of the White effect discussed in Chapter 3. This was studied extensively by von Bezold (1876) and is known as color assimilation. The effect is demonstrated in Figure 4–4. The words ANNUAL and REVIEW have the same wavelength composition, and so do the words OF and PSYCHOLOGY, but they appear to be very different colors. The lines making up the words are seen in contrast to the yellow and blue lines that form their continuation, and thus they appear to take on the colors of the blue and yellow lines above and below them—consequently the word *assimilation.*

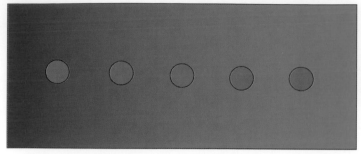

FIGURE 4–3. Color contrast. The right spot looks pinker than the left.

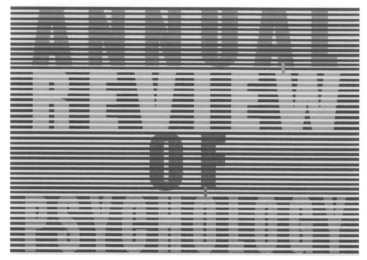

FIGURE 4–4. The words ANNUAL and REVIEW are the same wavelength composition, as seen by the connector between the A and the W. Similarly, the same is true for the words OF and PSYCHOLOGY, as seen by the connector between the letters F and O. However, the colors appear distinctly different—ANNUAL and OF are both seen in contrast to the horizontal yellow lines, whereas REVIEW and PSYCHOLOGY are seen in contrast to the horizontal blue lines, as seen by the connector between the letters F and O. (Reprinted from Shevell & Kingdom, 2008, with kind permission of Annual Reviews.)

Color Constancy

Simultaneous color contrast leads to color constancy, just as lightness contrast leads to lightness constancy. Color constancy is the property that the color of an object does not vary when placed in different immediate surroundings or in different illuminants. Thus, color constancy helps in the recognition of objects. This is not absolutely true in all circumstances, but it is largely true. Numerous authors have suggested various mechanisms by which color constancy may be achieved (Smithson, 2005). In particular, Helmholtz (1875/1962) suggested that the illuminant is discounted by unconscious inference. Similarly, Land suggested in his first version of the retinex theory that the visual system evaluates three numbers: the reflectance that an object has relative to a white object placed in the same position in red light, green light, or blue light (Land, 1959, 1983; see images C, D, and E in Fig. 4–5). He recognized that the visual system makes this calculation without placing a white object there, and in later versions of the retinex theory he came up with an algorithm for making the calculation by determining comparisons across boundaries between objects (Land, 1983, 1986). The essential concept here is that the visual system makes comparisons across the scene within the long-wave system, medium-wave system, and short-wave system, then combines the three comparisons. Unfortunately, what the visual system actually does is to make local comparisons between the L and M systems (H in Fig. 4–5) and the L + M and S systems (I in Fig. 4–5), then make the long-distance comparisons at a higher level of processing. Thus, the retinex hypothesis is not the way that the process works physiologically. Nearly all other quantifications of color constancy are similarly unable to predict how the calculations are actually made by the neurons in the retina, lateral geniculate, and cerebral cortex.

In color perception, as in lightness perception, the visual system has to distinguish a boundary due to a change in the illumination from a boundary between one object and another in the same illumination (Amano & Foster, 2004). Amazingly, this is accomplished, and it has been dramatically illustrated by Lotto and Purves (2000) as shown in Figure 4–6. In both upper and lower displays, the squares with a black dot in the center are physically identical. In the upper display, the square in the left circle is seen as bluish, and the square in the right circle is seen as brownish, as appropriate for a rosy illuminant on the left and a bluish illuminant on the right. In the lower display, the two squares are seen as much closer in color, as appropriate for two circles bathed with the same illuminant. How the visual system can achieve perceptions such as this is a mystery, leading Purves and his colleagues to suggest that it is due to empirical experience.

Color differences, like lightness differences, also appear more or less vivid, depending on the contrast of the surroundings (Brown & MacLeod, 1997). The six rectangles in the lower display can be seen to be different shades of gray when seen against a plain background (Fig. 4–7b). However, they appear to be almost identical when they are embedded in a more vivid surround in the upper display (Fig. 4–7a). The mean of the surrounds in the two displays are the same: it is just the variance that is different.

Processing of Color in the Brain

The fact that the visual system can accomplish all of this in an instant, largely independent of eye movements and without needing time to ponder, is a marvel. We do not yet understand how the higher levels of the visual system achieve color

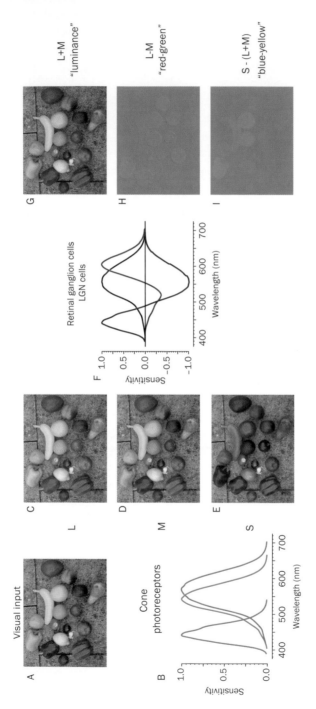

FIGURE 4–5. The original scene (*A*) is viewed through L, M, and S photoreceptors (*B*), giving three color separation images (*C*, *D*, and *E*). The photoreceptors feed into three channels, a blue/yellow, a luminance, and a red/green channel. L and M photoreceptors contribute to the luminance image (*G*), L-M photoreceptors to the red/green channel (*H*), and S-(L+M) photoreceptors to the blue/yellow channel (*I*). (Reprinted from Gegenfurtner, 2003, with kind permission of MacMillan Publishers.)

A

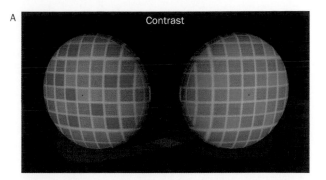

Contrast

B

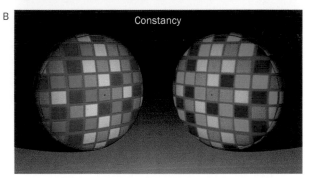

Constancy

FIGURE 4–6. Differences in illumination compared to differences with neighboring objects. In the upper display (*A*), the left disk appears to be illuminated by a rosy light, and the right by a bluish light, and the central square on the left appears bluish, and on the right appears brownish, as appropriate for the two different illuminations. In the lower display (*B*), the two disks appear to be in the same illumination, and the two central squares appear to be much closer in color. (Reprinted from Lotto & Purves, 2000, with kind permission of the National Academy of Sciences.)

A

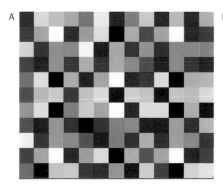

B

FIGURE 4–7. Six gray rectangles are seen. Against a brightly colored background they appear to be quite similar in color (*A*). Against a gray background, they are seen to be different (*B*). (Reprinted from Brown & MacLeod, 1997, with kind permission of Elsevier.)

constancy and distinguish illumination boundaries from reflectance boundaries. All we can do is describe what processing goes on at lower levels of the system, where cells are organized to produce opponency and contrast, and state which areas at higher levels of the system are particularly concerned with color, and what happens after lesions in those areas.

Processing in the Retina and Lateral Geniculate Nucleus

As described earlier, there are three classes of cone photoreceptor: L, M, and S cones, which absorb light in the red, green, and blue portions of the spectrum. They are most abundant in the center of the retina near the fovea; they fall off in abundance as one moves toward the periphery of the retina. Therefore, color vision becomes poor when one looks at objects in the periphery, and very poor in the far periphery (see Hansen, Pracejus, & Gegenfurtner, 2009, for details). In the very center of the fovea, the S cones are absent, avoiding problems from the chromatic aberration of the eye, and making vision in a small region there dichromatic.

Many ganglion cells in the retina give opponent color responses. These may be red/green (excited by L cones and inhibited by M cones, or vice versa) or yellow/blue (usually excited by S cones and inhibited by L and M cones, sometimes vice versa). The red/green cells are midget ganglion cells, receiving input from a single cone in the center of their receptive fields near the fovea and from a group of cones further in the periphery of their receptive fields, with opposing input from lateral inhibition through horizontal and/or amacrine cells (Fig. 4–8, left). Yellow/blue cells excited by blue light get input from two types of bipolar cell: one in the inner part of the inner plexiform layer, which deals with ON responses, the other in the outer part of the inner plexiform layer, which deals with OFF responses (Fig. 4–8, right). Large sparse bistratified cells and small bistratified cells give ON responses to blue light and OFF responses to yellow light; large sparse monostratified cells give ON responses to yellow light and OFF responses to blue (Dacey, 1996; see Fig. 2–6 in Chapter 2).

The responses to color in the lateral geniculate nucleus, where opponent color cells were first discovered in the primate (De Valois et al., 1966), are much the same as those in the retina. There are red/green cells, yellow/blue cells, and cells that respond to lightness (black/white). In some cases, the inhibitory influence extends further than the excitatory influence (types I and III; Fig. 4–9); in other cases, the inhibitory and excitatory influences have the same lateral extent (type II; Wiesel & Hubel, 1966). As described in Chapter 2, the lateral geniculate nucleus has six layers, and the top four (parvocellular or P) deal with color. There are also cells between the layers, called koniocellular, or K cells. The midget (red/green) ganglion cells tend to project to the P layers, and the blue ON bistratified cells tend to project to the K population (Hendry & Reid, 2000). A macaque with

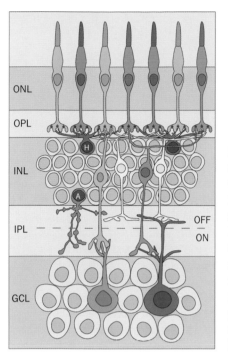

FIGURE 4–8. Connections of photoreceptors to opponent color cells in the retina. On the left, a green/red ganglion cell is connected to a midget bipolar cell and a single M cone in the center of its receptive field, and to both L and M cones in the periphery of its receptive field. On the right, a blue/yellow ganglion cell is connected to S cones through bipolar cells in the center of its receptive field, and to L and M cones through lateral connections for the periphery of its receptive field. (Reprinted from Calkins et al., 2004, with kind permission of MIT Press.)

a lesion of the P layers, which included the K cells between them, could not make the most basic discrimination of red, green, or blue spots from yellow spots in the area of the lesion (Schiller, Logothetis, & Charles, 1990). This shows that color signals all pass through these layers on their way to higher centers.

Color Responses in Primary Visual Cortex

The red/green cells in the upper layers of the LGN project to layer IVCβ in primary visual cortex, and from there to layers II and III (see Chapter 2). Within layers II and III, there are pegs of cytochrome oxidase staining known as blobs. Cells in these blobs are particularly concerned with color (Livingstone & Hubel, 1984; Lu & Roe, 2008); these cells receive input directly from the K cells in the lateral geniculate and indirectly through layer IVCβ from the P cells. Layer IVA, which is a very thin layer next to layers II and III, gets input from the blue OFF cells, with input from the blue ON cells above it (Chatterjee & Callaway, 2003).

In the blobs of V1 one finds a new class of color-coded cell called double opponent. These are cells that are opponent for color and also for space. As an example, a cell might give an ON response to red light and an OFF response to green light in the center of its receptive field, and an OFF response to red light and an ON response to green light in the periphery of the receptive field (Fig. 4–10). Such a cell gives little response to white light in any part of the

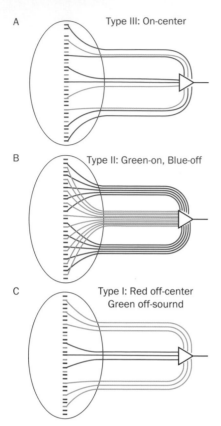

A   Type III: On-center

B   Type II: Green-on, Blue-off

C   Type I: Red off-center
     Green off-sournd

FIGURE 4–9. Three types of cell in the macaque lateral geniculate nucleus. Type I (C) is color coded, with ON input from one cone type in the center of its receptive field, and OFF input from another cone type in the periphery of its receptive field, or vice versa. Type II (B) is also color coded, with ON input from one cone type, and OFF input from another cone type with the same lateral extent. Type III (A) has a center-surround organization to its receptive field, but no color coding, although the input to the center of the receptive field may come from a single cone type. (Reprinted from Wiesel & Hubel, 1966, with kind permission of the American Physiological Society.)

receptive field (because the L and M inputs oppose each other) or to uniform illumination (because the inputs to the center and surround of the receptive field oppose each other). The largest response comes from contrasting colors in the center and surrounds of the receptive field. In particular, a gray spot in a red surround gives the same response as a green spot in a gray surround, corresponding to the phenomenon of simultaneous color contrast (Daw, 1967). Double opponent cells are found in the layer II and III blobs but not in layer IVCβ (Livingstone & Hubel, 1984).

We still do not know how inputs from the lateral geniculate nucleus converge to form the double opponent cells in V1. It is clear that Type I cells do not respond to simultaneous color contrast. Indeed, a red spot in a green surround will give little response in the type I cell illustrated in Figure 4–10: what is required for a color contrast response would be an ON response to red light in the center of the receptive field, and an ON response, not an OFF response, to a green light on the surround. Such cells have not been found. Double opponent cells may be formed by excitatory input from a Type II cell to the center of the receptive field, and by inhibitory input from similar Type II cells to the surround. However, few red/green Type II cells have been found, so the subject is unresolved.

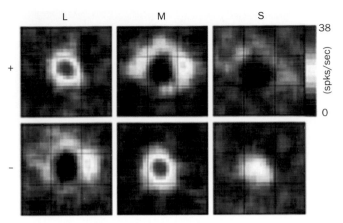

FIGURE 4–10. Response of a double opponent cell in a V1 blob from macaque visual cortex. The stimuli were devised to isolate the responses of the L, M, and S cones, respectively. + shows the response to turning the stimulus on, and – to turning it off. In the center of the receptive field, the response increased for turning L cones on, or M cones off. In the periphery of the receptive field, the response increased for turning M cones on, or L cones off. S cones acted like M cones, but less vigorously. Note that the colors denote the magnitude of the response, according to the scale at the right top, not the wavelengths of the stimulus. (Photograph courtesy of Bevil Conway.)

There has been controversy regarding how many of the cells in the blobs are double opponent, and as to whether there are separate blobs for red/green cells and yellow/blue cells. According to recent evidence using stimuli that isolate the contributions of L, M, and S cones, a significant percentage of color-coded cells in V1 are double opponent (Conway, 2001; Conway & Livingstone, 2006; Johnson, Hawken, & Shapley, 2001). Moreover, the areas responding to red, green, yellow, and blue partially overlap each other (Fig. 4–11; Roe, Lu, & Crewther, 2007; Xiao, Casti, Xiao, & Kaplan, 2007). There may not be separate blobs for red/green and yellow/blue, but there are places where a penetration with a microelectrode will encounter only red/green cells, places with only yellow/blue cells, and places with both.

The areas in layers II and III between the blobs are concerned with orientation (Chapter 7). Some of the cells in those areas respond to colors as well as orientation, whereas less than 50% of the cells in the blobs respond to orientation, depending on the stimulus. In some cases, the stimulus that gives a response can be quite complicated, for example, a bar with a particular orientation of limited length, moving in a particular direction but not the opposite direction, and with red light on one side and green on the other (Fig. 4–12; Michael, 1979). In the case of this particular cell, all these conditions had to be fulfilled. Lengthening the stimulus, changing the orientation or direction of movement, or removing either the red or green lights reduced the response.

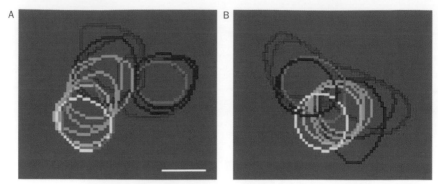

FIGURE 4–11. Areas responding to different colors around the blobs in V1 overlap each other. The scale marker represents 100 microns, which is somewhat smaller than the size of a blob. Two separate blobs (A and B) are shown. (Reprinted from Xiao et al., 2007, with kind permission of Elsevier.)

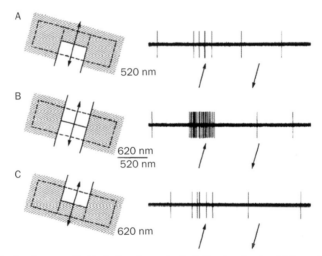

FIGURE 4–12. A cell responding to both color and orientation in primate striate cortex. The cell gives a vigorous response to a short boundary with red light above and green light below moving upward (B). Little response is seen for movement downward, or for movement of the red light alone (C), or for movement of the green light alone (A). (Reprinted from Michael, 1979, with kind permission of the American Physiological Society.)

Area V2

The blobs in V1 project to the thin stripes in V2, where color is also processed (Hubel & Livingstone, 1987). Like cells in the blobs of V1, the receptive fields of cells in these thin stripes tend not to be oriented. There is some segregation of different colors along the stripes, arranged in the order of colors in the spectrum (Xiao, Wang, & Felleman, 2003; see Fig. 3–14). The pale stripes in V2, which receive projections from the areas between the blobs in V1, also have a number of cells that are color coded. Indeed, the percentage of cells that are color coded in the thin stripes and pale stripes may not be too different (Friedman, Zhou, & von der Heydt, 2003). As in layers II/III of V1, the difference lies primarily in the orientation selectivity rather than in the color coding.

While many of the cells in the thin stripes respond to color contrast, like the double opponent cells in V1, they do not give a response that tallies with color constancy (Moutoussis & Zeki, 2002). This is probably coded at a higher level of the system (see later).

The nature of the receptive fields of cells in the pale stripes of V2 has not been studied carefully. One would assume that some further processing would take place, so that the stimuli required to give a response in some cells in V2 would be even more complicated than the cell found in V1 (illustrated in Fig. 4–12). How far this is true remains to be studied.

Area V4

Area V4 was first identified by Zeki (1973) as an area with a high percentage of color-coded cells. The actual percentage found depends on the stimuli used and the criteria applied; it has gone down over the years as different investigators have gone over the subject. There are a number of cells in V4 that respond to features other than color. However, there is no doubt that V4 has something to do with the perception of color.

Zeki and his colleagues have distinguished wavelength cells, which respond to a particular wavelength independent of the color perceived, and color cells, which respond to the color perceived independent of the wavelengths illuminating the center of the receptive field using "Mondrian" stimuli (Fig. 4–13). They have suggested that few color cells are found in V1, whereas color cells are found in V4 at a high percentage (Kusunoki, Moutoussis, & Zeki, 2006). This is logical, since cells in V4 have larger receptive fields with more extensive suppressive surrounds (Schein & Desimone, 1990) and more widespread connections across the corpus callosum. It makes sense that the double opponent cells in V1 should provide the local computations of contrast across boundaries suggested in Land's later versions of his retinex model, and that longer-range connections in V4 should coordinate these local computations to provide color constancy. However, the concept that all cells in V4 and none in V1 are color cells, as opposed to wavelength cells, is certainly an oversimplification. Inter alia, the size of the center of the receptive field, which is smaller in V1, has to be taken into account, and some cells in V1 are color cells by Zeki's definition if the stimuli are adjusted appropriately (Wachtler, Sejnowski, & Albright, 2003).

Lesions in V4 affect color discrimination a little, but they do not abolish it altogether as lesions of the P and K layers of the lateral geniculate nucleus do (Heywood & Cowey, 1987; Schiller & Lee, 1991). Moreover, lesions of V4 affect the

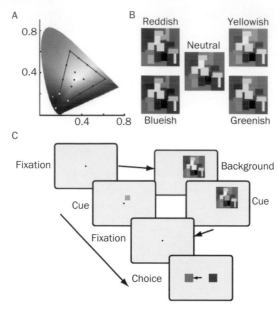

FIGURE 4–13. Macaque cells in V4 are tested for color constancy. The macaque is presented with a "Mondrian" stimulus in one of various illuminants centered over the receptive field of the cell. (*A*) The illuminants shown on the CIE chromaticity diagram. (*B*) The appearance of the Mondrian stimuli in the different illuminants. (*C*) The procedure—the macaque is shown the stimulus, and trained to match the color of the central square with one of two choices, by making a saccade to the choice. (Reprinted from Kusunoki et al., 2006, with kind permission of the American Physiological Society.)

perception of shape significantly. These observations make two points: first, that there are areas outside V4 dealing with color, and second, that there are components of V4 that deal with properties other than color. These points are supported by a recent study that finds groups of color-coded cells near V4 in the dorsal part of posterior inferotemporal cortex (PITd) and the posterior part of temporooccipital cortex (TEO) as well as in V4. The cells that are color coded form what the authors have named globs, interspersed with the cells dealing with other properties in the interglobs (Conway, Moeller, & Tsao, 2007; Tanigawa, Lu, & Roe, 2010). However, insofar as lesions of V4 do affect color vision, the effect is more on color constancy than on wavelength discrimination (Wild, Butler, Garden, & Kulikowski, 1985).

Inferotemporal Cortex

Inferotemporal cortex (IT) has been investigated more for its coding of complex shapes than for its coding for color (see Chapter 7). One study that looked at the responses of 492 cells in some detail found about 20% of them that responded to one group of colors more than others (Komatsu, Ideura, Kaji, & Yamane, 1992). Figure 4–14 shows some examples (the position of the color is given by the x-y coordinates of the CIE chromaticity diagram, and the size of the response is given by the size of the circle at that position). There is a cell responding to greens and yellows (*A*); a cell responding to reds (*B*); a cell responding to greens, yellows, and purples (*C*); and a cell responding to saturated stimuli of all hues, but not to whites or unsaturated stimuli (*D*). The stimuli were simple ones: circles, squares, or gratings. One assumes that cells in IT, which can give selective responses to complicated shapes, would also give selective responses to stimuli of a particular shape and a particular color, but it is time consuming to test for this; no study has attempted it yet. It seems likely that IT is divided into some regions that are concerned with color, and some that are not, just like V1, V2, and V4 (Harada et al., 2007; Tootell, Nelissen, Vanduffel, & Orban, 2004). Within the regions that

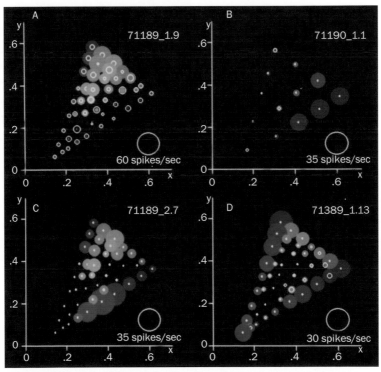

FIGURE 4–14. Responses of four cells in primate inferotemporal cortex. The responses are plotted at the position of the color in the CIE chromaticity diagram, and the size of the response is denoted by the size of the circle. (*A*) Cell responding to greens and yellows. (*B*) Cell responding to reds. (*C*) Cell responding to greens, yellows, and purples. (*D*) Cell responding to most saturated hues, but not to unsaturated ones. (Reprinted from Komatsu et al., 1992, with kind permission of the Society for Neuroscience.)

are concerned with color, color-tuned neurons are clustered according to color preference (Conway & Tsao, 2009).

Lesions of the inferotemporal cortex anterior to V4 in the macaque lead to more severe deficits in color perception than do lesions of V4 (Heywood, Gaffan, & Cowey, 1995). The macaques could perform achromatic discriminations adequately. The severity of the deficit depends on the extent and position of the lesion, and on the task that the macaque is asked to perform (see Merigan, Pasternak, Fahle, & Greenlee, 2003).

Deficits of Color Vision in Humans

COLOR BLINDNESS

The term *color blindness* is used to refer to a photoreceptor deficit in which one of the pigments in the L, M, or S cones is missing or has an abnormal spectral sensitivity. It is common, affecting 8% of males and 0.04% of females (the genes for the L and M cones are on the X chromosome), and it has been known at least since the time of the chemist John Dalton (1766–1844), who described his own case. Six L pigments have been found, with spectral sensitivity peaks ranging from 550 to 560 nm, and five M pigments, with spectral sensitivity peaks ranging from 530 to 536 nm (see Neitz, Neitz, Chalupa, & Werner, 2004). People with defects in the L pigment are known as protans, and people with defects in the M pigment are known as deutans. The pigment may be missing altogether, in which case the subject is a dichromat, or the subject may have two pigments from the L group, or two pigments from the M group, instead of one from the L group and one from the M group, in which case the subject is a trichromat but makes abnormal matches of wavelengths. Occasionally both L and M pigments are missing, leading to blue-cone monochromacy.

The gene for the S cone pigment is on chromosome 7, so deficits in this gene are not gender linked. Deficits are rare, and the condition is known as tritanopia. Sometimes there is a deficit in the ion channels in the cone photoreceptors, leading to complete color blindness. This is extremely rare except in a Micronesian population, where 5% of the population is affected (see Neitz, Neitz, Chalupa, & Werner, 2004).

ACHROMATOPSIA

Achromatopsia, more specifically called cerebral achromatopsia or cerebral color blindness, is a deficit in color vision caused by a lesion in extrastriate cortex. The lesions involve the anterior inferior cortex, in medial occipitotemporal (fusiform) gyrus and/or lingual gyrus (Bouvier & Engel, 2006; Meadows, 1974; Zeki, 1990). Needless to say, since these are human lesions that are not well controlled, there are a variety of results depending on the extent of the lesion. If it includes the lower lip of the calcarine sulcus, there will also be a scotoma in the upper field. If it extends anteriorly into the fusiform gyrus, there will also be an inability to recognize faces (prosopagnosia—see Chapter 8). Not many patients have been seen who have achromatopsia without prosopagnosia, but they do exist, showing that there is an area specifically dealing with color vision (Kolmel, 1988). This area is equivalent to an area in the macaque that is wider than V4 and probably anterior to it.

Patients with achromatopsia make the same wavelength matches as normal people. When asked to color a simple child's drawing with the appropriate colors, given a choice of a variety of crayons, they take a very long time and use the wrong colors (Pearlman et al., 1979; Fig. 4–15). However, they can name the colors of the objects (tomatoes, red; carrots, orange; and mushrooms, brown), even though the objects were all colored with the brown crayon. Tests of color vision designed to detect color blindness from the absence of one of the cone pigments (Ishihara or H-R-R plates) may be passed, while tests of color vision that depend on arranging hues (Farnsworth-Munsell test) may be failed. The common complaint is that everything looks dirty, or gray, illustrated by the woman who had all her curtains cleaned and said they that still looked dirty when they came back.

OTHER CORTICAL COLOR DEFICITS

Patients with lesions in the striate cortex may make matches appropriate for lightness constancy, but not for color constancy (Kentridge, Heywood, & Weiskrantz, 2007). In the display that was used, the circles in *a* have the same luminance, whereas the circles in *b* are adjusted to appear the same lightness (Fig. 4–16). This

FIGURE 4–15. Coloring of a child's diagram by an achromatopsic patient. Tomato, carrots, and mushrooms were all colored brown, even though red and orange crayons were available. The patient stated that the tomato was red, the carrots orange, and the mushrooms brown, although he hesitated and looked quizzical about this. The coloring took almost 30 minutes. (Reprinted from Pearlman et al., 1979, with kind permission of John Wiley & Sons.)

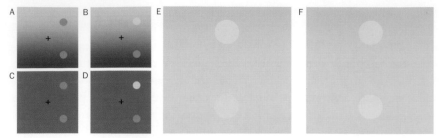

FIGURE 4–16. Stimuli used to test the perception of lightness constancy and color constancy. Two gray spots of the same luminance are shown against a gradient (a); the same spots against a uniform background are shown in (c). Two gray spots that are perceived to be the same lightness are shown against a gradient (b), and the same two spots are shown against a uniform background (d). In (e) two colored spots are seen against a gradient of color, and in (f) the colors of the two spots have been adjusted so that a normal observer judges them to be the same color. (Reprinted from Kentridge et al., 2007, with kind permission of the National Academy of Sciences.)

is demonstrated by viewing the same circles against uniform background (c and d). Similarly, the circles in e are the same wavelengths, whereas the circles in f are adjusted to appear the same color. A normal person, when asked which pairs of circles look the same, will choose b and f. The patient with a lesion of the striate cortex chose b and e. The explanation is that the process of lightness constancy is started in the retina and lateral geniculate nucleus, and these signals can bypass the striate cortex in the extrastriate pathways through the pulvinar. The process of color constancy, on the other hand, is started in striate cortex with double opponent cells and cannot be bypassed through extrastriate pathways.

There are also patients with lesions near the junction of occipital, parietal, and temporal cortex who can see colors, and would therefore not be defined as having achromatopsia, but do not match colors appropriately for color constancy (Clarke, Walsh, Schoppig, Assal, & Cowey, 1998; Ruttiger et al., 1999). They may also have deficits in color memory.

Other patients have specific difficulties in naming colors, but the world does not appear gray or dirty as in achromatopsia. Their problems are always associated with other difficulties, which vary from patient to patient, depending on the location of the lesion, but in all cases there are deficits specific to color, coming under the heading of color agnosia, or color anomia. There seem to be two general types: those that have specific visual difficulties, and those that pass visual tests and verbal tests but have problems in visuoverbal tests (see Beauvois & Saillant, 1985). The former presumably have lesions affecting the visual system; the latter likely have lesions affecting the connections between the visual system and the verbal system. In any case, the existence of these problems indicates a separation of areas dealing with color from areas dealing with other aspects of vision, and of the connections between these areas and verbal parts of the brain.

References

Amano, K., & Foster, D. H. (2004). Colour constancy under simultaneous changes in surface position and illuminant. *Proceedings of the Royal Society B, 271*, 2319–2326.

Beauvois, M-F., & Saillant, B. (1985). Optic aphasia for colours and colour agnosia: A distinction between visual and visuo-verbal impairments in the processing of colours. *Cognitive Neuropsychology 2*, 1–48.

Bouvier, S. E., & Engel, S. A. (2006). Behavioral deficits and cortical damage loci in cerebral achromatopsia. *Cerebral Cortex, 16*, 183–191.

Brown, P. K., & Wald, G. (1964). Visual pigments in single rods and cones of the human retina. Direct measurements reveal mechanisms of human night and color vision. *Science, 144*, 45–52.

Brown, R. O., & MacLeod, D. I. (1997). Color appearance depends on the variance of surround colors. *Current Biology, 7*, 844–849.

Calkins, D. J., Chalupa, L. M., & Werner, J. S. (2004). Linking retinal circuits to colour opponency. In L. M. Chalupa & J. S. Werner (Eds.), *The visual neurosciences* (pp. 989–1002). Cambridge, MA: MIT Press.

Chatterjee, S., & Callaway, E. M. (2003). Parallel colour-opponent pathways to primary visual cortex. *Nature, 426*, 668–671.

Clarke, S., Walsh, V., Schoppig, A., Assal, G., & Cowey, A. (1998). Colour constancy impairments in patients with lesions of the prestriate cortex. *Experimental Brain Research, 123*, 154–158.

Conway, B. R. (2001). Spatial structure of cone inputs to color cells in alert macaque primary visual cortex. *Journal of Neuroscience, 21*, 2768–2783.

Conway, B. R., & Livingstone, M. S. (2006). Spatial and temporal properties of cone signals in alert macaque primary visual cortex. *Journal of Neuroscience, 26*, 10826–10846.

Conway, B. R., Moeller, S., & Tsao, D. Y. (2007). Specialized color modules in macaque extrastriate cortex. *Neuron, 56*, 560–573.

Conway, B. R., & Tsao, D. Y. (2009). Color-tuned neurons are spatially clustered according to color preference within alert macaque posterior inferior temporal cortex. *Proceedings of the National Academy of Sciences USA, 106*, 18034–18039.

Dacey, D. M. (1996). Circuitry for color coding in the primate retina. *Proceedings of the National Academy of Sciences USA, 93*, 582–588.

Daw, N. W. (1967). Goldfish retina: Organization for simultaneous color contrast. *Science, 158*, 942–944.

De Valois, R. L. (1966). Analysis of response patterns of LGN cells. *Journal of the Optical Society of America – A, 56*, 966–977.

Friedman, H. S., Zhou, H., & von der Heydt, R. (2003). The coding of uniform colour figures in monkey visual cortex. *Journal of Physiology, 548*, 593–613.

Gegenfurtner, K. R. (2003). Cortical mechanisms of colour vision. *Nature Reviews Neuroscience, 4*, 563–572.

Hansen, T., Pracejus, L., & Gegenfurtner, K. R. (2009). Color perception in the intermediate periphery of the visual field. *Journal of Vision, 9*, 21–22.

Harada, T., Goda, N., Ogawa, T., Ito, M., Toyoda, H., Sadato, N., & Komatsu, H. (2009) Distribution of colour-selective activity in the monkey inferior temporal cortex revealed by functional magnetic resonance imaging. *European Journal of Neuroscience, 30*, 1960–1970.

Helmholtz, H. (1875/1962). *Treatise on physiological optics.* New York: Dover.

Hendry, S. H., & Reid, R. C. (2000). The koniocellular pathway in primate vision. *Annual Review of Neuroscience, 23,* 127–153.

Hering, E. (1878/1964). *Outlines of a theory of the light sense.* Cambridge, MA: Harvard University Press.

Heywood, C. A., & Cowey, A. (1987). On the role of cortical area V4 in the discrimination of hue and pattern in macaque monkeys. *Journal of Neuroscience, 7,* 2601–2617.

Heywood, C. A., Gaffan, D., & Cowey, A. (1995). Cerebral achromatopsia in monkeys. *European Journal of Neuroscience, 7,* 1064–1073.

Hubel, D. H., & Livingstone, M. S. (1987). Segregation of form, color, and stereopsis in primate area 18. *Journal of Neuroscience, 7,* 3378–3415.

Hurvich, L. M., & Jameson, D. (1957). An opponent-process theory of color vision. *Psychology Review, 64*(Pt 1), 384–404.

Johnson, E. N., Hawken, M. J., & Shapley, R. (2001). The spatial transformation of color in the primary visual cortex of the macaque monkey. *Nature Neuroscience, 4,* 409–416.

Judd, D. B. (1966). Fundamental studies of color vision from 1860 to 1960. *Proceedings of the National Academy of Sciences USA, 55,* 1313–1330.

Kentridge, R. W., Heywood, C. A., & Weiskrantz, L. (2007). Color contrast processing in human striate cortex. *Proceedings of the National Academy of Sciences USA, 104,* 15129–15131.

Kolmel, H. W. (1988). Pure homonymous hemiachromatopsia. Findings with neuro-ophthalmologic examination and imaging procedures. *European Archives of Psychiatry and Neurological Sciences, 237,* 237–243.

Komatsu, H., Ideura, Y., Kaji, S., & Yamane, S. (1992). Color selectivity of neurons in the inferior temporal cortex of the awake macaque monkey. *Journal of Neuroscience, 12,* 408–424.

Kusunoki, M., Moutoussis, K., & Zeki, S. (2006). Effect of background colors on the tuning of color-selective cells in monkey area V4. *Journal of Neurophysiology, 95,* 3047–3059.

Land, E. H. (1959). Color vision and the natural image. *Proceedings of the National Academy of Sciences USA, 45,* 115–129 & 636–644.

Land, E. H. (1983). Recent advances in retinex theory and some implications for cortical computations: Color vision and the natural image. *Proceedings of the National Academy of Sciences USA, 90,* 5163–5169.

Land, E. H. (1986). Recent advances in Retinex theory. *Vision Research, 26,* 7–21.

Livingstone, M. S., & Hubel, D. H. (1984). Anatomy and physiology of a color system in the primate visual cortex. *Journal of Neuroscience, 4,* 309–356.

Lotto, R. B., & Purves, D. (2000). An empirical explanation of color contrast. *Proceedings of the National Academy of Sciences USA, 97,* 12834–12839.

Lu, H. D., & Roe, A. W. (2008). Functional organization of color domains in V1 and V2 of Macaque monkey revealed by optical imaging. *Cerebral Cortex, 18,* 516–533.

Marks, W. B., Dobelle, W. H., & Macnichol, E. F., Jr. (1964). Visual pigments of single primate cones. *Science, 143,* 1181–1183.

Maxwell, J. C. (1855). Experiments on colour, as perceived by the eye, with remarks on colour-blindness. *Transactions of the Royal Society, Edinburgh, 21,* 275–298.

McCann, J. J. (1972). Rod-cone interactions: Different color sensations from identical stimuli. *Science, 176,* 1255–1257.

Meadows, J. C. (1974). Disturbed perception of colours associated with localized cerebral lesions. *Brain, 97,* 615–632.

Merigan, W. H., Pasternak, T., Fahle, M., & Greenlee, M. W. (2003). Lesions in primate visual cortex leading to deficits of visual perception. In M. Fahle & M. Greenlee (Eds.), *The neuropsychology of vision* (pp. 121–161). New York: Oxford University Press.

Michael, C. R. (1979). Color-sensitive hypercomplex cells in monkey striate cortex. *Journal of Neurophysiology, 42,* 726–744.

Moutoussis, K., & Zeki, S. (2002). Respnses of spectrally selective cells in macaque area V2 to wavelengths and colors. *Journal of Neurophysiology, 87,* 2104–2112.

Neitz, M., Neitz, J., Chalupa, L. M., & Werner, J. S. (2004). Molecular genetics of human color vision and color vision deficits. In L. M. Chalupa & J. S. Werner (Eds.), *The visual neurosciences* (pp. 974–988). Cambridge, MA: MIT Press.

Palmer, G. (1777). *Theory of colours and vision.* London: Leacroft.

Pearlman, A. L., Birch, J., & Meadows, J. C. (1979). Cerebral color blindness: An acquired defect in hue discrimination. *Annals of Neurology, 5,* 253–261.

Roe, A. W., Lu, H. D., & Crewther, D. P. (2007). Blue color activation in V1 and V2 of macaque monkey. *Society for Neuroscience Meeting Planner, 229.210.*

Ruttiger, L., Braun, D. I., Gegenfurtner, K. R., Petersen, D., Schonle, P., & Sharpe, L. T. (1999). Selective color constancy deficits after circumscribed unilateral brain lesions. *Journal of Neuroscience, 19,* 3094–3106.

Schein, S. J., & Desimone, R. (1990). Spectral properties of V4 neurons in the macaque. *Journal of Neuroscience, 10,* 3369–3389.

Schiller, P. H., & Lee, K. (1991). The role of the primate extrastriate area V4 in vision. *Science, 251,* 1251–1253.

Schiller, P. H., Logothetis, N. K., & Charles, E. R. (1990). Role of the color-opponent and broad-band channels in vision. *Visual Neuroscience, 5,* 321–346.

Shevell, S. K., & Kingdom, F. A. (2008). Color in complex scenes. *Annual Review of Psychology, 59,* 143–166.

Smithson, H. E. (2005). Sensory, computational and cognitive components of human colour constancy. *Philosophical Transactions of the Royal Society of London B: Biol Sciences, 360,* 1329–1346.

Tanigawa, H., Lu, H. D., & Roe, A. W. (2010). Functional organization for color and orientation in macaque V4. *Nature Neuroscience, 13,* 1542–1548.

Tootell, R. B., Nelissen, K., Vanduffel, W., & Orban, G. A. (2004). Search for color 'center(s)' in macaque visual cortex. *Cerebral Cortex, 14,* 353–363.

von Bezold, W. (1876). *The theory of color.* Boston, MA: Prang.

Wachtler, T., Sejnowski, T. J., & Albright, T. D. (2003). Representation of color stimuli in awake macaque primary visual cortex. *Neuron, 37,* 681–691.

Wiesel, T. N., & Hubel, D. H. (1966). Spatial and chromatic interactions in the lateral geniculate body of the rhesus monkey. *Journal of Neurophysiology, 29,* 1115–1156.

Wild, H. M., Butler, S. R., Garden, D., & Kulikowski, J. J. (1985). Primate cortical area V4 important for colour constancy but not wavelength discrimination. *Nature, 313,* 133–135.

Xiao, Y., Casti, A., Xiao, J., & Kaplan, E. (2007). Hue maps in primate striate cortex. *Neuroimage, 35,* 771–786.

Xiao, Y. P., Wang, Y., & Felleman, D. J. (2003). A spatially organized representation of colour in macaque cortical area V2. *Nature, 421,* 535–539.

Young, T. (1802). *On the theory of light and colours.* London: The Society.

Zeki, S. (1990). A century of cerebral achromatopsia. *Brain, 113*(Pt 6), 1721–1777.

Zeki, S. M. (1973). Colour coding in rhesus monkey prestriate cortex. *Brain Research, 53,* 422–427.

5

Perception of Motion

There are two aspects of the perception of motion. One is the perception of an object in relation to other objects around it. The other is the perception of the whole scene moving around us, as we navigate through the world. There are different neurons in different areas, or in some cases, different parts of the same area, to deal with these two aspects.

The Perception of Motion Is Relative

The perception of motion of objects, like everything else in visual perception, is a relative phenomenon. If one looks at a slowly moving dot in darkness, it is hard to tell whether it is moving. However, if a second dot is introduced, one knows immediately that one dot is moving relative to the other, although it may be hard to tell which one is moving (Duncker, 1929). The threshold to perceive motion of a dot by itself is 10–20 min arc/sec, whereas the threshold for motion against a background is 1–2 min arc/sec (Aubert, 1886). If the dot is surrounded by a rectangle, the dot is seen to move in relation to the rectangle, a phenomenon known as the surround effect. The surround is an important influence, because the dot is seen as moving even if it is stationary and the rectangle is moving slowly in the opposite direction (Duncker, 1929). Further complications can arise with a surround within a surround (Fig. 5–1). In this display, the rectangle is moving to the left and the circle is moving downward. The dot is seen as moving to the right, relative to the rectangle, as if the circle were not there, and the rectangle is seen as moving up and to the left, relative to the circle (Wallach, 1959).

There are also many examples of these effects outside the laboratory. When clouds are moving across the sky in front of the moon, one frequently sees the moon as moving rather than the clouds. There is also the barber pole illusion, in which the diagonal lines on a barber pole are seen to move upward (or to the left or right, if the barber pole is made horizontal), the edges of the barber pole providing the surround (Wallach, 1935). However, if one is sitting in a stationary train, and one sees a nearby train start to move through the window, it seems as though

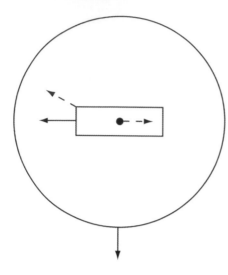

FIGURE 5–1. Surround effects on movement perception. The rectangle moves to the left, and the circle moves downward (solid arrows). The dot is seen as moving right (in relation to the rectangle), the rectangle is seen as moving up and to the left (in relation to the circle) and the circle is not seen as moving (dashed arrows).

one's own train is moving—an observation that does not tally with the surround effect. Thus, it is clear that the perception of motion is a higher order process that involves much more than stimulation of a series of photoreceptors in the retina.

Contribution of Eye Movements

Eye movements also influence the perception of motion. When the eyes move, the world appears to be stationary, even though the image on the retina changes. This is due to an efferent signal from the eye movement system, rather than to proprioceptive signals from the eye muscles, because the scene does appear to move when the observer is asked to move his or her eyes with the eye muscles paralyzed (Helmholtz, 1875/1962). Moreover, afterimages are seen to move when the eyes move. Thus, there can appear to be motion with the stimulus stationary on the retina, and no motion with the stimulus moving across the retina. The system for perception of motion is obviously extremely complicated.

Apparent Motion

Motion is seen when two nearby sparks are flashed in succession (Exner, 1875). This is known as apparent motion. With very slow alternation, the dots are seen as turning on and off sequentially. With slow alternation, there appears to be continuous motion between the two positions. With slightly faster alternation, the dot appears to move between the two positions without taking up any intermediate position, a perception known as the Phi phenomenon (Wertheimer, 1912). With very fast alternation, the dots appear to be flickering simultaneously. What kind of motion is seen depends on the intensity and separation of the dots as well as the rate of alternation (Korte, 1915).

More complicated perceptions occur with more complicated stimuli. For example, a pattern of three dots that is moved sideways by one dot between display 1 and display 2 may be seen either as three dots moving sideways together, or as two dots stationary in the center with a third dot moving from one end of the display to the other (Ternus, 1938; Fig. 5–2). The perception of motion as a group tends to occur with interstimulus intervals of more than 40 msec, whereas the perception of a single dot moving between the ends tends to occur with interstimulus intervals of less than 30 msec (Pantle & Picciano, 1976).

There are two processes in apparent motion: a short-range process and a long-range process (Braddick, 1974). The distinction can be illustrated using random dot displays in which a central rectangle of dots moves sideways. Apparent motion is only seen with small displacements (less than 0.25°) and rapid alternation rate (less than 80 msec). The short-range process is not seen if the displays are presented to different eyes, but the long-range process is. The suggestion is that the short-range

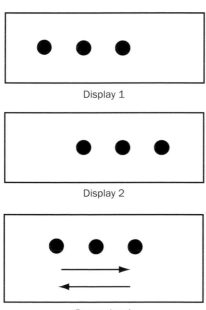

Display 1

Display 2

Perception 1

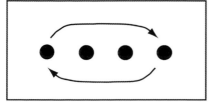

Perception 2

FIGURE 5–2. A pattern of three dots is moved from side to side between display 1 and display 2. With interstimulus intervals of more than 40 msec, they are seen as three dots moving together (perception 1). With interstimulus intervals of less than 30 msec, the two dots in the middle are seen as stationary and the end dots as moving from one end to the other (perception 2).

process occurs early in visual processing, whereas the long-range process involves higher levels, although the distinction may be as much a matter of the stimuli used (random dots versus single dots or lines) as the level of processing.

Component and Pattern Motion

The motion of a line, when one cannot see the ends of the line, is perceived as moving perpendicular to the orientation of the line. The line as a whole may, of course, be moving in any one of a wide variety of directions, but this can only be seen if the ends of the line are visible (Fig. 5–3). This is called the aperture problem.

Objects are composed of numerous contours. Even when the object as a whole has a definite direction of motion, the motion of contours within the object may be ambiguous because of the aperture problem. This has been investigated with a pair of gratings moving in different directions (Stoner, Albright, & Ramachandran, 1990; Fig. 5–4; see motion transparency 1 and 2 on http://viperlib.york.ac.uk/ for moving version). The brightness of the intersections of the gratings in the middle display is varied from dark to light. At intermediate brightness, the display is consistent with one transparent grating in front of the other, but at lighter or darker brightness, it is not. The gratings are seen as sliding past each other in two separate directions (component motion) when the display is consistent with transparency, and they are seen as a single plaid moving in one direction (pattern motion) when the display is not consistent with transparency. The intersections in the left display do not vary,

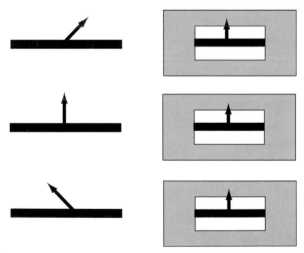

FIGURE 5–3. The three bars on the left are moved in three different directions: up right, straight up, and up left. When seen by themselves, they are seen to move in these directions. When moved behind an aperture (*right*), they all appear to be moving straight upward, because the ends of the lines cannot be seen.

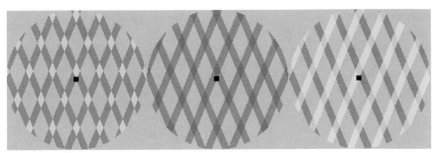

FIGURE 5–4. The two gratings are moved perpendicular to their lengths. In the left and right displays, the intersections are never consistent with transparency, and the gratings are seen to move together as a plaid. In the middle display, the lightness of the intersections is varied, and the gratings move as a plaid for light or dark intersections, but separately for intermediate lightnesses that are consistent with transparency. (Modified by Gene Stoner from Stoner et al., 1990, with kind permission of MacMillan Publishers.)

and it is always seen as a plaid; the right display does not vary either, and it is always seen as two component gratings sliding past each other. This implies a higher level of processing wherein the direction of motion of contours of an object is integrated into a perception of the direction of motion of the object as a whole.

Velocity and Direction Discrimination

The velocity of one stimulus can be discriminated from the velocity of another if there is more than a 5% difference in velocity—that is, with a Weber fraction of 5% (Nakayama, 1985). The direction of one stimulus can be discriminated from another with a difference of 1°. The perception of velocity also depends on the distance of an object. There is a tendency toward speed constancy, so that objects traveling at the same velocity at different distances appear to be traveling at the same speed. However, this is only true if there are cues to depth perception (Rock et al., 1968). In the absence of cues to depth, the perception of speed is determined by the velocity of motion across the retina. Thus, there also has to be input from the depth perception system into the motion perception system.

Motion in Depth

When an object moves in depth, the images on the two retinas move at different velocities (Cynader & Regan, 1978; Fig. 5–5). Indeed, for an object aimed to hit the head between the two eyes, the directions of motion in the two eyes are opposite. It is clearly important to detect objects that are going to hit the head, both to avoid them in everyday life as well as to hit or catch them in sports such as baseball and cricket.

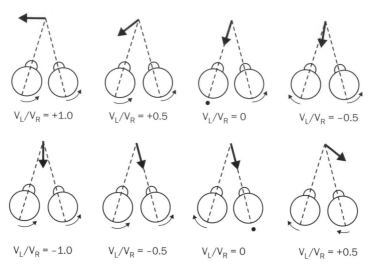

FIGURE 5–5. Movement in different directions in space produces different velocities on the two retinas, from opposite directions of movement for objects aimed between the eyes (displays 4, 5, and 6), to zero velocity in one eye for an object aimed at that eye (displays 3 and 7), to the same direction for objects aimed to pass the observer (displays 1, 2, and 8). (Reprinted from Cynader et al., 1982, with kind permission of Elsevier.)

Psychophysical experiments suggest that there are several channels in the visual system that are sensitive to different directions of motion in depth (Beverley & Regan, 1973). Four of these deal with motion very close to and toward the nose, within 1.5° of the center line. For objects that are moving toward the nose, a change of direction of 0.2° is detectable (Beverley & Regan, 1975). Experiments with cats show that the analysis of motion in depth, from different velocities in the two eyes, is separate from the analysis of static depth using disparity cues (Cynader & Regan, 1982).

Optic Flow

When an observer is looking at a point and moving toward it, as when driving a car or piloting an airplane, the whole scene around that point expands. More rarely, in moving away, the whole scene contracts. This is known as optic flow and was extensively investigated by Gibson (1950), who considered that it is critical for our orientation in space.

The perception of where an observer is headed, based on an analysis of the pattern of optic flow, is a complicated one (Fig. 5–6). The point to which the observer is headed may be moving; the observer may not be looking directly at it; the observer's eyes may be moving; the observer is also moving and may be rotating with activation of the vestibular system. While being bombarded by all this information, the

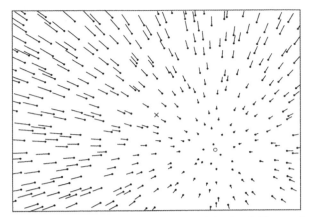

FIGURE 5–6. Optic flow when the observer is not looking straight ahead. Observer is moving toward X, while rotating to the right and downward to track the O. This produces a pseudo focus of expansion at the fixation point. (Reprinted from Warren, 2004, with kind permission of MIT Press.)

sensory systems have to detect the path that the observer is following, and also the heading at each instant of time tangent to the path, in order to be able to make decisions about what to do (Warren, 2004). It is a real feat that humans and animals are able to do this, to an accuracy of 1° or less. Patterns of optic flow across the retina are used, as well as extraretinal signals from the eye movement and vestibular systems.

Biological Motion

One of the most fascinating achievements of the motion system is that a person who cannot be seen but has lights attached to the joints and extremities of his or her limbs is seen as a person as soon as he or she starts moving (Johansson, 1975). Before moving, the pattern of lights is seen simply as a pattern of lights. After moving, a person is immediately apparent. Moreover, one can distinguish a male moving from a female moving, due to differences in shoulder and hip widths, arm swing, and speed of walking. This is known as biological motion, because animals with lights attached to their limbs are also seen as moving animals.

This phenomenon is undoubtedly related to the tendency to interpret moving contours and dots as part of a rigid structure moving in space (Johansson, 1975). For example, a square frame expanding and contracting is seen as a rigid square moving closer and further away in space, rather than as a square changing its size at a fixed distance. Similarly, two dots moving in an elliptical path are seen as the ends of a rigid rod rotating at an angle in space. Correspondingly, the lights on the limbs are seen as the ends of a rigid limb. However, there is clearly more to it than this, given the recognition of the moving lights as being human as opposed to animal, and male as opposed to female. For demonstrations of this and other motion phenomena, see http://www.psyk.uu.se/organisation/historia/?languageId=1.

First- and Second-Order Motion

Motion may be seen in displays where there are no obvious boundaries. This leads to the distinction between first-order motion, defined by boundaries of luminance or color, and second-order or non-Fourier motion, defined by boundaries of other characteristics such as contrast or depth (Cavanagh & Mather, 1989; Chubb & Sperling, 1988; Fig. 5–7). In some cases motion may be seen where there is nothing moving (see Wolfe et al., 2006; Chapter 7). This distinction may seem to be more a laboratory distinction than a perceptual distinction, although processes for second-order motion may be used in detecting the motion of camouflaged objects. However, as described later, there are separate areas of the brain for detection of first- and second-order motion, so the distinction must be of some practical importance.

Color and Motion

The perception of motion is degraded in equiluminant stimuli, for example, red/green stimuli where the red and green have the same brightness. When viewing chromatic gratings, the apparent speed of motion becomes slowed as the two colors approach equiluminance, and for gratings of low spatial frequency they may stop altogether (Cavanagh, Tyler, & Favreau, 1984). Where random dot stimuli are used, in displays designed to elicit Braddick's short-range process, no motion is seen at equiluminance (Ramachandran & Gregory, 1978). However, not all perception of motion is abolished at equiluminance, and psychophysical experiments suggest that there is an input from the opponent color system to the motion system (Cavanagh & Anstis, 1991).

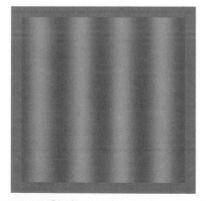 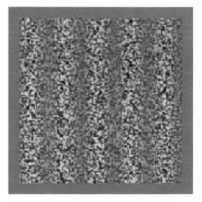

FIGURE 5–7. Displays used to test first-order and second-order movement. The grating on the left has variations in luminance (first-order motion), whereas the grating on the right has variations in contrast but not luminance (second-order motion). Second-order motion may also be defined by disparity and other parameters. (Reprinted from Blake et al., 2004, with kind permission of CRC Press.)

Mechanisms of Direction Selectivity

There is a clearly defined mechanism of direction selectivity in the rabbit retina, where the response for motion in the nonpreferred or null direction is abolished. Lateral inhibition from a previous position cancels the signal at the current position as the stimulus moves through the receptive field in this direction; the summation of excitatory signals for motion in the preferred direction plays little part (Barlow & Levick, 1965; Wyatt & Daw, 1976; Fig. 5–8). In the visual cortex, which is the first level at which directional selectivity is seen in higher mammals, it is more complicated than this. The difference in timing of excitatory and inhibitory signals adds up linearly to a larger response in the preferred direction, which is amplified by the nonlinearity due to spiking threshold (Priebe & Ferster, 2005).

Areas of the Brain Concerned With Motion

A number of areas associated with motion have been identified in both human and macaque brains (Orban & van Duffell, 2004; Sunaert, Van Hecke, Marchal, & Orban, 1999; Zeki, 1974, Zeki et al., 1991). Primary visual cortex (V1) has long been known to contain a large percentage of cells that respond to direction of motion, but it is not involved in more advanced aspects of motion perception. Motion in V2 is concentrated in the thick stripes, where there are columns for different

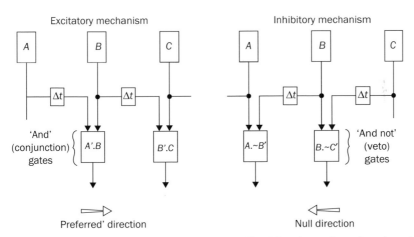

FIGURE 5–8. Two schemes for directional selectivity. The right scheme depends on lateral inhibition to prevent direct signals from getting through when the stimulus moves in the null direction. The left scheme depends on lateral excitatory signals, which combine in a nonlinear way with the direct signals to produce a significant response when the stimulus moves in the preferred direction. In the rabbit retina, where this was first studied, only the inhibitory mechanism applies, whereas in the cat visual cortex both apply. (Reprinted from Barlow & Levick, 1965, with kind permission of the Physiological Society.)

directions of motion (Lu, Chen, Tanigawa, & Roe, 2010). Areas in humans that are involved include hMT+/V5, V3A, the kinetic occipital region (KO), parts of the lateral occipital cortex (LO) between KO and hMT+/V5, the posterior part of the superior temporal sulcus (pSTS), and the fusiform face area (Fig. 5–9).

MT+/V5 corresponds to a complex of areas in the macaque—the middle temporal area (MT/V5): the medial superior temporal area around it (MST), which has a lateral (MSTl) and a dorsal component (MSTd); and another area nearby called the floor of the superior temporal sulcus (AKA fundus of superior temporal sulcus [FST]) (Fig. 5–10). This area is heavily myelinated and has been recognized in a wide variety of primates, with responses to motion in all of them. Area MT is retinotopically organized and has small receptive fields, but MST deals with motion of larger areas, enabling the homology to be made (Huk, Dougherty, & Heeger, 2002). Properties of these areas will be detailed later.

Functional magnetic resonance imaging (fMRI) studies show that area V3A in humans has responses to motion. On retinotopic criteria, it corresponds to V3A in macaque, but V3A in macaque does not respond to motion, whereas V3 in macaque does (Tootell et al., 1997). Thus, the homology as well as the exact function of these areas in both human and macaque remains to be evaluated.

The kinetic occipital region has been identified from fMRI studies. It is activated by kinetic boundaries (boundaries defined by the motion of random dot stimuli) (van Oostende et al., 1997). Several areas around hMT+/V5 respond to biological motion (Grossman et al., 2000). The posterior part of the superior temporal sulcus, in particular, responds to human motion more than to motion of mechanical objects with lights on them (Pyles, Garcia, Hoffman, & Grossman, 2007).

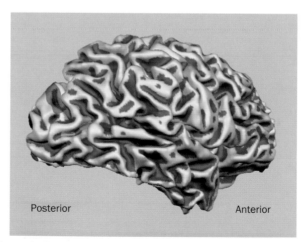

Posterior   Anterior

FIGURE 5–9. Human brain showing several movement areas. Purple is the small part of V1 visible on the lateral surface at the left tip of the diagram. Orange is V3A; cyan is the kinetic occipital region (KO); green is hMT+/V5; pink is the posterior part of the superior temporal sulcus (pSTS); and red is the fusiform face area. (Reprinted from Blake et al., 2004, with kind permission of CRC Press.)

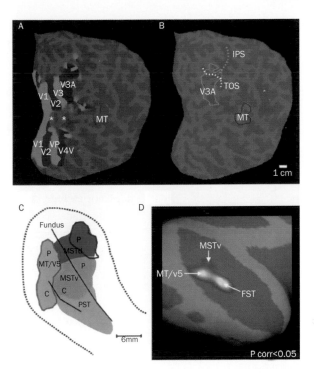

FIGURE 5–10. (*A* and *B*) Location of the middle temporal cortex (MT) in the macaque with respect to other visual areas on the flattened cortical surface. IPS, intraparietal sulcus; TOS, transverse occipital sulcus. (*C* and *D*) Subdivisions of hMT+/V5 in human. P and C denote peripheral and central representations, respectively. A portion of MSTv corresponds to MSTl as defined by Komatsu and Wurtz (1988). MST, medial superior temporal cortex; MSTv, medial superior temporal cortex, ventral; MSTl, medial superior temporal cortex, lateral. (Reprinted from Orban & van Duffel, 2004, with kind permission of MIT Press.)

Responses in Area MT/V5

Area MT was first identified in the owl monkey as a specialized area of vision; it is named MT because it is in the middle temporal cortex (Allman & Kass, 1971). Similar areas have been found in a variety of primates. In the macaque monkey it was renamed V5, since it is found at the junction between parietal and occipital cortex, rather than in the temporal cortex. The area has a high percentage of neurons responding to motion and direction of motion (Dubner & Zeki 1971; Zeki, 1974).

The cells in MT are arranged in a columnar fashion according to the preferred direction of motion (Albright, Desimone, & Gross, 1984; Zeki, 1974). Along a penetration perpendicular to the surface of the cortex, the cells tend to prefer the same direction of motion. Along a penetration parallel to the surface, the preferred direction varies steadily, with occasional jumps of 180°. Thus, columns for opposite directions of motion are found near each other, in

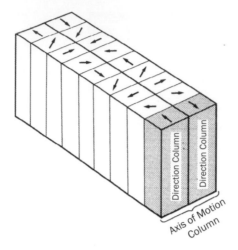

FIGURE 5–11. Schematic for columns for direction of movement in the medial temporal cortex (MT). Neighboring columns represent either opposite directions or a slow progression of directions around the clock. (Reprinted from Albright et al., 1984, with kind permission of the American Physiological Society.)

a general scheme in which the preferred direction moves around the clock through 180° (Fig. 5–11).

The cells are also specific for the speed of motion of the stimulus (Maunsell & Van Essen, 1983). Different cells prefer different speeds in a middle range of velocities between 2°/sec and 256°/sec—not too slow, and not too fast (Fig. 5–12). This range does not include the speeds seen in fast saccadic eye movements, or in the slow drifts seen during fixation.

MT is organized to respond to motion of patterns, rather than motion of the components of a pattern. This was first brought out in responses to a plaid, consisting of two gratings perpendicular to each other (Movshon, Adelson, Gizzi, & Newsome, 1985). Whereas the directional tuning curve of cells in V1 to such a plaid shows two lobes, corresponding to the direction of motion of the two gratings that comprise it, the directional tuning curve of many cells in MT shows a single lobe, corresponding to the motion of the pattern as a whole (Fig. 5–13). Moreover, when the brightness of the intersections in the plaid is varied, to simulate variations in transparency (Fig. 5–3), the direction sensitivity follows the components of the plaid when it appears to be two gratings sliding past each other, and it follows the plaid as a whole when it appears to be single pattern (Stoner & Albright, 1992). This experiment involved a comparison of human perception with macaque cell properties; nevertheless, it is strongly suggestive that MT signals the perception of the whole, rather than the perception of its components.

The response of cells in MT corresponds to the perception of motion in other ways (Britten, Shadlen, Newsome, & Movshon, 1992). Macaques can be taught to discriminate direction of motion in a display in which the difficulty of the discrimination is varied by changing the percentage of dots that are moving together (Fig. 5–14). The performance of the best cells in MT correlates well with the behavioral performance of the animal, when the psychophysical task is tailored to the properties of the neuron under study, in terms of size, speed, and direction of motion. Stated in the jargon of the field, both the absolute threshold and the shapes of the psychometric and neurometric functions match.

Two other points suggest that MT mediates the perception of motion. First, microstimulation of MT affects perceptual judgments of direction of motion

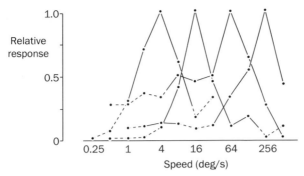

FIGURE 5–12. Speed-tuning curves for four neurons in the medial temporal cortex (MT). The overall range of speeds covered is 1–300 deg/sec, but each individual neuron only covers a fraction of that range. (Reprinted from Maunsell & Van Essen, 1983, with kind permission of the American Physiological Society.)

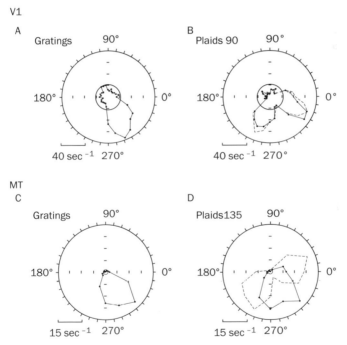

FIGURE 5–13. Component and pattern responses in primary visual cortex (V1) and the medial temporal cortex (MT). The response to a grating shows a single preferred direction in both V1 (*A*) and MT (*C*). The response to a plaid, consisting of two orthogonal gratings shows two preferred directions in V1 (*B*, component response) and a single preferred direction for some cells in MT (*D*, pattern response). In *B* and *D* the solid lines give the actual response, and the dashed lines give the sum of two responses to a single grating, taken from *A* and *C*, respectively. (Reprinted from Movshon et al., 1985, with kind permission of Springer-Verlag.)

(Salzman, Britten, & Newsome, 1990). In one experiment, a column with a particular preferred direction was identified, then stimulated with a small current that does not spread significantly to neighboring columns. Meanwhile the macaque was performing a discrimination of direction of motion with a stimulus like that shown in Figure 5–14. Microstimulation moved the perception of motion, as measured by the psychometric function, so as to increase the probability that motion in the preferred direction of the column is perceived. In another experiment, macaques were trained to choose the faster of two random dot patterns (Liu & Newsome, 2005). Microstimulation of a cluster of neurons with homogeneous speed-tuning properties biased speed judgment toward the speed of the stimulated cluster. These two experiments suggest that MT neurons play a role in the perception of both direction and speed of motion.

Finally, lesions of MT affect the perception of motion. Injections of ibotenic acid into MT produce striking elevations in the threshold for discrimination of direction, using displays such as those in Figure 5–14 (Newsome & Pare, 1988). Discrimination of small differences in speed and of small differences in direction is also affected (see Britten, 2004). However, there is recovery from these lesions, and even large lesions that include MST as well as MT do not abolish motion perception altogether (see Britten, 2004). Thus, MT is the most important area in the brain for perception of a variety of aspects of motion, but not the only one.

As described in Chapter 6, MT also plays an important role in depth perception. This interacts with motion perception, both in the properties of the cells in MT and also in the overall perception. The response of a cell in MT for a stimulus moving in the preferred direction can be inhibited by a stimulus moving in the opposite

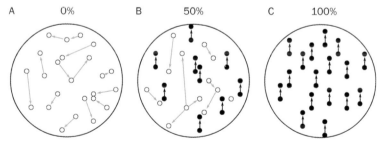

FIGURE 5–14. Stimulus used to test discrimination of direction of movement. The stimulus is a set of dots that may all move in the same direction (100% correlation, C) or may be mixed with noise, which is a set of dots moving in random directions (0% correlation, A). The center display (B) shows 50% moving in the same direction and 50% moving in random directions. In the figure the stimulus dots are black and the noise dots are white, but in the actual display stimulus dots and noise dots would be the same color, and, of course, there would be no arrows. The percentage of noise dots is varied, and threshold is the lowest percentage correlation where the subject can make a reliable discrimination. (Reprinted from Britten et al., 1992, with kind permission of the Society for Neuroscience.)

direction. This happens if the two stimuli are at the same depth, but not if they are at different depths (Bradley, Qian, & Andersen, 1995). This means that objects moving in different directions at different depths can be discriminated. The barber pole illusion is also affected by depth. If the edges of the barber pole are placed in front of the moving diagonal lines, the illusion is no longer seen, because the edges form an aperture through which the diagonal lines appear to move diagonally. This perception corresponds to the properties of cells in MT (Duncan, Albright, & Stoner, 2000). It appears that the input of depth signals to MT is designed to influence the perception of motion as much as to integrate signals related to motion in depth.

The receptive fields of cells in MT have surrounds (Allman, Miezin, & McGuinness, 1985). These may be antagonistic, so that the response of the cell is reduced when the stimulus extends into the surround (Fig. 5–15), or summative, so that the response of the cell increases when the stimulus extends into the surround (Born & Tootell, 1992). These two types of cell are segregated into separate bands within MT in the owl monkey, according to staining with 2–deoxyglucose using a large random dot stimulus. The cells with summative receptive fields are found in the stained bands, and cells with antagonistic surrounds are found between these bands. This means that the stained bands essentially deal with

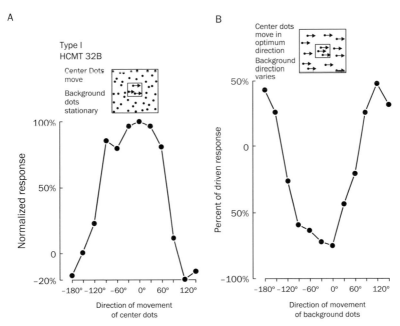

FIGURE 5–15. Responses from a cell with an antagonistic surround. The center is directionally sensitive, giving responses to directions between 60 deg and –60 deg (*A*). With dots in the center moving in the preferred direction, the response is inhibited by the surround moving in the same direction and by the surround moving in the opposite direction (*B*). (Reprinted from Allman et al., 1985, with kind permission of Annual Reviews.)

global motion, and the interbands deal with local motion, to discriminate an object moving against the background. Interestingly, these bands have different effects on eye movements (Born, Groh, Zhao, & Lukasewycz, 2000). Stimulation of the local motion interbands shifts pursuit eye movements in the preferred direction of the column stimulated, whereas stimulation of the global motion bands shifts pursuit eye movements opposite to the preferred direction. Thus, local motion signals are related to the motion and following of an object, while global motion is related to motion and following of the background.

Responses in Area MST

Area MST is heterogeneous. It can be divided into a dorsal part (MSTd), a lateral part (MSTl), and a part in between (Komatsu & Wurtz, 1988). Other authors have also recognized these divisions, using different names. The different cell types found in MT, classified by their surround responses, project to different parts of MST in the owl monkey (Berezovskii & Born, 2000), but how this works out in the macaque is not yet clearly understood due to species differences.

Cells in MSTd respond to large field stimuli (Komatsu & Wurtz, 1988). Presumably they get input from the cells in MT that have synergistic surrounds and deal with optic flow, although the motion of an object in a different direction from the optic flow may add to the response (Logan & Duffy, 2006). There are three types of cell responding to expansion or contraction of the scene, translation, or rotation (Saito et al., 1986) or to combinations of these (Duffy & Wurtz, 1991; Fig. 5–16). Some cells signal heading, irrespective of where the eyes are pointed (Bradley et al., 1996). When the eyes are still, this is the focus of expansion, but when the eyes are moving, the heading is displaced from the focus of expansion. Other cells simply signal the focus of expansion. Moreover, microstimulation affects the perception of heading (Britten & van Wezel, 1998).

Cells in MSTd also get input from the vestibular system. They respond to a combination of optic flow and translational or rotational movement of the animal (Duffy, 1998; Fig. 5–17). Nearly all cells in this area have visual optic flow input, and two-thirds of them also have vestibular input (Gu, Watkins, Angelaki, & DeAngelis, 2006). Deciding where one is headed can get extremely complicated with visual responses from expansion or contraction, translation, and rotation combined with vestibular responses from rotation and translation, and movements of the head. Much of this is done in MSTd (Bremmer et al., 2010; Gu, Angelaki, & Deangelis, 2008; Takahashi et al., 2007).

Cells in MSTl respond to small objects and to pursuit of a small object in darkness (Komatsu & Wurtz, 1988). The response is increased if the surround moves in the opposite direction to the center, and decreased if it moves in the same direction (Eifuku & Wurtz, 1998; Tanaka, Sugita, Moriya, & Saito, 1993). Moreover, stimulation of cells in MSTl affects smooth pursuit eye movements,

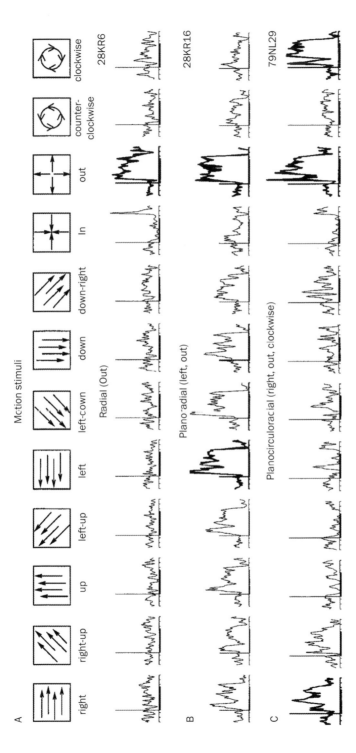

FIGURE 5–16. Examples of optic flow responses from three neurons in the medial superior temporal cortex, dorsal (MSTd). The first example responds to movement outward, called a radial neuron. The second example responds to movement outward, and movement left—a planoradial neuron. The third example responds to movement outward, movement right, and clockwise rotation—a planocirculoradial neuron. (Reprinted from Duffy & Wurtz, 1995, with kind permission of the Society for Neuroscience.)

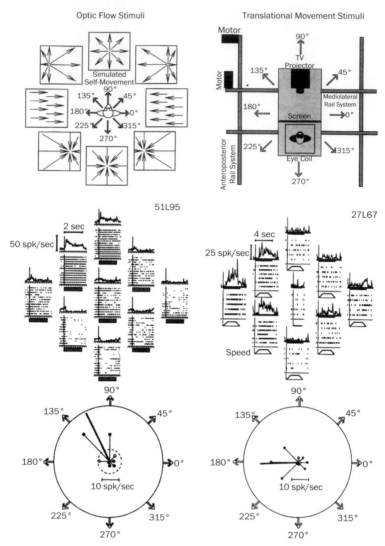

FIGURE 5–17. Responses of a medial superior temporal cortex, dorsal (MSTd) neuron to optic flow and translational stimuli. The best optic flow response is given when the observer moves forward and to the left. The best vestibular translational response is given when the observer moves to the left. A shows the visual stimuli; D, the vestibular stimuli, B and E, Raster displays of the responses with summaries; and C and F, the magnitude of the responses as a function of direction. (Reprinted from Duffy, 1998, with kind permission of the American Physiological Society.)

whereas stimulation in MSTd does not (Komatsu & Wurtz, 1989). MSTl also controls hand movements in response to a moving stimulus (Ilg & Schumann, 2007). Thus, MTSl deals with movement of an object across the field of view, rather than movement of the observer through the field of view, which is the province of MSTd.

Other Areas

Responses to motion are found in a variety of other areas around the parieto-occipital-temporal junction. These include areas 7a, lateral interparietal area (LIP), ventral interparietal area (VIP), anterior superior temporal polysensory area (aSTP), and others. Many details of the responses in these areas remain to be worked out. A summary can be found in Duffy (2004).

Patients With Deficits in Motion Perception

Patients with deficits in motion perception are rare. The most studied was a woman known as LM with an extensive lesion in the lateral occipitotemporal cortex, including human MT+/V5 (Zihl, von Cramon, & Mai, 1983). She either did not notice moving objects or saw them as a series of static images. When filling a glass of water, she overflowed it. When a new person entered the room, she did not immediately notice. Having more than one person moving in the room was uncomfortable for her. She could not cross the street, because she could not judge the speed of approaching cars. Testing showed normal acuity and color vision and perception of depth by stereopsis with reduced stereoscopic acuity. However, she did not see the Phi phenomenon or motion aftereffects.

There are also patients with deficits in one aspect of motion perception, but not another. One with a lesion in the caudal portion of the superior temporal sulcus, dorsal to but not including human MT, could see first-order motion but not second-order motion (Vaina & Cowey, 1996). Another with a lesion superior to the calcarine fissure in the medial third of the occipital cortex, near V2 and well away from MT, could see second-order motion but not first-order motion (Vaina, Makris, Kennedy, & Cowey, 1998). Other patients had biological motion either selectively impaired or selectively not impaired (see Blake, Sekular, & Grossman, 2004). Another intriguing patient did not incorporate eye movement signals into the perception of motion system, and thus saw the world as moving during eye movements (Haarmeier, Their, Repnow, & Petersen, 1997).

These various patients show that motion perception is processed in a different area of the brain from color, acuity, and depth perception. They also show that different aspects of motion are processed in different areas. Moreover, there have to be parallel pathways: not all the motion signals pass through MT, and not all of them pass through V2, since lesions in these areas do not abolish all perception of motion. While the lesions in human patients are not well localized and may affect fibers of passage as well as the cells in the area, studies in patients agree with the experimental studies in macaques about the localization of various aspects of motion perception.

References

Albright, T. D., Desimone, R., & Gross, C. G. (1984). Columnar organization of directionally selective cells in visual area MT of the macaque. *Journal of Neurophysiology, 51*, 16–31.

Allman, J., Miezin, F., & McGuinness, E. (1985). Stimulus specific responses from beyond the classical receptive field: Neurophysiological mechanisms for local-global comparisons in visual neurons. *Annual Review of Neuroscience, 8*, 407–430.

Allman, J. M., & Kaas, J. H. (1971). A representation of the visual field in the caudal third of the middle temporal gyrus of the owl monkey (Aotus trivirgatus). *Brain Research, 31*, 85–105.

Aubert, H. (1886). Der Bewegungsempfindung. *Archiv fur den Gesamte Physiologie, 39*, 347–370.

Barlow, H. B., & Levick, W. R. (1965). The mechanism of directionally selective units in rabbit's retina. *Journal of Physiology, 178*, 477–504.

Berezovskii, V. K., & Born, R. T. (2000). Specificity of projections from wide-field and local motion-processing regions within the middle temporal visual area of the owl monkey. *Journal of Neuroscience, 20*, 1157–1169.

Beverley, K. I., & Regan, D. (1973). Evidence for the existence of neural mechanisms selectively sensitive to the direction of movement in space. *Journal of Physiology, 235*, 17–29.

Beverley, K. I., & Regan, D. (1975). The relation between discrimination and sensitivity in the perception of motion in depth. *Journal of Physiology, 249*, 387–398.

Blake, R., Sekular, R., Grossman, E. (2004). Motion processing in human visual cortex. In J. H. Kaas & C. E. Collins (Eds.), *The primate visual system* (pp. 311–344). New York: CRC Press.

Born, R. T., Groh, J. M., Zhao, R., & Lukasewycz, S. J. (2000). Segregation of object and background motion in visual area MT: Effects of microstimulation on eye movements. *Neuron, 26*, 725–734.

Born, R. T., & Tootell, R. H. (1992). Segregation of global and local motion processing in primate middle temporal visual area. *Nature, 357*, 497–499.

Braddick, O. (1974). A short-range process in apparent motion. *Vision Research, 14*, 519–527.

Bradley, D. C., Maxwell, M., Andersen, R. A., Banks, M. S., & Shenoy, K. V. (1996). Mechanisms of heading perception in primate visual cortex. *Science, 273*, 1544–1547.

Bradley, D. C., Qian, N., & Andersen, R. A. (1995). Integration of motion and stereopsis in middle temporal cortical area of macaques. *Nature, 373*, 609–611.

Bremmer, F., Kubischik, M., Pekel, M., Hoffmann, K. P., & Lappe, M. (2010). Visual selectivity for heading in monkey area MST. *Experimental Brain Research, 200*, 51–60.

Britten, K. H. (2004). The middle temporal area: motion processing and the link to perception. In L. M. Chalupa & J. S. Werner (Eds.), *The visual neurosciences* (pp. 1203–1216). Cambridge, MA: MIT Press.

Britten, K. H., Shadlen, M. N., Newsome, W. T., & Movshon, J. A. (1992). The analysis of visual motion: a comparison of neuronal and psychophysical performance. *Journal of Neuroscience, 12*, 4745–4765.

Britten, K. H., & van Wezel, R. J. (1998). Electrical microstimulation of cortical area MST biases heading perception in monkeys. *Nature Neuroscience, 1*, 59–63.

Cavanagh, P., & Anstis, S. (1991). The contribution of color to motion in normal and color-deficient observers. *Vision Research, 31,* 2109–2148.

Cavanagh, P., & Mather, G. (1989). Motion: The long and short of it. *Spatial Vision, 4,* 103–129.

Cavanagh, P., Tyler, C. W., & Favreau, O. E. (1984). Perceived velocity of moving chromatic gratings. *Journal of the Optical Society of America – A, 1,* 893–899.

Chubb, C., & Sperling, G. (1988). Drift-balanced random stimuli: A general basis for studying non-Fourier motion perception. *Journal of the Optical Society of America – A, 5,* 1986–2007.

Cynader, M., & Regan, D. (1978). Neurones in cat parastriate cortex sensitive to the direction of motion in three-dimensional space. *Journal of Physiology, 274,* 549–569.

Cynader, M., & Regan, D. (1982). Neurons in cat visual cortex tuned to the direction of motion in depth: Effect of positional disparity. *Vision Research, 22,* 967–982.

Dubner, R., & Zeki, S. M. (1971). Response properties and receptive fields of cells in an anatomically defined region of the superior temporal sulcus in the monkey. *Brain Research, 35,* 528–532.

Duffy, C. J. (1998). MST neurons respond to optic flow and translational movement. *Journal of Neurophysiology, 80,* 1816–1827.

Duffy, C. J. (2004). The cortical analysis of optic flow. In L. M. Chalupa & J. S. Werner (Eds.), *The visual neurosciences* (pp. 1260–1283). Cambridge, MA: MIT Press.

Duffy, C. J., & Wurtz, R. H. (1991). Sensitivity of MST neurons to optic flow stimuli I A continuum of response selectivity to large stimuli. *Journal of Neurophysiology, 65,* 1329–1345.

Duffy, C. J., & Wurtz, R. H. (1995). Response of monkey MST neurons to optic flow stimuli with shifted centers of motion. *Journal of Neuroscience, 15,* 5192–5208.

Duncan, R. O., Albright, T. D., & Stoner, G. R. (2000). Occlusion and the interpretation of visual motion: Perceptual and neuronal effects of context. *Journal of Neuroscience, 20,* 5885–5897.

Duncker, K. (1929). Uber induzierte Bewegung. *Psychologische Forschung, 12,* 180–259.

Eifuku, S., & Wurtz, R. H. (1998). Response to motion in extrastriate area MSTl: Center-surround interactions. *Journal of Neurophysiology, 80,* 282–296.

Exner, S. (1875). Experimentelle Untersuchungen der Einfachsten Psychischen Processe. *Archiv fur den Gesamte Physiologie, 11,* 403–432.

Gibson, J. J. (1950). *The perception of the visual world.* Boston, MA: Houghton Mifflin.

Grossman, E., Donnelly, M., Price, R., Pickens, D., Morgan, V., Neighbor, G., & Blake, R. (2000). Brain areas involved in perception of biological motion. *Journal of Cognitive Neuroscience, 12,* 711–720.

Gu, Y., Angelaki, D. E., & Deangelis, G. C. (2008). Neural correlates of multisensory cue integration in macaque MSTd. *Nature Neuroscience, 11,* 1201–1210.

Gu, Y., Watkins, P. V., Angelaki, D. E., & DeAngelis, G. C. (2006). Visual and nonvisual contributions to three-dimensional heading selectivity in the medial superior temporal area. *Journal of Neuroscience, 26,* 73–85.

Haarmeier, T., Thier, P., Repnow, M., & Petersen, D. (1997). False perception of motion in a patient who cannot compensate for eye movements. *Nature, 389,* 849–852.

Helmholtz, H. (1875/1962). *Treatise on physiological optics.* New York: Dover.

Huk, A. C., Dougherty, R. F., & Heeger, D. J. (2002). Retinotopy and functional subdivision of human areas MT and MST. *Journal of Neuroscience, 22,* 7195–7205.

Ilg, U. J., & Schumann, S. (2007). Primate area MST-l is involved in the generation of goal-directed eye and hand movements. *Journal of Neurophysiology, 97,* 761–771.

Johansson, G. (1975). Visual motion perception. *Scientific American, 232,* 76–88.

Komatsu, H., & Wurtz, R. H. (1988). Relation of cortical areas MT and MST to pursuit eye movements. I. Localization and visual properties of neurons. *Journal of Neurophysiology, 60,* 580–603.

Komatsu, H., & Wurtz, R. H. (1989). Modulation of pursuit eye movements by stimulation of cortical areas MT and MST. *Journal of Neurophysiology, 62,* 31–47.

Korte, A. (1915). Kinematoskopische Untersuchungen. *Zeitschrift Psychologie, 72,* 193–206.

Liu, J., & Newsome, W. T. (2005). Correlation between speed perception and neural activity in the middle temporal area. *Journal of Neuroscience, 25,* 711–722.

Logan, D. J., & Duffy, C. J. (2006). Cortical area MSTd combines visual cues to represent 3-D self-movement. *Cerebral Cortex, 16,* 1494–1504.

Lu H. D., Chen G., Tanigawa H., & Roe A. W. (2010). A motion direction map in macaque V2. *Neuron, 68,* 1002–1013.

Maunsell, J. H., & Van Essen, D. C. (1983). Functional properties of neurons in middle temporal visual area of the macaque monkey. I. Selectivity for stimulus direction, speed, and orientation. *Journal of Neurophysiology, 49,* 1127–1147.

Movshon, J. A., Adelson, E. H., Gizzi, M. S., & Newsome, W. T. (1985). The analysis of moving visual patterns. In C. Chagas, R. Gattass, & C. Gross (Eds.), *Pattern recognition mechanisms* (pp. 117–151). Vatican City: Pontifical Academy of Sciences.

Nakayama, K. (1985). Biological image motion processing: A review. *Vision Research, 25,* 625–660.

Newsome, W. T., & Pare, E. B. (1988). A selective impairment of motion perception following lesions of the middle temporal visual area (MT). *Journal of Neuroscience, 8,* 2201–2211.

Orban, G. A., & van Duffel, W. (2004). Functional mapping of motion regions. In L. M. Chalupa & J. S. Werner (Eds.), *The visual neurosciences* (pp. 1229–1246). Cambridge, MA: MIT Press.

Pantle, A., & Picciano, L. (1976). A multistable movement display: Evidence for two separate motion systems in human vision. *Science, 193,* 500–502.

Priebe, N. J., & Ferster, D. (2005). Direction selectivity of excitation and inhibition in simple cells of the cat primary visual cortex. *Neuron, 45,* 133–145.

Pyles, J. A., Garcia, J. O., Hoffman, D. D., & Grossman, E. D. (2007). Visual perception and neural correlates of novel 'biological motion.' *Vision Research, 47,* 2786–2797.

Ramachandran, V. S., & Gregory, R. L. (1978). Does colour provide an input to human motion perception? *Nature, 275,* 55–56.

Rock, I., Hill, A. L., & Fineman, M. (1968). Speed constancy as a function of size constancy. *Perception and Psychophysics, 4,* 37–40.

Saito, H., Yukie, M., Tanaka, K., Hikosaka, K., Fukada, Y., & Iwai, E. (1986). Integration of direction signals of image motion in the superior temporal sulcus of the macaque monkey. *Journal of Neuroscience, 6,* 145–157.

Salzman, C. D., Britten, K. H., & Newsome, W. T. (1990). Cortical microstimulation influences perceptual judgements of motion direction. *Nature, 346,* 174–177.

Stoner, G. R., & Albright, T, D, (1992). Neural correlates of perceptual motion coherence. *Nature, 358,* 412–414.

Stoner, G. R., Albright, T. D., & Ramachandran, V. S. (1990). Transparency and coherence in human motion perception. *Nature, 344,* 153–155.

Sunaert, S., Van Hecke, P., Marchal, G., & Orban, G. A. (1999). Motion-responsive regions of the human brain. *Experimental Brain Research, 127,* 355–370.

Takahashi, K., Gu, Y., May, P. J., Newlands, S. D., DeAngelis, G. C., & Angelaki, D. E. (2007). Multimodal coding of three-dimensional rotation and translation in area MSTd: Comparison of visual and vestibular selectivity. *Journal of Neuroscience, 27,* 9742–9756.

Tanaka, K., Sugita, Y., Moriya, M., & Saito, H. (1993). Analysis of object motion in the ventral part of the medial superior temporal area of the macaque visual cortex. *Journal of Neurophysiology, 69,* 128–142.

Ternus, J. (1938). The problem of phenomenal identity. In W. D. Ellis (Ed.), *A source book of Gestalt psychology* (pp. 149–160). London: Routledge & Kegan Paul.

Tootell, R. B., Mendola, J. D., Hadjikhani, N. K., Ledden, P. J., Liu, A. K., Reppas, J. B., … Dale, A. M. (1997). Functional analysis of V3A and related areas in human visual cortex. *Journal of Neuroscience, 17,* 7060–7078.

Vaina, L. M., & Cowey, A. (1996). Impairment of the perception of second order motion but not first order motion in a patient with unilateral focal brain damage. *Proceedings of the Royal Society of London B: Biological Sciences, 263,* 1225–1232.

Vaina, L. M., Makris, N., Kennedy, D., & Cowey, A. (1998). The selective impairment of the perception of first-order motion by unilateral cortical brain damage. *Visual Neuroscience, 15,* 333–348.

Van Oostende, S., Sunaert, S., Van Hecke, P., Marchal, G., & Orban, G. A. (1997). The kinetic occipital (KO) region in man: An fMRI study. *Cerebral Cortex, 7,* 690–701.

Wallach, H. (1935). Uber visuelle Wahrgenommene Bewegungrichtung. *Psychologische Forschung, 20,* 325–380.

Wallach, H. (1959). The perception of motion. *Scientific American, 201,* 56–60.

Warren, W. H. (2004). Optic flow. In L. M. Chalupa & J. S. Werner (Eds.), *The visual neurosciences* (pp. 1247–1259). Cambridge, MA: MIT Press.

Wertheimer, M. (1912). Experimentelle Studien Uber das Sehen von Bewegung. *Zeitschrift Psychologie, 61,* 161–265.

Wolfe, J. M., Kluender, K. R., Levi, D. M., Bartoshuk, L. M., Herz, R. S., Klatzky, R. L., & Lederman, S. J. (2006). *Sensation and perception.* Sunderland, MA: Sinauer Associates.

Wyatt, H. J., & Daw, N. W. (1976). Specific effects of neurotransmitter antagonists on ganglion cells in rabbit retina. *Science, 191,* 204–205.

Zeki, S. M. (1974). Functional organization of a visual area in the posterior bank of the superior temporal sulcus of the rhesus monkey. *Journal of Physiology, 236,* 549–573.

Zeki, S. M., Watson, J. G., Lueck, C. J., Friston, F. J., Kennard, C., & Frackowiak, R. J. (1991). A direct demonstration of functional specialization in human visual cortex. *Journal of Neuroscience, 11,* 641–649.

Zihl, J., von Cramon, D., & Mai, N. (1983). Selective disturbance of movement vision after bilateral brain damage. *Brain, 106*(Pt 2), 313–340.

6

Depth Perception

There are a number of cues to depth perception. Disparity is the most power-ful and well known, but by no means the only one. Helmholtz (1867/1925) listed nine of them, and his list has been brought up to date by Gibson (1950) and others. The list can be divided into ocular or physiological cues, depending on the position of the eye and the lens; kinetic cues, depending on the movement of the scene or the observer; pictorial cues, employed by painters (mostly since the fifteenth century) to represent depth on a two-dimensional surface; and ste-reopsis, depending on disparity (Table 6–1). Our sense of depth in the normal world depends on these various cues working together to give an integrated perception.

Ocular Cues

The two ocular cues are accommodation and convergence. Accommodation is the change in focus of the lens to bring the object looked at into sharp focus on the retina. Convergence is a disjunctive eye movement, where the eyes move in different directions, to bring a near object onto corresponding points of the two retinas, usually the foveas. Accommodation and convergence are normally linked, so that focus and binocular fusion occur together. They are weak cues to depth perception. Indeed, Gibson (1950) raised the question as to whether depth is a cue for accommodation and convergence more than the reverse, and this is probably true. However, they are the prime cues for distance from the observer, as opposed to depth of one object relative to another.

Accommodation is a monocular cue, since it can be used with one eye open. It is of little use for objects more than 6–8 feet away because there is little change in lens thickness beyond this. It is used at distances less than this to judge the size of objects (Wallach & Floor, 1971). The best evidence that it can be a cue for depth perception actually comes from experiments with chameleons, rather than humans. A chameleon uses it to gauge the distance of an insect when sticking out its tongue to catch it (Harkness, 1977).

Convergence is the only binocular cue for depth besides stereopsis. Subjects can judge the distance of a small dot accurately when starting from a point of rest

TABLE 6–1.
Cues to Depth Perception

Ocular or physiological	Accommodation
	Convergence
Kinetic	Motion parallax
	Optic flow
	Kinetic depth effect
	Interocular velocity differences
Pictorial	Perspective
	Size
	Texture gradients
	Aerial perspective
	Superposition
	Shading
Stereopsis	Disparity

(von Hofsten, 1976). As with accommodation, this works up to a distance of 6–8 feet. There is little in the way of signals from the eye muscles going to the cortex to convey the state of convergence, so most authors suggest that a copy of the signals going to the eye muscles (efference copy) leads to the sensation of depth associated with convergence. If so, then this signal has to be generated as a result of some command to converge coming from other cues to depth perception, or from the experimenter's instruction in a rather abnormal experimental situation. This emphasizes the point that convergence is a weak cue to depth perception, and probably contributes little in a real-life situation.

Kinetic Cues

MOTION PARALLAX

Helmholtz noticed that if you lie on your back in the forest and look up at the branches with one eye closed, the scene of the leaves appears comparatively flat. If you then move your head from side to side, you can see which leaves are in front of the others. This is motion parallax. It occurs whenever the observer is moving laterally, for example, looking out of the side window in a car or train. If you fixate on an object in the middle distance, and you are moving to the left, objects nearer than the point of fixation will move to the right, and objects further than the point of fixation will move to the left (Fig. 6–1 top). The further the object is from the point of fixation, the faster it moves. This is an important cue for objects in the distance, where accommodation, convergence, and stereopsis do not work. Macaque monkeys respond to motion parallax, as do humans (Cao & Schiller, 2002), so mechanisms of single-unit responses recorded from these animals can be generalized to other species.

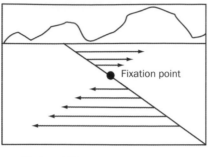

Motion of Observer ⟶

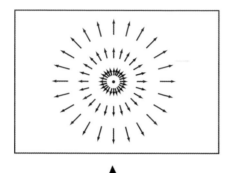

Motion of Observer

FIGURE 6–1. (*Top*) Observer is moving to the right and fixating on the middle distance. Objects nearer than the fixation point move left, and objects further than the fixation point move right. This is called motion parallax. (*Bottom*) Observer is moving toward a point straight ahead. Everything else in the field of view moves outward, creating optic flow.

OPTIC FLOW

Optic flow occurs when the observer moves directly toward or away from an object (Fig. 6–1 bottom), for example, the driver of a car or train. Investigations of optic flow became particularly important when people started to fly aircraft. It was studied extensively by Gibson (1950), who advised the Air Force on the subject. As with motion parallax, objects further from the fixation point move faster than objects near it. This is a cue primarily for the direction in which the observer is headed, but it can also be used to detect how far away the observer is by combining cues about the size of the objects in the scene with the speed with which the scene expands (or contracts).

KINETIC DEPTH EFFECT

In some cases depth will be seen when a set of lines moves on a flat surface. This is called the kinetic depth effect (Wallach & O'Connell, 1953), or more generally structure from motion. It can be demonstrated by rotating a three-dimensional wire frame behind a translucent screen while illuminating it from behind as it rotates (Fig. 6–2; see also nowobbleglobe at http://viperlib.york.ac.uk/). The observer, in front of the screen, will perceive a rotating frame rather than a set of

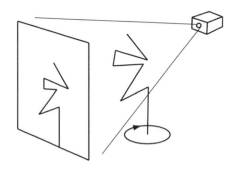

FIGURE 6–2. Kinetic depth effect. A three-dimensional wire structure is rotated, and a light projects its image onto a flat screen. The image on the screen is seen as rotating in depth, as long as the wire structure is not a simple object such as a horizontal line.

lines moving in the plane of the screen. The frame has to be sufficiently complex—a single horizontal bar will appear to be a line expanding and contracting, rather than a bar rotating in space—but for a sufficiently complicated frame the effect is very powerful. Frames with corners work better than frames with curves.

INTEROCULAR VELOCITY DIFFERENCES

When an object moves in depth, the disparity changes; thus, the velocity of its image on the two retinas is different. Both the change in disparity (Cumming & Parker, 1994) and the difference in velocity on the two retinas (Fernandez & Farell, 2005; Rokers, Cormack, & Huk, 2008; Shioiri, Saisho, & Yaguchi, 2000) are used as cues to the motion in depth.

Pictorial Cues

PERSPECTIVE

Linear perspective and a technique for achieving it were described by the painter Alberti in 1436 and also by Leonardo da Vinci half a century later. Parallel lines are represented by lines converging to a vanishing point on the horizon (Fig. 6–3A). Where there is more than one set of parallel lines, there will be more than one vanishing point (Fig. 6–3B). This is an artistic device familiar to anybody today, but not before the fifteenth century, as attested by the flatness of many paintings before that date.

SIZE

Objects of the same size appear smaller with distance. This is an important cue for relative depth and also for absolute depth where the size of an object is known, such as an adult human.

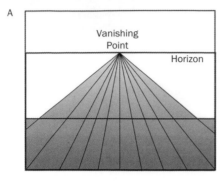

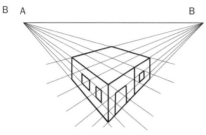

FIGURE 6–3. (*A*) Linear perspective with a single vanishing point. (*B*) Linear perspective with two vanishing points.

TEXTURE GRADIENTS

Since parallel lines get closer together with distance, and objects get smaller with distance, putting the two together gives a powerful impression of depth. This is called a texture gradient (Fig. 6–4).

AERIAL PERSPECTIVE

Because of the atmosphere in front of them, objects that are a long distance away appear hazy (Fig. 6–5). This can be taken as an indication of distance, particularly for mountains or for tall buildings in a polluted city, but it also works for artificial objects. Distant objects, as well as being hazy, are also bluer because of the scattering of light by the atmosphere.

SUPERPOSITION

An object in front will occlude an object that is partially behind it. In Figure 6–6, people invariably perceive a circle in front and a square behind it, rather than a square beside it with a quarter circle cut out of it. Of course, this cue simply determines which object is in front and which behind, and it does not say how far behind.

SHADING

Shading is a cue to depth, based on the assumption that the illumination comes from above. In Figure 6–7, the top row of circles appears convex and the bottom

FIGURE 6–4. The fence has parallel rails, which converge with distance. Underneath, the stones get smaller with distance, also giving an impression of depth (a texture gradient).

FIGURE 6–5. Mountain scene. Blue haze makes the hills above appear to be further away.

row appears concave. If the figure is turned upside down, this perception is reversed. This has long been an important cue in drawing. It is a cue for depth within an object, rather than the position of one object relative to another.

STEREOPSIS

Disparity

Stereopsis depends on disparity, which is due to the fact that we have two eyes looking at the world from different positions about 6.5 cm apart. If the eyes are

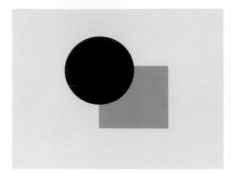

FIGURE 6–6. Superposition makes the gray shape appear to be a square with a circle in front of it.

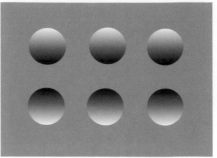

FIGURE 6–7. Shading makes the top row appear convex and the bottom row appear concave, based on the assumption that illumination comes from above.

looking at an object F at the fixation point, then the image of another object (A) at the same distance will fall on corresponding points in the two retinas (Fig. 6–8), meaning that the two images are the same distance from the fovea. Such an object has zero disparity. The images of an object (B) that is closer than the fixation point will fall on noncorresponding points of the two retinas. It is said to have crossed disparity, since the lines of sight cross each other before reaching the horopter (see below). The images of an object (C) that is further away than the fixation point will also fall on noncorresponding points of the two retinas; it is said to have uncrossed disparity. The magnitude of the disparity is an indication of how near or how far away the object is for a particular viewing distance.

Horopter

The horopter is the location of all objects that are the same distance away as the fixation point, that is, objects that will fall on corresponding points of the two retinas. In theory, it is a circle going through the fixation point and the nodal points of the two eyes, called the Vieth-Muller circle. In practice, it is a little flatter than this (Fig. 6–8) and moves further away above the horizontal, and closer below the horizontal.

Stereograms

The first person to investigate stereopsis extensively was Wheatstone (1838). He invented the stereoscope, in which separate figures or photographs are presented to the two eyes. Wheatstone's stereoscope consisted of a mirror in front of each eye at 45°, with two separate images reflected into the two eyes by the two mirrors (Fig. 6–9A). The first stereograms were line drawings, with one example shown in Figure 6–9B. This can be visualized without a stereoscope by converging the eyes until there are three images side by side, with the middle one fused, then allowing accommodation to relax so that it is in focus on the retina. You will see the inner square above the outer one, as though looking down on a lampshade

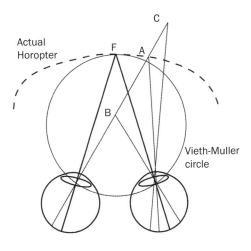

FIGURE 6–8. Crossed and uncrossed disparity. Subject is fixating on point F, with images that fall on the foveas of the two eyes. The images of point A, which is at the same distance as F, fall on two points the same distance away from the fovea, called corresponding points. The images of point B are at different distances from the fovea (noncorresponding points with crossed disparity), and so are the images of point C (noncorresponding points with uncrossed disparity). In theory, the Vieth-Muller circle is the locus of points in space that fall on corresponding points on the two retinas. In practice, the actual locus (the horopter is indicated by a dashed line) is flatter than this.

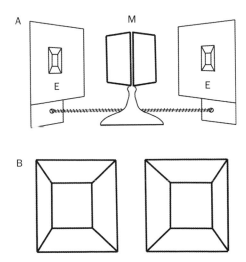

FIGURE 6–9. (*A*) Wheatstone's stereoscope. The apparatus is arranged so that the left eye looks at the left half of the instrument, and the right eye at the right half. Two images (*E*) are reflected by two mirrors (*A*) into the observer's eyes. (*B*) One of Wheatstone's stereograms. When fused with convergent fusion, the inner square appears above the outer one. (Redrawn from Wheatstone, 1838, with kind permission of the Royal Society.)

from above. It may also be viewed by bringing the page close to your face, then moving it away without converging, although this is harder. In this case, you see a lampshade from below.

Random Dot Stereograms

It is possible to see stereo in a pattern of dots that has no outline of an object when seen with either eye alone. Known as a random dot stereogram, this was investigated extensively by Julesz (1971). An example of one of Julesz's random dot stereograms is shown in Figure 6–10. If you converge your eyes to fuse the two images, you will see two rectangles, one in front of the background in the lower half and one behind the background in the upper half. The stereogram consists of a background that is a pattern of dots in the same place for both eyes. Then there is a square pattern of dots in the lower half of the image that is again the same for both eyes, but displaced to the left in the right eye image and to the right in the left eye image, and another square pattern of dots in the upper half of the image that is displaced to the right in the right eye image, and to the left in the left eye image. On one side of the square patterns of dots, the displacement covers the background. On the other side, a new group of random dots is inserted to fill the space.

The success of random dot stereograms in creating a sensation of depth shows that one does not need to outline an object prior to creating depth from stereo. It helps us understand why stereo is useful in detecting camouflaged objects. Random dot stereograms are also a useful device for investigating stereo by itself as a cue to depth perception, since there are no other cues present. Thus, they have been used extensively in both human and animal experiments.

Fusion and Suppression in Stereopsis, and Double Vision

Stereopsis involves both fusion and suppression. As described later, there are cells in the visual cortex that respond to zero disparity, and also cells that respond to positive disparity (uncrossed disparity for objects further away than the fixation point) and cells that respond to negative disparity (crossed disparity for objects nearer than the fixation point). There is fusion in the random dot stereogram in Figure 6–10, where cells with zero disparity fire in the background area but "near" cells and "far" cells do not; in the region of the upper square where far cells fire, but near cells and cells with zero disparity do not; and in the region of the lower square where near cells fire, but far cells and cells with zero disparity do not. Suppression occurs in the strips on each side of the squares, where there is no correspondence between the pattern of dots seen in the left eye and those seen in the right eye, so that none of the near cells, far cells, or cells with zero disparity will fire. When images fall on noncorresponding points of the two eyes, one may get suppression,

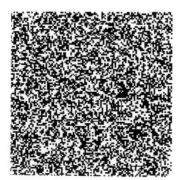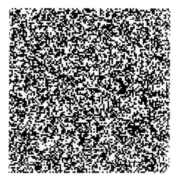

FIGURE 6–10. A random dot stereogram. When fused with convergent fusion, one sees a square at the top behind the background, and a square at the bottom in front of the background.

where the image in one eye is suppressed by the image in the other eye, or one may get double vision, known as diplopia. Diplopia tends to occur when one has incompatible contours in the two eyes, and suppression occurs when the contours are high contrast in one eye and low contrast in the other.

There is a limit to the extent of fusion. The area over which images can be fused is known as Panum's fusional area. It is an ellipse, wider in the horizontal dimension than in the vertical dimension. The size depends on the method of measurement, and it is of the order of several minutes to a degree. Once a pair of images is fused, they can be moved apart and will continue to be fused until a disparity of 2° or so is reached; then one gets double vision. However, they will not be fused again until brought back to within Panum's fusional area. The fusional area, like stereoscopic acuity, increases with eccentricity.

Fine and Coarse Stereopsis

As noted by Helmholtz, images that are not fused and produce diplopia can also give a sensation of depth (see Ogle, 1953). This is limited to a perception of whether one object is in front of or behind the other: there is not much judgment of how far. This was called coarse stereopsis (Bishop & Henry, 1971). It can occur with a disparity up to 7–10°. Some authors have suggested that coarse stereopsis is used primarily to control vergence, so that the two images of an object can be fused, and fine stereopsis will operate to give a more precise judgment of the depth of the object.

da Vinci Stereopsis

When one object is in front of another, there is a strip of the background on the right of the object that can be seen by the right eye but not the left, and a strip of the background on the left of the object that can be seen by the left eye but not the right. These "unpaired" strips can be used to tell that one object is in front of another and to give some indication of how far. It works only with valid strips (on the right of the foreground object, seen in the right eye, or on the left of the foreground object seen in the left eye) and not with invalid strips (on the right of the foreground object, seen in the left eye, or on the left of the foreground object seen in the right eye). This situation was investigated by Nakayama and Shimojo (1990) and named da Vinci stereopsis after Leonardo, who first pointed it out.

The Correspondence or Matching Problem

In scenes in the real world, there is never much doubt about which left eye image should be correlated with which right eye image. Each object is characterized by a variety of attributes—color, orientation of edges, shading, and so on—which are the same in both images, and there are few other images nearby with the same attributes to confuse the situation. However, it is easy to produce displays in which the correspondence or matching between the images in the two eyes is ambiguous. An example is shown in Figure 6–11. When one fuses the two crosses, the set of vertical lines below appears like a Venetian blind. There is a tendency to

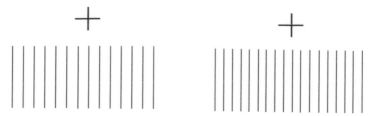

FIGURE 6–11. Correspondence or matching problem. Fixate on the two crosses above the displays, one with the left eye, and one with the right. There is some ambiguity about which line in the left display should be matched up with which line in the right display. Usually nearest neighbors are matched up with each other. This leads in the above display to three neighboring lines tallied with each other, and perception of a slanting surface over the three lines, and a sharp jump back to the next three lines, giving a Venetian blind effect.

match lines close to each other, so that three neighboring lines will be matched, to produce a slanting surface, followed by a sharp jump back to fusion of the next three lines, giving another slanting surface. There are considerable complications to the problem, discussed in Howard and Rogers (2002, Chapter 16).

An interesting situation occurs when a black-on-white version of an object is paired with a white-on-black version of the same object. This can be seen in depth, depending on the width of the lines in the object and various other factors (Howard & Rogers, 2002). However, a random dot object, paired with the same pattern of dots of opposite contrast, is almost never seen in depth. This has been used as a test in experiments in the visual cortex to suggest whether a cell is signaling some aspect of the stereogram that represents disparity rather than depth perception.

Stereoscopic Acuity

Stereoacuity has been measured with three rods, asking the subject to say whether the center one is in front or behind the lateral ones. Good subjects, under the best conditions, produce values of a few seconds of arc (see Howard & Rogers, 2002). This is called a hyperacuity, because it is 10 times better than grating or letter acuity, and the value is close to that for the other hyperacuity, vernier acuity. Since it is difficult to make such fine measurements with random dot stereograms, because the dots have to be large enough to be seen, random dot tests do not go below tens of seconds of arc. Stereoscopic acuity drops off rapidly as one moves away from the fovea. Also, it varies with the conditions under which it is measured, making the topic very complicated (see Howard & Rogers, 2002). How cells in the visual system produce such fine discriminations has generated models and theories but is not definitely known.

Other Properties of Stereo

Stereo can be seen in a brief flash of light. This was noticed by Dove (1841) shortly after Wheatstone introduced the stereoscope. The point applies to simple stick diagrams and also to simple random stereograms. Stereograms that are ambiguous may take longer to process, and complicated shapes such as a spiral or a torus in a random dot stereogram can take many seconds (Julesz, 1971). There is some variability from individual to individual in the length of time that it takes to do this.

People have difficulty in seeing depth in a stereogram when the boundaries in the scene are defined by two different colors—say, red and green—at the same luminance. While there is no doubt that it is more difficult, there has been considerable disagreement over whether the perception of depth is completely gone, complicated by the technical point that equiluminance varies across the retina because of the macular pigment (for a discussion see Livingstone, 1996). Summing all the evidence, it seems reasonable to conclude that stereo signals are carried primarily by cells that are not color coded.

Interaction of Cues to Depth Perception

In the real world, there are several cues to depth perception that usually agree with each other. In the laboratory, one can devise innumerable situations where one cue can affect another, or even oppose another, in the perception of depth (Howard & Rogers, 2002, Chapter 27). One cue may be ambiguous, for example, the direction of rotation in the kinetic depth effect, with the perception affected by the introduction of another cue. Superposition as a cue can certainly be affected by disparity. In Figure 6–12, all three displays are seen as a black square behind a gray square by superposition. When the right pair of stereograms is combined by convergent fusion, one sees a black square behind a gray square, and when the left two stereograms are combined, one sees a black square with a corner cut out in front of the gray square.

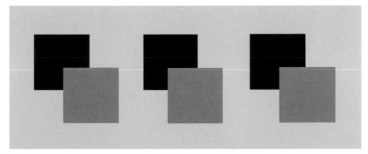

FIGURE 6–12. Interaction of stereopsis and superposition. The three displays, without stereo, are usually each seen as gray squares in front of black squares. When the right two displays are combined with convergent fusion, the stereo cue agrees with this interpretation. When the left two displays are fused, however, the stereo cue leads one to see a gray square behind a black square with a corner cut out of it.

Perspective and disparity may interact in displays of a trapezoidal window, which may be seen as either trapezoidal or rectangular (Brouwer, van Ee, & Schwarzbach, 2005). Faces may be seen as either normal (convex) or inverted (concave), depending on the disparity of a texture superimposed on them (van den Enden & Spekreijse, 1989). The perception in cases of ambiguity such as these has turned out to be a useful test to discover whether responses in areas of cortex, and cells within them, are related to the perception of depth, or just the perception of a cue such as disparity (Brouwer et al., 2005).

The Pulfrich Phenomenon

An interesting illusion that produces a perception of depth is the Pulfrich phenomenon. A pendulum swinging in the frontoparallel plane appears, of course, to be a swinging pendulum. However, if one introduces a neutral density filter in front of one eye, it appears to swing in an ellipse. Transfer of the filter to the other eye reverses the direction of rotation of the pendulum (Pulfrich, 1922). The explanation is that the signal in the filtered eye is delayed because it is dimmer; thus, the cortex correlates the signal in the filtered eye with a slightly later signal in the unfiltered eye (Fig. 6–13). Various experiments have tested predictions that the effect depends on the density of the filter, the velocity of the pendulum, and the overall level of illumination (Lit, 1949). While cells that code for both motion and disparity explain the phenomenon, one can in fact explain it with separate motion and disparity detectors (Read & Cumming, 2005).

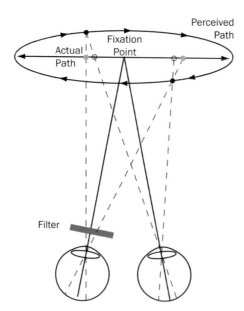

FIGURE 6–13. Pulfrich phenomenon. An observer views a pendulum swinging in a straight line. A filter is placed over the left eye, with slowed transmission from photoreceptors to visual cortex in this eye, as a result of which the signal from the left eye is correlated with a signal from the right eye when the pendulum has swung a little further. Thus, the pendulum appears to swing in an ellipse, clockwise when the filter is over the left eye, and counterclockwise when the filter is over the right eye.

Border and Wallpaper Capture

There is an interesting phenomenon known as border and wallpaper capture, where the cue of disparity can affect the perception of an object (Ramachandran & Cavanagh, 1985). The well-known illusion of a square defined by subjective contours is seen as a white square rather than four circles with quarters cut out of them. If disparity is introduced into the quarters cut out of the circles, viewing stereoscopically one sees a white square floating in space in front of four circles (Fig. 6–14, top). One can then superimpose a wallpaper pattern onto the display, and view it stereoscopically, and the wallpaper pattern in the region of the square appears to come forward, even though the actual pattern of dots in this region has zero disparity (Fig. 6–14, middle). Moreover, a pattern of vertical lines super-imposed onto the display makes the lines appear to have breaks in them at the top and bottom edges of the square, even though the lines are actually continuous (Fig. 6–14, bottom). This shows disparity to be a very powerful cue that can affect the perception of edges, shapes, and location of objects and patterns on them.

Areas of the Brain Concerned With Depth Perception

Most of the work on the areas of the brain concerned with depth perception has been done with stereopsis, because the stimuli (random dot stereograms) are easy

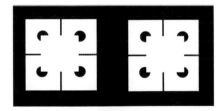

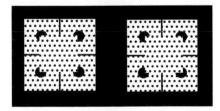

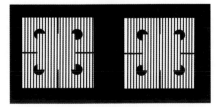

FIGURE 6–14. The top display, when fused convergently, is seen as a square floating in front of four black circles.In the second display, the black dots within the square come forward with the square, even though the nearest correspondence leaves them on the background. In the bottom display, the lines appear to be broken at the top and bottom edges of the square, and to come forward with the square, even though they are in reality continuous. (Redrawn from Ramachandran & Cavanagh, 1985, with kind permission of MacMillan Publishers.)

to apply. Cells that respond to disparity are found in primary visual cortex (V1), and many other areas of cortex are also concerned with stereopsis. Indeed, Holmes and Horrax (1919) reported a soldier with a bullet wound through both parietal cortices who had good acuity in his upper visual fields, but no sensation of depth at all, from any cues, including stereopsis. Using PET (positron emission tomography) and random dot stimuli, Gulyas and Roland (1994) reported activation of a number of areas in occipital cortex, parietal cortex, frontal cortex, and cerebellum by stereo. This has since been confirmed by a number of studies using functional magnetic resonance imaging (fMRI). Area 3A is particularly well activated (Backus, Fleet, Parker& Heeger, 2001; Tsao et al., 2003).

There is a distinction between absolute disparity and relative disparity. Relative disparity gives a perception of the depth of one object in relation to another object nearby. Absolute disparity gives a perception of the depth of an object relative to the point of fixation. Early visual areas (V1, V2, and V3) give small fMRI signals in response to stimuli for both absolute and relative disparity. Dorsal visual areas (V3A, MT, and V7) respond better to stimuli for absolute disparity than stimuli for relative disparity; ventral areas (human V4, V8/V4a) respond equally to stimuli for both (Neri, Bridge, & Heeger, 2004). Insofar as absolute disparity drives vergence eye movements, and relative disparity is used to judge the three-dimensional layout and shape of objects, this fits in with the general point that the dorsal pathway is involved with where an object is, and the ventral pathway is involved with what an object is (Minini, Parker, & Bridge, 2010).

More recent work has started to analyze contributions of various cues to the three-dimensional shape of an object. This is a complicated process, and the analysis is at an early stage. However, it is clear that various areas in temporal cortex are involved as well as those in occipital cortex (Sereno, Trinath, Augath, & Logothetis, 2002).

Experiments with fMRI and PET can tell us only so much about the processing of depth perception, because these signals have limited resolution and average the response over a number of neurons. For further information, we have to turn to recordings from single cells, carried out mostly in macaque monkey and cat. The areas concerned with stereo in macaque are a little different from those in man (Tsao et al., 2003), and the areas in cat are considerably different; nevertheless, a considerable amount has been learned from recordings in those two species. We will describe the main findings, concentrating on recordings from macaque.

STEREO SIGNALS IN V1

Recordings in macaque striate cortex have distinguished a variety of types of cells sensitive to disparity (Poggio & Talbot, 1981; Fig. 6–15). Cells that are excited by a particular disparity with a narrow tuning curve are called tuned excitatory (TE). These may be divided into those that respond best to zero disparity (To), those that respond best to objects beyond the horopter (tuned far,

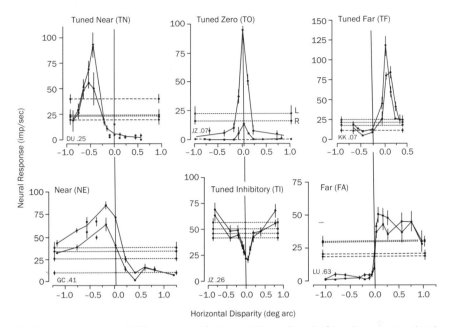

FIGURE 6–15. Examples of different types of cell sensitive to disparity from the macaque visual cortex. Tuned near cells respond to a narrow range of negative disparities, tuned zero cells to a narrow range around zero disparity, and tuned far cells to a narrow range of positive disparities. Near cells respond to a wide range of negative disparities, far cells to a wide range of positive disparities, and tuned inhibitory cells are inhibited over a narrow range of disparities near zero. (Reprinted from Poggio et al., 1988, with kind permission of the Society for Neuroscience.)

TF), and those that respond best to objects nearer than the horopter (tuned near, TN). Cells that are inhibited by a particular disparity are called tuned inhibitory (TI)—a small class, mostly tuned to zero disparity. Cells that respond to a wide range of disparities beyond the horopter are called far cells (FA), and those that respond to a wide range of disparities nearer than the horopter are called near cells (NE). The tuned cells tend to have symmetric tuning curves (the curve of response as a function of disparity), and the near and far cells tend to have asymmetric tuning curves. The suggestion is that tuned cells are responsible for the fine details of depth perception, corresponding to fine stereopsis, and that near and far cells control vergence movements, corresponding to coarse stereopsis (Poggio & Talbot, 1981).

Experiments first done in the cat show that there are two types of disparity sensitivity, known as position disparity and phase disparity (DeAngelis, Ohzawa, & Freeman, 1991). In position disparity, the structure of the receptive fields in the two eyes is the same, and the position of the receptive field in one eye is displaced relative to the other (Fig. 6–16). In phase disparity, the receptive fields in the two eyes have the same position, but areas that are excited are displaced relative to each other, and so are areas that are inhibited. Either position or phase disparity

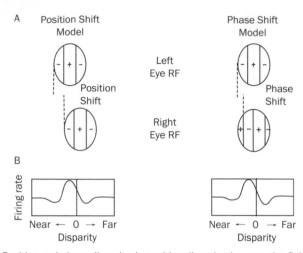

FIGURE 6–16. Position and phase disparity. In position disparity the receptive fields in the two eyes lie on noncorresponding points of the two retinas, one displaced laterally from the other (A left). In phase disparity, the receptive fields lie on corresponding points of the retinas, but the substructure of the receptive field in one eye is displaced relative to the other (A right). Both types of cell have disparity tuning curves with a peak (B).

can be used to produce ordinary stereopsis. Having both is useful for da Vinci stereopsis (Tsao et al., 2003).

There is a relationship between the various tuned, near, and far categories, and the phase and position disparity (Prince, Cumming, & Parker, 2002). However, study of a large sample of cells from macaque V1 has shown that the categories are not distinct. There is a continuum of responses, so that one category blends into another (Fig. 6–17). How this fits into the function of the various disparity-sensitive cells, and what aspects of vision they control, remains to be determined.

DEPTH SIGNALS IN V2

As described in Chapter 2, V2 can be divided into thin, thick, and pale stripes (Hubel & Livingstone, 1987). Cells selective for disparity are concentrated in the thick stripes. There are also disparity-selective cells in the other stripes, but the concentration is lower: 38% of cells in thick stripes, 18% in thin, and 15% in pale (Peterhans & von der Heydt, 1993). However, nearly all the disparity cells with narrow tuning curves recorded by Peterhans and von der Heydt were found in thick stripes, so the two studies are actually in substantial agreement. Within the thick stripes, the disparity cells are clustered into groups of near, far, tuned excitatory, and tuned inhibitory cells (Ts'o, Roe, & Gilbert, 2001). The original work claimed little relationship between disparity and orientation sensitivity (Hubel & Livingstone, 1987), but more recent work, using microelectrode penetrations guided to the appropriate location by optical imaging (Ts'o et al., 2001), suggests

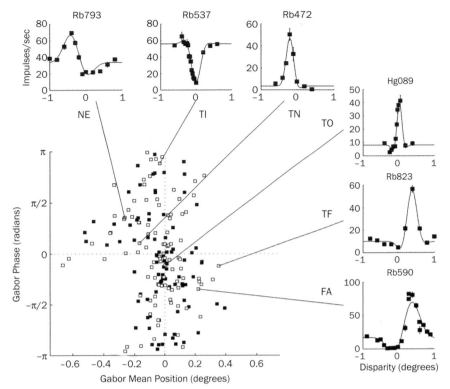

FIGURE 6–17. Position and phase disparity, related to types of cell defined by Poggio and colleagues. Far cells tend to have positive position disparity and negative phase disparity, and near cells the reverse. There is clearly a continuum of position and phase disparities, and most investigators would say that there is also a continuum between tuned cells and cells responding to a wider range of disparities. Stimulus used to elicit the response was a Gabor, which is a sine-wave grating that falls off in intensity from center to periphery. Open and closed squares represent cells from two different macaques (Reprinted from Prince et al., 2002, with kind permission of the American Physiological Society.)

that many disparity cells have an orientation selectivity close to vertical, and that the orientation sensitivity varies little as the electrode is lowered through the layers of cortex.

As described in Chapter 7, V2 is the area where cells respond to illusory contours as well as real contours, and the response of a cell to an edge depends on whether the edge belongs to an object located to the left or the right of the edge—a phenomenon known as border capture. There is a correlation between stereopsis and border capture, so that the cell will associate "object left" with "left surface in front." This is illustrated in Figure 6–18, from a cell recorded by Qiu and von der Heydt (2005) in V2. The cell responded to a dark/light border with the dark on the left when the boundary belonged to an object to the left (Fig. 6–18A), but not when it belonged to an object on the right (Fig. 6–18B). It did not respond

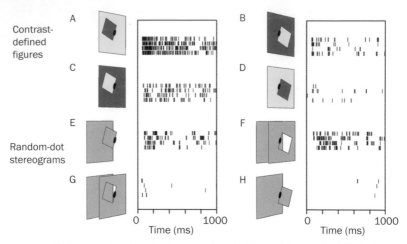

FIGURE 6–18. Cell responding to a border associated with an object to the left. Cell responds to a border (black on left, gray on right) when the border is part of an object to the left (*A*), but less when the object is to the right (*B*). It does not respond as vigorously to a border with black on the right and gray on the left, with the object either to the left (*C*) or to the right (*D*). It also responds to a border defined by a random dot stereogram when the border belongs to the surface in front (*E* and *F*), but not when the border belongs to the surface behind (*G* and *H*). (Reprinted from Qiu & von der Heydt, 2005, with kind permission of Cell Press.)

to a light/dark border with the dark on the right, either for an object on the left (Fig. 6–18C) or for an object on the right (Fig. 6–18D). It also responded to a disparity border when the area to the left was in front (Figs. 6–18Eand F), but not when the area to the left was behind (Figs. 6–18G and H). The association between "object left," which usually occurs when the object to the left is a small one seen against a background, and "left surface in front" makes sense, because small objects usually are in front of the background. Here again, the disparity cue is the powerful one, and it will override other cues about which object is in front and which is behind (Qiu & von der Heydt, 2005).

Disparity can also affect the perception of a line as being complete. When a broken line is partly obscured by an orthogonal bar in front of the gap, it appears continuous. If the orthogonal bar is behind, however, it appears broken. The response of some cells in V2 correlates with this phenomenon (Bakin, Nakayama, & Gilbert, 2000). The response of the cell illustrated in Figure 6–19 shows that the response to a bar in the receptive field is enhanced by a bar outside the receptive field in line with it, but with a gap. This enhancement also occurs when the gap is covered by an orthogonal bar in front of the display, but not when there is an orthogonal bar located in the same plane as the gap or behind the gap (Fig. 6–19). This kind of result is seen in a reasonable percentage of disparity-sensitive cells in V2, but in very few cells in V1. These various results show that V2

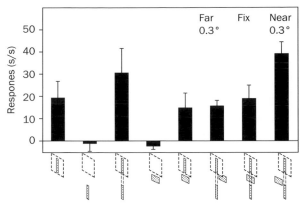

FIGURE 6–19. Cell responds to a vertical bar in the receptive field, outlined with dashes (left histogram), but not to a bar outside the receptive field (second histogram). The bar outside the receptive field, although it gives no response by itself, enhances the response of the bar in the receptive field (third histogram). A horizontal bar outside the receptive field does not change the response of the vertical bar inside the receptive field, or give a response by itself (fourth and fifth histograms). The horizontal bar also does not change the response of the broken vertical bar when it is in the same plane or behind (sixth and seventh histograms), but enhances it when it is in front (eighth histogram), which would lead to the perception of a continuous vertical bar. (Reprinted from Bakin et al., 2000, with kind permission of the Society for Neuroscience.)

plays a significant role in how disparity affects the perception of contours, edges, and shapes in three dimensions.

STEREO AND DEPTH PERCEPTION IN AREAS V3 AND V3A

Although fMRI studies, listed earlier, have identified area V3A as an area in human brain that is activated particularly well by stereoscopic stimuli, there are few single-cell studies in macaque V3A that elucidate how the responses might differ from those in V1 and V2. Recordings have been made in V3, which probably included cells from V3A (Adams & Zeki, 2001). These recordings, as well as those from Poggio (Poggio, Gonzalez, & Krause, 1988) have identified tuned, near, and far cells in these areas, and confirm the fMRI studies that disparity responses are common. V3A signals absolute disparity rather than relative disparity (Anzai & de Angelis, 2010). More detailed studies about the nature of those responses remains to be done.

DORSAL AND VENTRAL PATHWAYS

As described in Chapter 2, there are two streams of processing of visual information after V3, the dorsal stream, leading to V3A, V5/MT, MST, and V7 (human), concerned with where an object is, and the ventral stream, leading to V4, inferotemporal cortex (IT), and V8 (human), concerned with what an object is. Magnocellular layers in the lateral geniculate nucleus feed the dorsal stream, and parvocellular layers feed the ventral stream. Despite early studies suggesting that stereopsis is primarily on the magnocellular/dorsal stream (Livingstone & Hubel, 1987), and lesion studies suggesting that it is primarily on the parvocellular/ventral stream (Schiller, Logothetis, & Charles, 1990), there is abundant evidence that it plays a significant role in both streams. We will describe evidence for its role first in the dorsal stream (V5/MT, MST, and LIP) and then in the ventral stream (V4 and IT).

DEPTH PERCEPTION IN MT

In addition to its well-known response to moving stimuli (Chapter 5), MT has a significant response to depth. Two-thirds of the cells in the area respond to disparity (Maunsell & van Essen, 1983). They are clustered into areas with disparity tuning and areas without (DeAngelis & Newsome, 1999). Within the areas with disparity tuning, there are regions for near cells, far cells, and cells for zero disparity (Fig. 6–20). This diagrammatic drawing is a suggestion of how the organization might look, and it has not been definitely proved. For one thing, it does not take account of the fact that there are some cells in MT that respond to disparity but not movement (Palanca & DeAngelis, 2003). Nevertheless, it points out the clustering in a dramatic way.

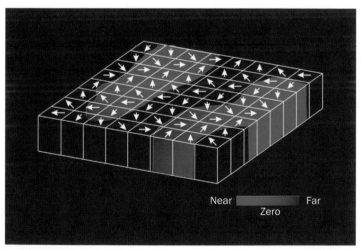

FIGURE 6–20. Schematic diagram of disparity tuning in medial temporal cortex (MT). There are columns for direction of motion (see arrows). Superimposed on this is a clustering of cells sensitive to near, zero, and far disparity, interspersed with areas that are not sensitive to disparity. (Reprinted from DeAngelis & Newsome, 1999, with kind permission of the Society for Neuroscience.)

The clustering of disparity tuning enables a test of the function of MT. Once the position of a cluster, for example, a group of near cells, has been identified, they can be stimulated. This biases the animal to perceive a pattern of dots as being closer than they really are (DeAngelis, Cumming, & Newsome, 1998), showing that MT is clearly involved in the perception of depth, in addition to any role that it plays in perception of motion.

Cells in MT respond to differences in disparity between an object located in the receptive field and the surround outside the receptive field (Bradley & Andersen, 1998). This is in addition to a response to differences in direction of movement between the object in the center and the surround, and differences in velocity between these two areas. These three aspects of the response all add up to identify objects moving in front of the background.

Furthermore, cells in MT respond to structure from motion. A cylinder with dots on it can be rotated and its image projected onto a screen (Fig. 6–21), and the two-dimensional image viewed from the other side. The image is seen as a rotating cylinder, but the direction of rotation is ambiguous. Sometimes it appears to rotate clockwise, and sometimes it appears counterclockwise. When macaques view such an image, they can be trained to report the direction of movement of the front surface of the cylinder (Bradley, Chang, & Andersen, 1998). The perception correlates with an increase in firing of cells responding to near objects moving in the appropriate direction.

Thus, MT responds to several aspects of the movement and location of objects in space. Depth cues are one of these aspects. Disparity is involved, and so is structure from motion, and depth from motion parallax (Nadler, Angelaki, & DeAngelis, 2008). The orientation of objects in depth (tilt and slant) is another

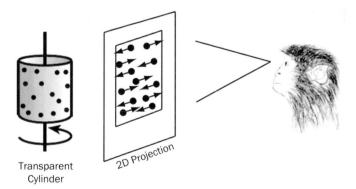

Transparent
Cylinder

2D Projection

FIGURE 6–21. Macaque monkey responding to structure from motion. A rotating cylinder with dots on it is located behind a flat screen, and its image is projected onto the screen. The image is seen as a rotating cylinder of dots, but the direction of motion is ambiguous. The monkey signals the direction of motion of the front surface of the cylinder, and the response of cells in medial temporal cortex (MT) corresponds to the perception. (Reprinted from Bradley et al., 1998, with kind permission of MacMillan Publishers.)

aspect included (Nguyenkim & DeAngelis, 2003). The motion information probably comes in the direct projection from V1 to MT, whereas the disparity information comes through V2 (Ponce, Lomber, & Born, 2008). Although MT is identified as being on the dorsal pathway, the activity of cells there is related to, and affects, both perception and eye movements.

DEPTH IN AREA MST

MT projects to the area close by called MST, which is divided into three parts: MSTd, MSTi, and MTSl. Nearly all the cells in this area are sensitive to disparity, have broad tuning curves, and are near or far cells—the number of tuned cells is comparatively small (Roy, Komatsu, & Wurtz, 1992). About half the cells in MSTd and MSTi have an interesting combination of properties: they respond to one direction of movement for objects nearer than the point of fixation, and in the opposite direction of movement for objects further away than the point of fixation (Fig. 6–22). This, of course, is exactly what should happen when the observer is moving in relation to the point of fixation. These cells are called disparity-dependent direction cells (DDD). The hypothesis is that these cells deal with the movement of an observer past an object, and the remainder of the cells that are not DDD deal with the movement of an observer toward or away from an object, which leads to optic flow (Chapter 5). This area is likely to be involved in the short-latency vergence eye movements investigated by Miles and his colleagues (Miles, 1998).

The cells in MSTl are not DDD. Instead, they have a clear center-surround separation in their receptive fields (Eifuku & Wurtz, 1999). They may respond to

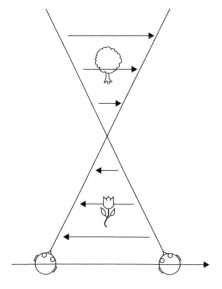

FIGURE 6–22. Disparity-dependent direction (DDD). When an observer is moving to the right, objects nearer than the fixation point move to the left, and objects further away than the fixation point move to the right. There are cells with properties like this in the medial superior temporal cortex, dorsal portion (MSTd). These cells presumably represent motion of the observer in relation to the world around. (Reprinted from Roy et al., 1992, with kind permission of the Society for Neuroscience.)

differences in relative disparity, or to differences in absolute disparity between center and surround. These properties—in addition to the point that MSTl cells respond to movement of a small object, whereas MSTd cells respond to movement of a large pattern—make the cells in MSTl appropriate for the segmentation of an object from its background.

PARIETAL CORTEX

Parietal cortex is where sensory inputs are combined to control movement. Several of the areas there are visuomotor, receiving input from V3/V3A and MT. The visual input has not been studied in great detail, but where it has been studied, there are some interesting findings. For example, cells in the caudal part of the lateral intraparietal sulcus (CIP) respond to gradients of texture and also to gradients of disparity, to code for surfaces oriented in depth (Tsutsui, Sakata, Naganuma, & Taira, 2002). Whether these two cues to depth perception come together in prior visual areas, or whether this is the first area where they are combined, is not known. Seventy-two percent of the cells in the lateral intraparietal sulcus (LIP) that fire before saccades, and that project to the superior colliculus, are coded for depth (Gnadt & Mays, 1995), emphasizing the visuomotor nature of the area. How various other cues to depth perception are combined in these areas, and how the response varies between the various subdivisions of the intraparietal sulcus (AIP, LIP, MIP, CIP), both remain to be investigated.

DEPTH IN V4

A high percentage of the cells recorded in V4 are sensitive to disparity. Several different authors have studied them, and their conclusions are largely the same. There is a preponderance of cells preferring crossed disparities (Hinkle & Connor, 2005; Watanabe, Tanaka, Uka, & Fujita, 2002). Compared to MT, there are more symmetric (tuned excitatory and inhibitory) cells than asymmetric (near and far) cells (Tanabe et al., 2005). Cells with like disparity are clustered together (Tanabe, Doi, Umeda, & Fujita, 2005; Watanabe et al., 2002). The response to disparity is largely independent of the position of the stimulus within the receptive field (Watanabe et al., 2002). Measuring the response to relative disparity compared to the response to absolute disparity, it is higher than in V2, but not as high as expected for a response that is totally dependent on relative disparity (Umeda, Tanabe, & Fujita, 2007). Moreover, the response to random dot stereograms is different from the response to bar stereograms, although the significance of this observation is not clear (Hegde & van Essen 2005a; Tanabe et al., 2005).

Size constancy has also been studied in V4 (Dobbins, Jeo, Fizer, & Allman, 1998). The response of many cells correlates with size constancy, although some cells respond better to distant objects, and some better to nearby objects, and in that sense can be said to respond to nearness or farness. Cells in V4 also respond to the slant of an object in space (Hegde & van Essen, 2005b; Hinkle & Connor, 2005). However, neither of these observations has been related to the disparity sensitivity of the cells.

All of these observations support the role of V4 as a way station between striate cortex and inferotemporal cortex, responsible for analyzing the structure of objects. However, at this point there is little study in V4 of the other cues to depth perception, or how the various cues might be integrated to provide the depth perception. This will depend on further work.

INFEROTEMPORAL CORTEX

Inferotemporal cortex (IT) is known as the area where cells respond to the shape of objects (see Chapter 7). More than half of them also respond to disparity (Uka et al., 2000) in the lower bank of the superior temporal sulcus—the percentage is lower in the anterior part of IT (Janssen, Vogels, & Orban, 2000a). A number respond to both shape and disparity (Uka et al., 2000; Fig. 6–23). The shape may be defined by luminance or by random dot stereograms (Fig. 6–24), and many cells respond to the shape independent of how the shape is specified (Tanaka et al., 2001).

Most cells respond to near or far disparities and are clustered according to this (Uka et al., 2000). There may be some tuned cells, but if they did not respond to zero disparity, the investigators would not have noticed them, and in any case the stimuli required to activate IT cells can be very complicated.

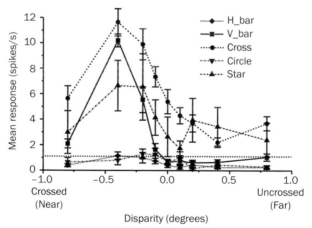

FIGURE 6–23. A cell responding to both shape and disparity in inferotemporal cortex. It responds best to a cross and a vertical bar, somewhat less to a star, and very little to a circle or a horizontal bar. For all objects that give a response, the response is greater for crossed disparities than for uncrossed disparities. (Reprinted from Uka et al., 2000, with kind permission of the American Physiological Society.)

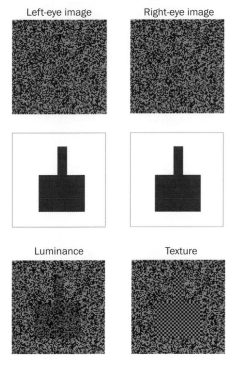

FIGURE 6–24. Three ways of specifying a shape, in this case the outline of a basket with a handle. (*A*) Defined by disparity in a random dot stereogram. (*B*) Defined by outline. (*C*) Defined by luminance (*left*), or density of texture (*right*). Cells in inferotemporal cortex will respond to the shape, independent of how it is specified. (Reprinted from Tanaka et al., 2001, with kind permission of the American Physiological Society.)

Some cells respond to planar slanting surfaces (second-order disparity) and some to surfaces curved in space (third-order disparity) (Janssen, Vogels, & Orban, 2000b). Examples are shown in Figure 6–25. This selectivity is somewhat independent of position in the frontoparallel plane and of size of the object. Cells in IT also respond to correlated random dot stereograms (RDS), but not to anti-correlated RDS, unlike cells in V1, MT, and MST (Janssen, Vogels, Liu, & Orban, 2003). This is what is expected if the matching problem has been solved in IT, but not in V1, MT, or MST (the problem is partly solved in V4; Watanabe et al., 2002). Thus, cells in IT can be said to signal depth perception, not just simply disparity. In summary, signals for disparity and shape finally come together in IT to define a three-dimensional object. Undoubtedly shading also plays a role, but how this happens awaits further experiments.

EYE MOVEMENT AREAS

About two-thirds of the cells in the frontal eye fields respond to disparity (Ferraina, Pare, & Wurtz, 2000). They are broadly tuned to near or far disparities. Although this area was originally related primarily to saccades, it also has cells related to smooth pursuit eye movements and vergence (Fukushima et al., 2002). Two-thirds of the cells in the superior colliculus, at least in the cat, also

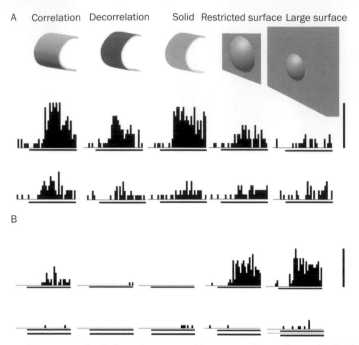

FIGURE 6–25. Responses of cells to surfaces curved in space and to surfaces slanting in space. (*A*) A cell in inferotemporal cortex that responds best to a curved surface, in a convex configuration (top row of histograms), and less in a concave configuration (second row of histograms). The response is reduced for a slanting surface, for both convex and concave configurations. (*B*) A cell that responds better to the slanting surface than to the curved surfaces, and to convex configurations, but not to concave configurations. (Reprinted from Janssen et al., 2003, with kind permission of Cell Press.)

respond to disparity with broad tuning (Mimeault, 2004). Presumably the cells with disparity sensitivity have to do with vergence movements, or saccades in three-dimensional space. Thus, it is interesting that the percentage is as high as it is in both these areas.

ROLE OF THE CORPUS CALLOSUM AND OPTIC CHIASM

There is a complication in the perception of objects straight ahead of the subject, because the images project to different hemispheres of the brain. For an object nearer than the fixation point, the image will fall on the temporal retinas of both eyes, and the right eye image will project to the right hemisphere while the left eye image will project to the left hemisphere. Connections between the two hemispheres through the corpus callosum coordinate the signals and provide perception of disparity (Fig. 6–26). For an object further away than the fixation point, the image will fall on the nasal retinas of both eyes, and the left eye image

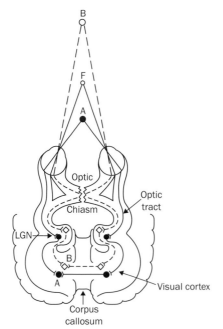

FIGURE 6–26. Point A projects to both temporal retinas, with ipsilateral projections to the cortex. Signals from the two eyes are combined through the corpus callosum. Point B projects to both nasal retinas, with contralateral connections to the cortex through the optic chiasm. Again signals from the two eyes are combined through the corpus callosum. Thus, cutting the corpus callosum will disrupt coordination for point A, and cutting either the optic chiasm or the corpus callosum will disrupt coordination for point B. (Reprinted from Blakemore, 1970, with kind permission of Elsevier.)

will project to the right hemisphere through the optic chiasm while the right eye image will project to the left hemisphere, also through the optic chiasm. Again, connections through the corpus callosum coordinate the two signals. Thus, section of the optic chiasm should disrupt depth perception of far objects in the midline, and section of the corpus callosum should disrupt perception of both far and near objects in the midline. Both these predictions are supported by animal experiments and by human patients who have section of the optic chiasm (Blakemore, 1970) or section of the corpus callosum (Mitchell & Blakemore, 1970).

People Who Lack Stereopsis

There are not many studies on people who lack stereopsis. The three main causes of lack of stereopsis are strabismus (which occurs when the eyes look in different directions), albinism, and lesions of the brain. In the case of lesions, the deficit is greater when the lesion affects the superior visual fields (Rizzo, Boller, & Grafman, 1989). One such case was the soldier studied by Holmes and Horrax (1919), discussed earlier. The lesion needs to be bilateral. The loss of stereopsis is often associated with deficits in motion sensitivity and attention. Suggestions that the right hemisphere is more important are controversial. Temporal cortex plays a particular role in random dot stereograms (Cowey & Porter, 1979).

Strabismus is a particular problem in children before puberty. With the eyes looking in different directions and a lack of correspondence between the images on the two retinas, there is a loss of cells with binocular input in the visual cortex (Hubel & Wiesel, 1965), which leads to a loss of stereopsis (Daw, 2006). A similar problem may occur where the two eyes are focused at different distances (anisometropia). From 2% to 5% of the population is at risk for these problems if they are not corrected by optical means or surgery. These children also have a loss of acuity in the deviating eye (amblyopia).

Albinism leads to a misrouting of fibers at the optic chiasm, so that there are more fibers projecting to the contralateral side of the brain than the ipsilateral side. Therefore, many albinos have no stereoscopic vision, but some show coarse stereopsis, perhaps from callosal connections (Apkarian & Reites, 1989). Siamese cats, which have a form of albinism, show deficits in stereopsis (Packwood & Gordon, 1975). They also show an absence of single cells in the visual cortex with binocular input (Guillery, Casagrande, & Oberdorfer, 1974), and this is likely to be true of human albinos as well.

A population of 150 students at MIT was studied by Richards for ability to detect depth in random dot stereograms (1970). He found that about 4% were unable to see depth at all, and another 10% had great difficulty and incorrectly reported the depth relative to the background. Some had trouble with near objects and others with far objects. The percentage totally lacking stereopsis is not far from the percentage with amblyopia (poor vision) from strabismus and other causes. However, Richards did not test for amblyopia, or take a history of their visual abilities, so we do not know how many of his subjects previously had strabismus or anisometropia. He suggested that there may be three classes of people: those lacking near cells, those lacking far cells, and those lacking both, and that there is a genetic component to stereo vision. There is certainly a genetic component to albinism and to strabismus, but the point needs to be studied in other people lacking stereopsis, and nobody has replicated Richards's observation that some people lack near cells only, and others lack far cells only.

References

Adams, D. L., & Zeki, S. (2001). Functional organization of macaque V3 for stereoscopic depth. *Journal of Neurophysiology, 86*, 2195–2203.

Anzai A., & DeAngelis. G. C. (2010) Neural computations underlying depth perception. *Current Opinion in Neurobiology, 20*, 367–375.

Apkarian, P., & Reites, D. (1989). Global stereopsis in human albinos. *Vision Research, 29*, 1359–1370.

Backus, B. T., Fleet, D. J., Parker, A. J., & Heeger, D. J. (2001). Human cortical activity correlates with stereoscopic depth perception. *Journal of Neurophysiology, 86*, 2054–2068.

Bakin, J. S., Nakayama, K., & Gilbert, C. D. (2000). Visual responses in monkey areas V1 and V2 to three-dimensional surface configurations. *Journal of Neuroscience, 20,* 8188–8198.

Bishop, P. O., & Henry, G. H. (1971). Spatial vision. *Annual Review of Psychology, 22,* 119–160.

Blakemore, C. (1970). Binocular depth perception and the optic chiasm. *Vision Research, 10,* 43–47.

Bradley, D. C., & Andersen, R. A. (1998). Center-surround antagonism based on disparity in primate area MT. *Journal of Neuroscience, 18,* 7552–7565.

Bradley, D. C., Chang, G. C., & Andersen, R. A. (1998). Encoding of three-dimensional structure-from-motion by primate area MT neurons. *Nature, 392,* 714–717.

Brouwer, G. J., van Ee, R., & Schwarzbach, J. (2005). Activation in visual cortex correlates with the awareness of stereoscopic depth. *Journal of Neuroscience, 25,* 10403–10413.

Cao, A., & Schiller, P. H. (2002). Behavioral assessment of motion parallax and stereopsis as depth cues in rhesus monkeys. *Vision Research, 42,* 1953–1961.

Cowey, A., & Porter, J. (1979). Brain damage and global stereopsis. *Proceedings of the Royal Society of London B: Biological Sciences, 204,* 399–407.

Cumming, B. G., & Parker, A. J. (1994). Binocular mechanisms for detecting motion-in-depth. *Vision Research, 34,* 483–495.

Daw, N. W. (2006). *Visual development.* New York: Springer.

DeAngelis, G. C., Cumming, B. G., & Newsome, W. T. (1998). Cortical area MT and the perception of stereoscopic depth. *Nature, 394,* 677–680.

DeAngelis, G. C., & Newsome, W. T. (1999). Organization of disparity-selective neurons in macaque area MT. *Journal of Neuroscience, 19,* 1398–1415.

DeAngelis, G. C., Ohzawa, I., & Freeman, R. D. (1991). Depth is encoded in the visual cortex by a specialized receptive field structure. *Nature, 352,* 156–159.

Dobbins, A. C., Jeo, R. M., Fizer, J., & Allman, J. M. (1998). Distance modulation of neural activity in the visual cortex. *Science, 281,* 552–555.

Dove, H. W. (1841). Uber die Combination der Eindrucke beider Ohren und beider Augen zu einem Eindruck. *Monatsberichte der Berliner Akadamie,* 251–252.

Eifuku, S., & Wurtz, R. H. (1999). Response to motion in extrastriate area MST1: Disparity sensitivity. *Journal of Neurophysiology, 82,* 2462–2475.

Fernandez, J. M., & Farell, B. (2005). Seeing motion in depth using inter-ocular velocity differences. *Vision Research, 45,* 2786–2798.

Ferraina, S., Pare, M., & Wurtz, R. H. (2000). Disparity sensitivity of frontal eye field neurons. *Journal of Neurophysiology, 83,* 625–629.

Fukushima, K., Yamanobe, T., Shinmei, Y., Fukushima, J., Kurkin, S., & Peterson, B. W. (2002). Coding of smooth eye movements in three-dimensional space by frontal cortex. *Nature, 419,* 157–162.

Gibson, J. J. (1950). *The perception of the visual world.* Boston, MA: Houghton Mifflin.

Gnadt, J. W., & Mays, L. E. (1995). Neurons in monkey parietal area LIP are tuned for eye-movement parameters in three-dimensional space. *Journal of Neurophysiology, 73,* 280–297.

Guillery, R. W., Casagrande, V. A., & Oberdorfer, M. D. (1974). Congenitally abnormal vision in Siamese cats. *Nature, 252,* 195–199.

Gulyas, B., & Roland, P. E. (1994). Binocular disparity discrimination in human cerebral cortex: Functional anatomy by positron emission tomography. *Proceedings of the National Academy of Sciences USA, 91,* 1239–1243.

Harkness, L. (1977). Chameleons use accommodation cues to judge distance. *Nature, 267,* 346–349.

Hegde, J., & Van Essen, D. C. (2005a). Stimulus dependence of disparity coding in primate visual area V4. *Journal of Neurophysiology, 93,* 620–626.

Hegde, J., & Van Essen, D. C. (2005b). Role of primate visual area V4 in the processing of 3-D shape characteristics defined by disparity. *Journal of Neurophysiology, 94,* 2856–2866.

Helmholtz, H. (1867/1925). *Treatise on physiological optics.* New York: Dover.

Hinkle, D. A., & Connor, C. E. (2005). Quantitative characterization of disparity tuning in ventral pathway area V4. *Journal of Neurophysiology, 94,* 2726–2737.

Holmes, G., & Horrax, G. (1919). Disturbances of spatial orientation and visual attention, with loss of stereoscopic vision. *Archives of Neurology and Psychiatry, 1,* 389–407.

Howard, I. P., & Rogers, B. J. (2002). *Seeing in depth: Depth perception.* Thornhill, ON: Porteous, I.

Hubel, D. H., & Livingstone, M. S. (1987). Segregation of form, color, and stereopsis in primate area 18. *Journal of Neuroscience, 7,* 3378–3415.

Hubel, D. H., & Wiesel, T. N. (1965). Binocular interaction in striate cortex of kittens reared with artificial squint. *Journal of Neurophysiology, 28,* 1041–1059.

Janssen, P., Vogels, R., Liu, Y., & Orban, G. A. (2003). At least at the level of inferior temporal cortex. the stereo correspondence problem is solved. *Neuron, 37,* 693–701.

Janssen, P., Vogels, R., & Orban, G. A. (2000a). Selectivity for 3D shape that reveals distinct areas within macaque inferior temporal cortex. *Science, 288,* 2054–2056.

Janssen, P., Vogels, R., & Orban, G. A. (2000b). Three-dimensional shape coding in inferior temporal cortex. *Neuron, 27,* 385–397.

Julesz, B. (1971). *Foundations of cyclopean perception.* Chicago, IL: University of Chicago Press.

Lit, A. (1949). The magnitude of the Pulfrich stereophenomenon as a function of binocular differences of intensity at various levels of illumination. *American Journal of Psycholology, 62,* 159–181.

Livingstone, M. S. (1996). Differences between stereopsis, interocular correlation and binocularity. *Vision Research, 36,* 1127–1140.

Livingstone, M. S., & Hubel, D. H. (1987). Psychophysical evidence for separate channels for the perception of form, color, movement and depth. *Journal of Neuroscience, 7,* 3416–3468.

Maunsell, J. R., & Van Essen, D. C. (1983). Functional properties of neurons in middle temporal area of the macaque monkey II. Binocular interactions and sensitivity to binocular disparity. *Journal of Neurophysiology, 49,* 1148–1167.

Miles, F. A. (1998). The neural processing of 3-D visual information: Evidence from eye movements. *European Journal of Neuroscience, 10,* 811–822.

Mimeault, D., Paquet, V., Molotchnikoff, S., Lepore, F., & Guillemot, J. P. (2004). Disparity sensitivity in the superior colliculus of the cat. *Brain Research, 1010,* 87–94.

Minini, L., Parker, A. J., & Bridge, H. (2010). Neural modulation by binocular disparity greatest in human dorsal visual stream. *Journal of Neurophysiology, 104,* 169–178.

Mitchell, D. E., & Blakemore, C. (1970). Binocular depth perception and the corpus callosum. *Vision Research, 10,* 49–54.

Nadler, J. W., Angelaki, D. E., & DeAngelis, G. C. (2008). A neural representation of depth from motion parallax in macaque visual cortex. *Nature, 452,* 642–645.

Nakayama, K., & Shimojo, S. (1990). da Vinci stereopsis: Depth and subjective occluding contours from unpaired image points. *Vision Research, 30,* 1811–1825.

Neri, P., Bridge, H., & Heeger, D. J. (2004). Stereoscopic processing of absolute and relative disparity in human visual cortex. *Journal of Neurophysiology, 92,* 1880–1891.

Nguyenkim, J. D., & DeAngelis, G. C. (2003). Disparity-based coding of three-dimensional surface orientation by macaque middle temporal neurons. *Journal of Neuroscience, 23,* 7117–7128.

Ogle, K. N. (1953). On the perception and validity of stereoscopic depth judgements from diplopic stimuli. *Journal of the Optical Society of America – A, 43,* 906–913.

Packwood, J., & Gordon, B. (1975). Stereopsis in normal domestic cat, Siamese cat, and cat raised with alternating monocular occlusion. *Journal of Neurophysiology, 38,* 1485–1499.

Palanca, B. J. A., & DeAngelis, G. C. (2003). Macaque middle temporal neurons signal depth in the absence of motion. *Journal of Neuroscience, 23,* 7647–7658.

Peterhans, E., & von der Heydt, R. (1993). Functional organization of area V2 in the alert macaque. *European Journal of Neuroscience, 5,* 509–524.

Poggio, G. F., Gonzalez, F., & Krause, F. (1988). Stereoscopic mechanisms in monkey visual cortex: Binocular correlation and disparity selectivity. *Journal of Neuroscience, 8,* 4531–4550.

Poggio, G. F., & Talbot, W. H. (1981). Mechanisms of static and dynamic stereopsis in foveal cortex of the rhesus monkey. *Journal of Physiology, 315,* 469–492.

Ponce, C. R., Lomber, S. G., & Born, R. T. (2008). Integrating motion and depth via parallel pathways. *Nature Neuroscience, 11,* 216–223.

Prince, S. J. D., Cumming, B. G., & Parker, A. J. (2002). Range and mechanism of encoding of horizontal disparity in macaque V1. *Journal of Neurophysiology, 87,* 209–221.

Pulfrich, C. (1922). Die stereoskopie im Dienste der isochromen und heterochromen Photometrie. *Naturwissenschaften, 10,* 553–564.

Qiu, F. T. T., & von der Heydt, R. (2005). Figure and ground in the visual cortex: V2 combines stereoscopic cues with Gestalt rules. *Neuron, 47,* 155–166.

Ramachandran, V. S., & Cavanagh, P. (1985). Subjective contours capture stereopsis. *Nature, 317,* 527–528. Read, J. C. A., & Cumming, B. G. (2005). All Pulfrich-like illusions can be explained without joint encoding of motion and disparity. *Journal of Vision, 5,* 901–927.

Richards, W. (1970). Stereopsis and stereoblindness. *Experimental Brain Research, 10,* 380–388.

Rizzo, M., Boller, F., & Grafman, J. (1989). Astereopsis. In F. Boller & J. Grafman (Ed.), *Handbook of neuropsychology* (pp. 415–427). Amsterdam, The Netherlands: Elsevier.

Rokers, B., Cormack, L. K., & Huk, A. C. (2008). Strong percepts of motion through depth without strong percepts of position in depth. *Journal of Vision, 8,* 6 1–10.

Roy, H. H., Komatsu, H., & Wurtz, R. H. (1992). Disparity sensitivity of neurons in monkey extrastriate area MST. *Journal of Neuroscience, 12,* 2478–2492.

Schiller, P. H., Logothetis, N. K., & Charles, E. R. (1990). Role of the color-opponent and broad-band channels in vision. *Visual Neuroscience, 5,* 321–346.

Sereno, M. E., Trinath, T., Augath, M., & Logothetis, N. K. (2002). Three-dimensional shape representation in monkey cortex. *Neuron, 33,* 635–652.

Shioiri, S., Saisho, H., & Yaguchi, H. (2000). Motion in depth based on inter-ocular velocity differences. *Vision Research, 40,* 2565–2572.

Tanabe, S., Doi, T., Umeda, K., & Fujita, I. (2005). Disparity-tuning characteristics of neuronal responses to dynamic random-dot stereograms in macaque visual area V4. *Journal of Neurophysiology, 94,* 2683–2699.

Tanaka, H., Uka, T., Yoshiyama, K., Kato, M., & Fujita, I. (2001). Processing of shape defined by disparity in monkey inferior temporal cortex. *Journal of Neurophysiology, 85,* 735–744.

Ts'o, D. Y., Roe, A. W., & Gilbert, C. D. (2001). A hierarchy of the functional organization for color, form and disparity in primate visual area V2. *Vision Research, 41,* 1333–1349.

Tsao, D. Y., Vanduffel, W., Sasaki, W., Fize, D., Knutsen, T. A., Mandeville, J. B., ... Tootell, R. H. (2003). Stereopsis activates V3A and caudal intraparietal areas in macaques and humans. *Neuron, 39,* 555–568.

Tsutsui, K. I., Sakata, H., Naganuma, T., & Taira, M. (2002). Neural correlates for perception of 3D surface orientation from texture gradient. *Science, 298,* 409–412.

Uka, T., Tanaka, H., Yoshiyama, K., Kato, M., & Fujita, K. (2000). Disparity selectivity of neurons in monkey inferior temporal cortex. *Journal of Neurophysiology, 84,* 120–132.

Umeda, K., Tanabe, S., & Fujita, I. (2007). Representation of stereoscopic depth based on relative disparity in macaque area V4. *Journal of Neurophysiology, 98,* 241–252.

Van den Enden, A., & Spekreijse, H. (1989). Binocular depth reversals despite familiarity cues. *Science, 244,* 959–961.

von Hofsten, C. (1976). The role of convergence in visual space perception. *Vision Research, 16,* 193–198.

Wallach, H., & Floor, L. (1971). The use of size matching to demonstrate the effectiveness of accommodation and convergence as cues for distance. *Perception and Psychophysics, 10,* 423–428.

Wallach, H., & O'Connell, D. N. (1953). The kinetic depth effect. *Journal of Experimental Psychology, 45,* 205–217.

Watanabe, M., Tanaka, H., Uka, T., & Fujita, I. (2002). Disparity-selective neurons in area V4 of macaque monkeys. *Journal of Neurophysiology, 87,* 1960–1973.

Wheatstone, C. (1838). Contributions to the physiology of vision—On some remarkable, and hitherto unobserved, phenomena of binocular vision. *Philosophical Transactions of the Royal Society of London B: Biological Sciences,* 371–394.

7

Objects and Faces

The perception of objects and faces is complicated. We are able to recognize a face in a fraction of a second, distinguishing it from numerous other faces. Experts on birds and cars can do the same for examples in their area of expertise. This is true despite variations in the viewpoint or in light and shadow across the object. It also holds for silhouettes and cartoons of a face. No machine has ever been devised that comes close to these capabilities. How the visual system accomplishes this is a mystery.

When neurophysiologists first started to record from single cells in the visual system, they discovered that the stimulus giving the best response becomes more complicated as one moves up the system from bipolar cell to ganglion cell in the retina, to lateral geniculate nuclcus, to striate cortex, and beyond. This led Horace Barlow (1972) to hypothesize that the process might continue, with fewer and fewer cells responding to more and more restricted sets of stimuli at higher and higher levels of the system, culminating in a cell that responds to one very particular stimulus—the grandmother cell or pontifical cell. Perception of a scene at any moment would be represented by a group of cardinal cells, each responding to a particular aspect of the scene, feeding into the pontifical cell.

However, the concept of a grandmother cell is now discredited by experiments that show that a particular face or object activates a number of cells in every area that has been studied. Scientists now refer to distributed coding of face and object identity (Rolls, 2004). Nevertheless, there is a hierarchy to the responses found, starting with responses to spots of light in the retina, going to responses to contours and edges in striate cortex, and on through intermediate areas to responses to faces in temporal cortex. We will discuss the phenomena that have been investigated and then go on, as far as we know, to how it is all processed.

Perception of Edges

Objects are defined by their edges. As pointed out in Chapter 3, we tend to ignore the variations in shading across an object. This is why a cartoon is as recognizable as a photograph. It is the edges that matter, for object perception as well as lightness perception.

An edge is usually defined by a difference in brightness, but edges can be seen even where there is no difference in brightness. Going back to Figure 3–1 in Chapter 3, one sees a rectangle inside another rectangle. The fact that there is a point where the edge of the inside rectangle has the same brightness as the point across the edge in the outside rectangle does not disturb the perception of the inside area as a rectangle with continuous boundaries.

Edges are also seen in displays where there is no difference in brightness across a significant length of the edge (illusory contours). Indeed, the illusion of an edge can create the perception of a difference in lightness where there is no difference in luminance. The most famous examples were illustrated by Kanisza (1979). There appears to be a white triangle in Figure 7–1A, bounded by the three Pacmen and the black outline of a triangle. The outlines do not have to be geometrical for the illusion to occur—it can also be seen in curved lines defining a curved object (Figure 7–1B).

These illusory contours occur because the visual system likes to complete objects. The Pacmen are interpreted as complete black disks rather than segments of a disk, and the lines are also interpreted as the edges of a complete triangle, without gaps, with a solid white triangle in front that is obscuring them. Thus, the obscuring object in front is sometimes seen as lighter than the background.

Where an object is seen in front of its inducer elements (i.e., the Pacmen), it is known as modal completion (Fig. 7–2A). An object may also be seen as behind, which is known as amodal completion (Kanisza, 1979; Ringach & Shapley, 1996; Fig. 7–2B). Amodal completion can also occur with a variety of curved objects as well as straight lines. In all cases, where possible, a complete object is detected.

Edges may also be signified by differences in texture. This is sometimes obvious (see the rectangle of Xs embedded in a sea of Ls; Fig. 7–3 left) and sometimes not very obvious (try to see the rectangle of Ts; Fig. 7–3 right). Matching texture to the background is one way of concealing an object—in other words, camouflaging it (Fig. 7–4).

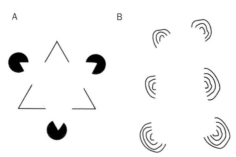

FIGURE 7–1. (*A*) Kanisza triangle. There appears to be a white triangle bounded by the three Pacmen and the lines. It may also appear whiter than the background. (*B*) There appears to be a curved shape concealing part of the lined figures around and behind it.

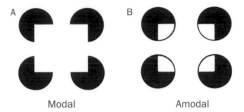

Modal   Amodal

FIGURE 7–2. (*A*) Modal completion. A white square is seen in front of four black circles. (*B*) Amodal completion. A white square in a black background is seen behind three circular holes. (Reprinted from Ringach & Shapley, 1996, with kind permission of Elsevier.)

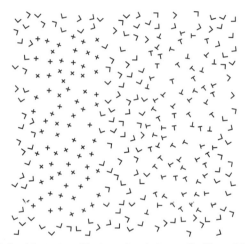

FIGURE 7–3. Edges defined by texture. The boundary between the X's and the L's can be seen easily. The boundary between the L's and the T's is not so obvious. (Reprinted from Landy & Graham, 2004, with kind permission of MIT Press.)

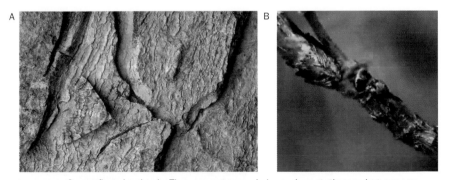

FIGURE 7–4. Camouflaged animals. They are not very obvious when stationary, but appear immediately as soon as they start to move. (*A*) A moth on a rock. (*B*) An insect on a tree branch.

Camouflage is typically broken by movement—once a camouflaged object begins to move, it becomes readily visible (see spider camouflage at http://viperlib. york.ac.uk and camouflage & motion at http://psy2.ucsd.edu/~sanstis/SASlides. html). This is true of any of the animals illustrated in Figure 7–4. Therefore, movement of a series of points along a contour also outlines the edge of an object. Common motion can define the edges of an object. Similarly, common depth can delineate object boundaries. One way of detecting camouflaged buildings is to have an aircraft fly over them and take two pictures separated by some distance, then view them stereoscopically.

In summary, edges can be defined by a variety of cues: a difference in luminance, perception of points along a contour as being part of the same edge, completion of contours that seem to belong together, movement together of components of the edge, and contiguity of the components of the edge in depth.

Grouping of Components

The Gestalt psychologists early in the twentieth century studied how visual elements are perceived as belonging together in larger groups (Wertheimer, 1923/1938). They adopted a number of principles, suggesting that grouping may occur because of proximity of the elements; similarity of color, size, or orientation; a common direction of movement; symmetry; parallelism; continuity; and closure (Fig. 7–5). Their overall principle was Pragnanz, a word that is hard to translate but essentially means the most regular, ordered, stable, and balanced state possible, sometimes abbreviated as "good form" or, in the case of contours, "good continuation." In practice it is not too hard to devise situations where the application of this principle leads to a prediction that is not what is seen (Kanisza, 1979). However, their general theories led to a large number of experiments that illuminated the field.

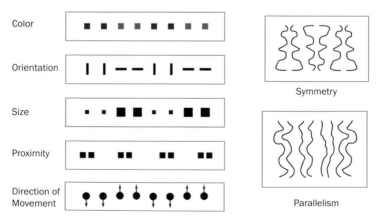

FIGURE 7–5. Gestalt principles of grouping, by color, orientation, size, proximity, direction of movement, symmetry, or parallelism.

Transparency

The tendency to see contours as part of a single object sometimes leads to the perception of one object overlying another, and to the object on top as being transparent (Fig. 7–6). The requirement in Figure 7–6 is that the luminance of regions C and D should be between the luminances of A and B. C has to be darker than A, because the object in front has to reduce the light from A somewhat. D has to be lighter than B, because the light from the transparent object has to add to the light from a dark object behind it. Also C has to be lighter than D, because there is more light coming from A than B. If these conditions are fulfilled, then the rectangle in front may be seen as transparent rather than as simply a solid object in front (see also Fig. 3–9 in Chapter 3).

Recognition of Complete Objects

An important point in the recognition of complete objects is the concept of border ownership and figure/ground relationships. This was also studied extensively by the Gestalt psychologists (Rubin, 1921). The figure is the object that appears closer, and the ground is the background. The figure tends to be bounded by a contour, and the border between figure and ground is said to belong to the figure. People tend to remember the figure more than the ground.

Smaller objects tend to be seen as the figure. Symmetric objects and convex objects also tend to be seen as the figure. In agreement with the point that closer objects are taken to be the figure, stereo cues assigning an object as nearby determine unambiguously which object is figure (Nakayama, Shimojo, & Silverman, 1989).

Another factor that plays a role in assignment to figure versus ground is recognition of one side of a border as belonging to a familiar object (Peterson, 2003). The right side of Figure 7–7A is recognized as a pineapple, the left side of B as a sea horse, and the left side of C as the outline of a woman. Thus, white is figure in A and C, black in B. If the displays are turned upside down so that the outlines are no longer recognized, then white and black are assigned to figure equally often. It

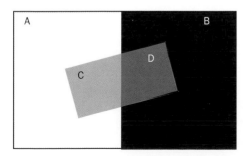

FIGURE 7–6. Transparency. The slanted rectangle appears to be transparent with the white and black rectangles seen through it, if C is darker than A, D is lighter than B, and C is lighter than D.

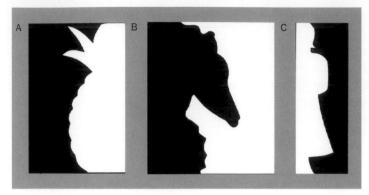

FIGURE 7–7. Figure and ground. The white area in (A) is seen as a pineapple, and the white area in (C) as a woman; thus, the white areas appear to be the figure and the black the ground. In (B), the black area is seen as a seahorse, so the black is figure and the white the ground. (Reprinted from Palmer, 2004, with kind permission of MIT Press.)

is not surprising that memory plays a role in object recognition: indeed, it would be very surprising if it did not. However, all of this shows that object recognition must take place before figure/ground assignment, or that it feeds back to figure/ground assignment.

Object recognition and figure/ground assignment are sometimes ambiguous. Famous examples are Rubin's vase/face, Boring's wife/mother, and Jastrow's duck/rabbit (Fig. 7–8). In all these cases, more than one outline can be recognized. Most people see one figure, then it switches to the other, and back again. However, both figures are never seen simultaneously.

Recognition of Complete Objects Compared to Their Components

The Structuralists believed that an object is first decomposed into its component parts before being recognized, whereas the Gestalt psychologists believed that the whole was recognized first (see Kimchi, 2003). An illustration of how this can be addressed experimentally is provided by the patterns investigated by Navon (1977). These were large letters made up of components that consisted of small letters (Fig. 7–9). The question was whether the large letters (global level) would be recognized before or after the small ones (local level). All other things being equal, the larger letters were recognized first. However, numerous other experiments show that this is not an absolute rule (Kimchi, 2003). There is increasing evidence that neither components nor complete objects take precedence, and that the whole system works together to recognize both. There is also some evidence that the right hemisphere deals with global perception, and the left with local perception (Delis, Robertson, & Efron, 1986; Fig. 7–10).

FIGURE 7–8. (*A*) This figure may be seen as a vase or as two faces looking at each other. (*B*) This figure may be seen as an old woman or as a young woman. (*C*) This figure may be seen as a duck or as a rabbit.

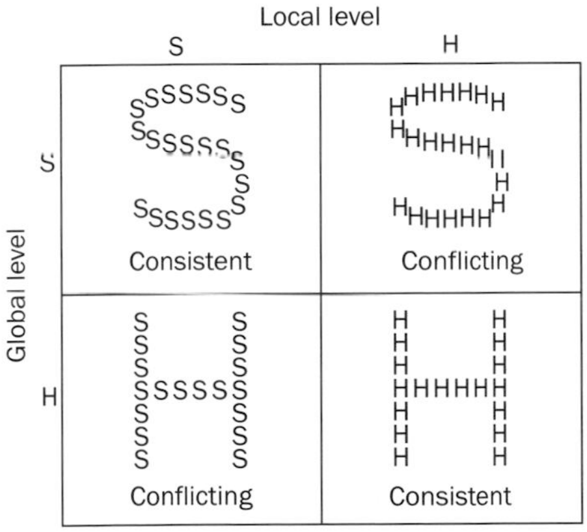

FIGURE 7–9. Navon figures, used to test whether local components or the global figure are recognized. (Reprinted from Kimchi, 2003, with kind permission of Oxford University Press.)

Recognition of Categories of Objects, Compared to Recognition of Individual Examples

We know the differences between faces, animals, houses, and chairs. We can also recognize a variety of examples of each of these, particularly faces. Some of this is innate, and some of it is learned. A child will know its mother's face soon after birth, but recognition of other relatives and strangers comes with experience. Moreover, some of us become experts in a particular category of objects—birds for bird watchers, cars for racetrack fanatics, and so on. Psychologists talk about distinguishing categories as opposed to exemplars. This distinction will

Stimulus   Right Damage   Left Damage

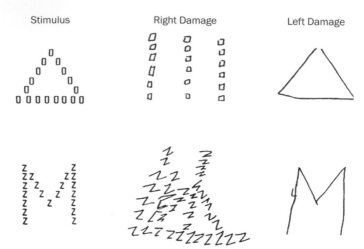

FIGURE 7–10. Differences in damage to the right hemisphere from damage to the left hemisphere. When asked to copy Navon figures, the patient with right damage copied the small symbols, and the patient with left damage copied the overall symbol. (Reprinted from Delis et al., 1986, with kind permission of Elsevier.)

become important when we discuss where in the occipitotemporal cortex various distinctions are made.

Illusions

We have discussed illusory contours. There are also illusions about the geometry of objects (Fig. 7–11). These include the T illusion (A), where the vertical line appears longer than the horizontal; the Hering illusion (B), where the two vertical lines appear bowed; the Ponzo illusion (C), where the lower line appears shorter than the upper; the Muller-Lyer illusion (D), where the upper line appears longer than the lower; and the Poggendorff illusion (E), where the slanted line appears not to be continuous. These figural illusions can even be seen in relation to illusory contours (Fig. 7–12). Howe and Purves (2005) would claim that these illusions, like most other perceptions in vision, are the result of empirical experience.

Faces

It has been known for some time that there is something special about the recognition of faces. We can recognize faces in an instant, no matter whether they are real, photographs, portraits, or cartoons. We can ignore some distortions. This is true of our family, friends, and famous people seen on TV, the Internet, and

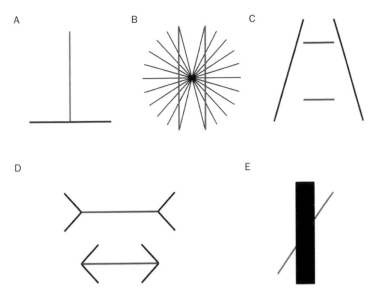

FIGURE 7–11. Illusions of geometry. (*A*) T illusion. (*B*) Hering illusion. (*C*) Ponzo illusion. (*D*) Muller-Lyer illusion. (*E*) Poggendorff illusion.

FIGURE 7–12. The illusory white triangle creates the further illusion that the two vertical lines are of different lengths.

newspapers. Hundreds, maybe thousands, of faces can be distinguished. Some people are better at it than others (Russell, Duchaine, & Nakayama, 2009), but every normal person has this ability. It is much harder to recognize faces of other races that we do not have daily contact with, so this is an ability that depends on experience.

Upside-down faces are harder to recognize than faces in their normal orientation (the inversion effect). This is true of faces upside-down on the retina, rather than faces upside down in the world but right side up on the retina (Kohler, 1940). The inversion effect applies particularly to faces, and not to most other objects (Yin, 1969), but it does apply to cursive writing (Rock, 1974), although not to Chinese characters (McCleery et al., 2008), and maybe to experts who have studied or have long experience with a particular class of objects, such as dogs (Diamond & Carey, 1986), although this is controversial. A striking example is illustrated by a painting by Arcimboldo of a scene that looks like a bowl of vegetables in one orientation, and a face when turned upside down (Fig. 7–13).

The expression on a face is also lost by inversion. This is illustrated particularly by the well-known Thatcher illusion (Thompson, 1980), which can be replicated with the face of any famous politician. In this illusion, two copies of the face are created, one smiling, and the other with the eyes and mouth inverted to give a sour look (Fig. 7–14). The recognition of expression is disrupted by inversion even more than the recognition of identity: indeed, Kohler (1940) suggested that the inversion effect occurs primarily because of the loss of expression.

There is something about the face seen as a whole that assists in its recognition, which is known as holistic or configural processing (Peterson & Rhodes, 2003). In composites of faces, with the top half from one person and the bottom from another, it is not easy to recognize the parts, because the face is seen as a whole new face (Young, Hellawell, & Hay, 1987). However, when the face is inverted, recognition of the components becomes much easier. The internal features (eyes, nose, and mouth) are more important than the external features (hairline and chin) in the recognition of faces (Hosie, Ellis, & Haig, 1988), and internal features are recognized more easily when seen as part of the whole face than when seen by themselves (Tanaka & Farah, 2003).

As expected from the experience required to recognize faces, it is a process that develops over time in children. The gender of the primary caregiver is

FIGURE 7–13. *The Vegetable Gardener* by Arcimboldo. In this orientation it appears as a bowl of vegetables. When inverted, a face is seen. (Reprinted from Hulten & Pontus, 2004.)

FIGURE 7–14. Thatcher illusion. The difference in expression is much more apparent when the face is right side up than when it is upside down. (Reprinted from Thompson, 1980, with kind permission of Pion.)

preferred by infants. Infants exposed to pictures of Barbary monkeys between 6 and 9 months of age are better able to discriminate such pictures than infants not exposed (Pascalis, de Haan, & Nelson, 2005). The inversion effect develops between 6 and 10 years of age (Carey & Diamond, 1977). Thus, the development of face perception is a long process depending on experience. Indeed, it is a lifelong process, continuing as new faces are learned, until old age starts to reverse it.

Dependence on Viewpoint

Another capability of the visual system is that it can recognize objects as the same when seeing them from different points of view. This is certainly true of faces. It is largely based on experience (Tarr, 2003). Macaques can recognize an object rotated up to 40° from the view in which it was initially presented, but if they are trained with three different images at 120° from each other, they can recognize it at all angles (Logothetis, Pauls, Bulthoff, & Poggio, 1994). It helps to move around a scene in order to recognize the various objects in it (Bulthoff & Bulthoff, 2003).

Single Neuron Recordings in Macaque

EARLY VISUAL AREAS

The original work by Hubel and Wiesel (1968) showed that cells in primary visual cortex respond to the orientation of an edge, particularly moving edges. Cells responsive to similar orientations are arranged in columns, with a regular progression of orientations all the way around the clock for each part of the retina (see Chapter 2). Numerous cells also respond to edges of color (Friedman, Zhou, & von der Heydt, 2003).

It has become apparent over the years that visual cortex also responds to edges defined by other cues. Thus, cells in V2 respond to illusory contours with the same orientation selectivity as real contours, even when the illusory contour is composed of lines running perpendicular to the contour (von der Heydt, Peterhans, & Baumgartner, 1984; Fig. 7–15). Lee and Nguyen (2001) also found a response to illusory contours in V1, weaker than that in V2, and starting later. Presumably the V2 signal feeds back to V1. Experiments with functional magnetic resonance imaging (fMRI) in humans show that responses to illusory contours are found also in human primary visual cortex, but they are not as strong as those in other visual areas, particularly V3A and V4 (Mendola et al., 1999).

Cells in V2 also respond to edges defined by disparity (von der Heydt, Zhou, & Friedman, 2000). The preferred orientation of the cyclopean edge is the same as that for a luminance contrast edge, and the preferred location is the same, but the response with one side of the edge in front may differ from the response for the other side in front. Also the cyclopean edge response was sometimes abolished by small changes in disparity (Bredfeldt & Cumming, 2006). The latter authors therefore suggested that the responses support a cue-invariant representation of edges at a higher level of the pathway, fed back to V2.

Cells may also respond to a kinetic edge, defined by dots moving in one direction on one side of the edge and in the opposite direction on the other side. Some such cells are found in V2, and a few in V1 (Marcar, Raiguel, Ziao, & Orban, 2000). The preferred orientation of the motion edge is the same as the preferred orientation of a luminance edge, but the response to the motion edge is a little slower. The response does not depend on the direction of movement of the dots, which may be parallel to the edge or perpendicular to it.

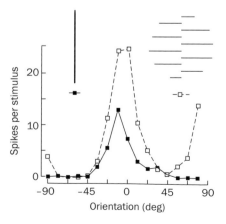

FIGURE 7–15. A neuron responsive to illusory contours. The orientation tuning curve to movement of a line is shown by a solid line, and the orientation tuning curve to movement of a boundary defined by lines perpendicular to the boundary is shown by dashed lines. In both cases the largest response is seen when the line, or boundary, is vertical. (Reprinted from von der Heydt et al., 1984, with kind permission of AAAS.)

Like luminance- and motion-defined borders, texture-defined borders can also generate oriented edges (Leventhal, Wang, Schmolesky, & Zhou, 1998). In Figure 7–16, the tuning of such a cell is shown, in response to a grating as well as a luminance stimulus and a texture stimulus. The authors suggested that cue-invariant cells are first found in primary visual cortex in both cat and macaque—a point that everybody would now agree with, even if the cue invariance may be provided in part by feedback from higher areas.

Some cells in V1 also appear to perform amodal completion, in the sense that they respond to both an isolated bar and a bar partially obscured by an object. These cells, however, do not respond to a bar with a gap in it (Bakin, Nakayama, & Gilbert, 2000; Sugita, 1999; Fig. 7–17). A stereoscopic signal is involved here—what is required for the response is a bar with a gap in it, combined with a stereo signal showing that the bar is behind the occluding object (see Fig. 6–21 in Chapter 6).

Not only does primary visual cortex respond to edges and borders, it also integrates them, a process known as contour integration. Monkeys were trained to saccade to one of two targets, both of which had a central element with a specified orientation; one had the central element as part of a contour, while in the other the central element had random elements around it (Li, Piech, & Gilbert, 2006; Fig. 7–18). At the same time, records were made from a cell in primary visual cortex whose preferred orientation matched that of the central element.

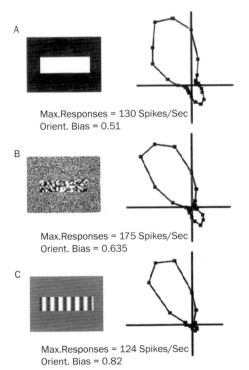

A

Max.Responses = 130 Spikes/Sec
Orient. Bias = 0.51

B

Max.Responses = 175 Spikes/Sec
Orient. Bias = 0.635

C

Max.Responses = 124 Spikes/Sec
Orient. Bias = 0.82

FIGURE 7–16. Direction tuning curves for a neuron in V1 for movement of a white rectangle (*A*), a rectangle defined by a difference in texture (*B*), and a rectangle formed by a grating on a grey background (*C*). The tuning curves show that the neuron responds to movement in the same direction of the rectangle for all three stimuli. (Reprinted from Leventhal et al., 1998, with kind permission of Cambridge University Press.)

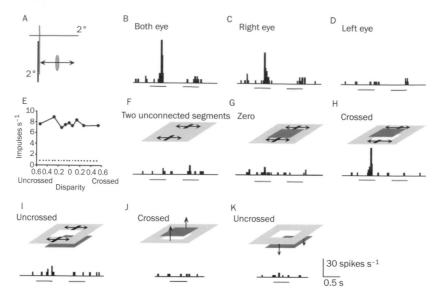

FIGURE 7–17. Response appropriate for amodal completion. The cell responds to stimulation by a complete bar in the right eye or both eyes (*b* and *c*), and to a bar behind a patch (*h*). It did not respond to a bar with a gap in it without the patch (*f*), or in front of the patch (*g*), or to the patch by itself, either in front or behind the background, without a bar (*i, j,* and *k*). (Reprinted from Sugita, 1999, with kind permission of MacMillan Publishers.)

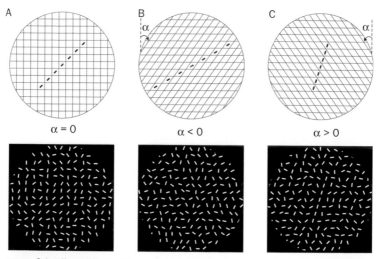

FIGURE 7–18. Stimuli used to test for perception of elements as part of a line. The elements are seen as a line most clearly when they are close (*C*), less clearly as they are moved apart somewhat (*A*), and even less clearly when they are moved apart a lot (*B*). (Reprinted from Li et al., 2006, with kind permission of Cell Press.)

The macaques were rewarded for making a saccade toward the display with a contour in it, and the cell gave an enhanced response when the animal was attending and made a saccade to the correct display. The behavioral response and the single-unit response varied together when the saliency of the contour was changed (compare Figs. 7–18B and C with 7–18A). This V1 response to contour integration is related to lateral connections within V1, and also subject to top-down influences—it is enhanced by learning, and it is reduced by anesthesia (Li, Piech, & Gilbert, 2008).

Finally, border ownership is coded in primary visual cortex (Zhou, Friedman, & von der Heydt, 2000). This is illustrated in Figure 7–19. The cell responds to an edge with red below and gray above, but only when the red is part of a square that is figure rather than ground. The cell is said to respond to contrast polarity as well as border ownership. A cell that responds to C and D but not A and B is said to have contrast polarity alone, and a cell that responds to C and A but not to B and D is said to have border ownership alone. In V2 and V4, half the cells had border ownership; in V1, the percentage was rather less. The finding that figure-ground segmentation and border ownership are properties of primary visual cortex is supported by the experiments of Lamme (1995) showing that some cells respond to a pattern of textures when it is placed against a background, but not when the pattern of textures covers a large part of the field of view. As already pointed out in Chapter 6, for cells that are sensitive to both border ownership and disparity, the two properties agree in placing the figure in front of the ground (see Fig. 6–20).

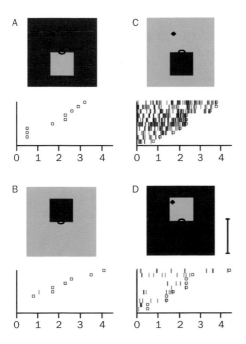

FIGURE 7–19. Border ownership. The cell responds most vigorously to an edge that is grey above and red below, when the edge is part of a small rectangle (*C*), much less when the edge is part of the background (*D*), and not at all when the edge is red above and gray below (*A* and *B*). (Reprinted from Zhou et al, 2000, with kind permission of the Society for Neuroscience.)

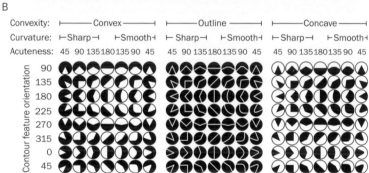

FIGURE 7–20. (*A*) Shapes used by Gallant and colleagues to test the responses of cells in V4. (Photograph courtesy of Jack Gallant.) (*B*) Shapes used by Connor and colleagues. (Reprinted from Pasupathy & Connor, 2001, with kind permission of the American Physiological Society.) In both cases the shapes were largely geometrical.

We have come some distance since Hubel and Wiesel first showed the selectivity of cells in primary visual cortex for luminance borders. We now know that the border can be defined by motion, disparity, texture, illusions, and contours that are outside the receptive field of the cell being recorded. Undoubtedly the list of properties will expand as more ingenious experiments are done.

V4

Although V4 has long been known to be anatomically positioned midway between primary visual cortex and the temporal cortex, surprisingly little is known about the nature of the underlying representation of visual form in V4. Many recent studies have sought to use mathematically derived stimuli to characterize visual selectivity in V4 (Gallant, Braun, & van Essen, 1993;

Pasupathy & Connor, 2001). Some of the stimuli used by Gallant and his colleagues are shown in Figure 7–20A. V4 neurons are responsive to polar, hyperbolic, and Cartesian stimuli; however, at the population level, there is a bias toward the more complex non-Cartesian polar and hyperbolic. Interestingly, nearly all cells conveyed significant information about all three classes. Some of the stimuli used by Connor and his colleagues are shown in Figure 7–20B. They found that many cells are tuned for the curvature and object-centered position of boundary fragments. These were not the only ones that these two groups used, but most of the other stimuli were also geometrical. V4 cells also respond to textures (Hanazawa & Komatsu, 2001), checkerboards defined by patterns of lines (Kastner, De Weerd, & Ungerleider, 2000), and kinetic boundaries (Mysore, Vogels, Raiguel, & Orban, 2006). Responses of V4 neurons to natural scene stimuli can be partially accounted for by the spectral receptive field, which constitutes a quasi-linear model of first-order selectivity based on joint orientation and spatial frequency tuning (David, Hayden, & Gallant, 2006). However, the broader impact of V4 studies to date is limited by the range of stimuli employed. Just as a lot more has been learned about primary visual cortex in the 45 years since 1965, a lot more will be learned about V4 in the years ahead; it should take more than 45 years, because it is a higher area! What we can say at the present time is that V4 cells respond to more complicated stimuli than V1 and V2 cells and to less complicated stimuli than inferotemporal cortex (IT) cells (Kobatake & Tanaka, 1994), and that the representation of the scene is spread all over V4.

TEMPORAL CORTEX

Early recordings from inferotemporal cortex (IT) revealed some cells with surprising specificity (Desimone, Albright, Gross, & Bruce, 1984; Gross, Rocha-Miranda, & Bender, 1972). Many had broad specificity, but some responded more particularly to hands in any orientation (Fig. 7–21), some to flowers, some to snakes, and some to faces. The most specific responses were observed in those neurons responding to faces. The receptive fields were large, typically not well organized retinotopically, and usually covered the center of gaze as well as portions of both the contralateral and ipsilateral visual fields.

Tanaka and his colleagues have studied how the responses of IT neurons can be predicted based on responses to an object's component features (see Tanaka, 2004 and Tanifuji, Kaas, & Collins, 2004 for summary). The cell illustrated in Figure 7–22 responded equally to a bottle, the outline of a bottle, and an oval with a stick on the end like a bottle, but not to a circle or rectangle in place of the oval, or to the oval or stick by themselves. Another example is shown in Figure 7–23 (Kobatake & Tanaka, 1994). This cell responded to a face and the outline of a face, but not when components or the outline were removed. No cells like this have ever been described in V1, V2, or V4.

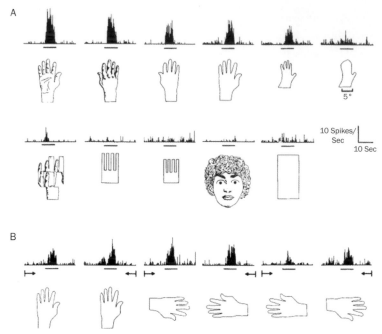

FIGURE 7–21. Response of a cell in macaque IT to hands, with less response to a mitten, and an obscured hand, and little response to combs, a face, or a rectangle (*A*). The orientation of the hand did not matter (*B*). (Reprinted from Desimone et al, 1984, with kind permission of the Society for Neuroscience.)

Not surprisingly, responses in IT specific for shape are independent of the cue that defines the shape, much like specificity for orientation in V1 (Sary, Vogels, & Orban, 1993). The cell shown in Figure 7–24 responded to a star, as opposed to a grating, an arrow, an H, a cross, a triangle, an octagon, or a simple figure, and this was true whether the shape was defined by luminance, movement, or texture. The responses vary with the size and position of the object over a narrow range in some cells and over a broad range in others (Ito, Tamura, Fujita, & Tanaka, 1995). As pointed out in Chapter 6, cells are also responsive to shape in three dimensions, distinguishing concave from convex objects (Janssen, Vogels, Liu, & Orban, 2001). Cells are responsive to both global and local shapes, as illustrated earlier with Navon figures; interestingly, the global response is about 30 msec faster than the local response (Sripati & Olson, 2009).

The discovery by Gross and his colleagues that a few cells in IT respond specifically to faces is what first stimulated interest in this area (Gross et al., 1972). The authors found some responses that were independent of inversion or rotation of the face, its size, covering up part of the face, making an outline of the face, and changing color or distance. This invariant face selectivity was restricted to a subset of IT face neurons (Perrett, Rolls, & Caan, 1982). For example, making a profile of the face generally reduced the response considerably. Similarly,

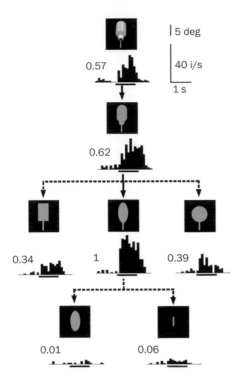

FIGURE 7–22. Analysis of the response to a bottle with a handle. The response was the same to an outline of the stimulus; was reduced by making the bottle rectangular or circular; and was eliminated when either the handle or the bottle was removed. (Reprinted from Tanaka, 2004, with kind permission of MIT Press.)

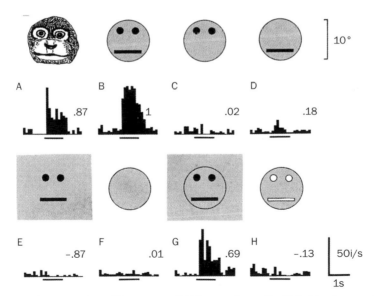

FIGURE 7–23. Response of a cell in macaque IT. This was a face cell, which did not respond when the internal features of the face were removed (C, D, F), or when the outline was removed (E), and had a reduced response when the contrast of the internal features was changed (F). (Reprinted from Kobatake & Tanaka, 1994, with kind permission of the American Physiological Society.)

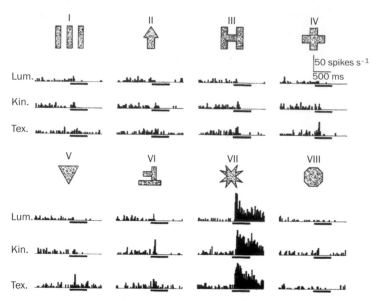

FIGURE 7–24. Response of a cell in macaque IT to stimuli defined by luminance, kinetic movement, or texture. In all cases the cell responded to a star, but not to a grating, arrow, H, cross, triangle, upside-down F, or octagon. (Reprinted from Sary et al., 1993, with kind permission of AAAS.)

the response was reduced when there was another stimulus in the field of view, particularly when the other stimulus was at the fovea (Rolls & Tovee, 1995). There may be a short-latency response, depending on whether the stimulus is a human face or a macaque face or some other object, and a longer latency response depending on the expression on the face (Fig. 7–25; Sugase, Yamane, Ueno, & Kawano, 1999). Thus, cells in IT can signal the changes in emotion represented by changes in shape.

There are columns in IT, as in all other parts of the cortex. In a vertical penetration, cells tended to respond to the same shape, and in an oblique penetration, there was a cluster of cells responding to the same shape, followed by a cluster responding to a different shape (Fujita, Tanaka, Ito, & Cheng, 1992). The columnar organization was illustrated particularly clearly when imaging was combined with single-unit recording (Wang, Tanaka, & Tanifuji, 1996). After the properties of a column had been determined by single-unit recording, imaging with the best stimulus for the column showed that several other patches nearby also responded. Different stimuli activated different columns (Fig. 7–26; Tsunoda, Yamane, Nishizaki, & Tanifuji, 2001). Sometimes simplification of the stimulus would reduce the number of columns activated, and sometimes simplification would activate new columns. The conclusion is that objects are represented in IT by activation of several columns in a sparsely

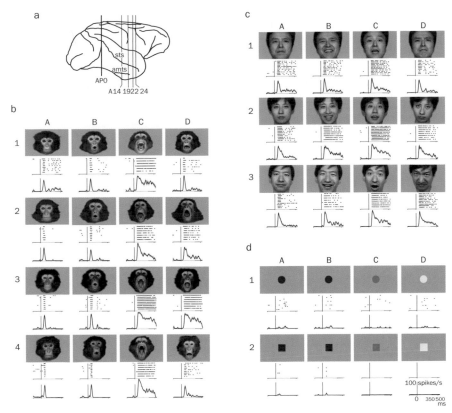

FIGURE 7–25. Response of a cell in macaque IT to the expression on a face. The initial response depends on the face. The longer latency response depends on the expression on the face. (Reprinted from Sugase et al., 1999, with kind permission of MacMillan Publishers.)

distributed manner, and that lack of activity in other columns may play a role in recognizing the object.

The responses of cells in IT can also be shaped by learning and visual experience. We have already described how macaques can learn to recognize an object from different viewpoints, after the initial recognition was for a limited selection of viewpoints. This is reflected in the responses of cells in IT (Logothetis, Pauls, & Roggio, 1995). After training in distinguishing a variety of trees and other objects, some cells were found that responded to trees rather than other objects, and a few to specific examples of trees (Vogels, 1999). Moreover, macaques must learn recognition in the periphery of the visual field, because they regard looking straight at another macaque as a sign of dominance and aggression (Perrett et al., 1985), although this is not known to be a property of IT.

In this discussion, we have lumped together the subdivisions of inferotemporal cortex (IT). In fact it is divided into various parts: anterior and posterior IT by

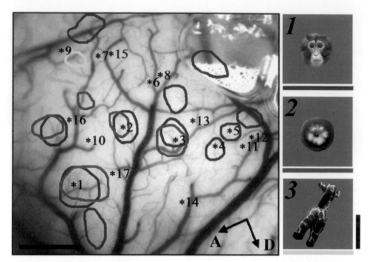

FIGURE 7–26. A monkey face activated the columns outlined in red; a red apple with a yellow bottom the columns outlined in green; and a toy giraffe the columns outlined in yellow. Notice that these were overlapping columns, with a different set activated by each stimulus. (Reprinted from Tsunoda et al., with kind permission of MacMillan Publishers.)

some groups, and TE and TEO by other groups. The general flow of information is from V4 to posterior IT to anterior IT. Moving along the pathway, the receptive fields of the cells become larger, their responses become more specific, and their dependence on size and position decreases. Face cells are found particularly in anterior IT. How the responses vary with specific parts of cortex will be dealt with in more detail in a discussion of human cortex and results with fMRI. The homologies between human and macaque cortex here are not yet clear, so to bring in variations with area in the macaque could be confusing (see Pinsk et al., 2009; Tsao, Moeller, & Freiwald, 2008).

PARIETAL CORTEX

Because the overall generalization is that the ventral pathway deals with perception of objects, there are very few investigations of responses to the shape of objects in the dorsal pathway that projects to parietal cortex. One of the few studies directly compared responses in lateral intraparietal cortex (LIP) with responses in anterior IT (AIT) (Lehky & Sereno, 2007). There was lower selectivity in LIP than in AIT, and responses in the LIP population were less distinct than in AIT and showed a more poorly differentiated grouping of similar shapes. The suggestion is that shape selectivity in LIP does not come from IT, but rather arises independently, in agreement with the function of LIP, which is to integrate signals from various senses to control eye movements. The suggestion is that the dorsal stream analyzes 3-D cues to shape, to be integrated with the cue invariance and viewpoint invariance found in the ventral stream (Farivar, 2009).

Areas Dealing With Objects and Faces in Humans

There are several areas in human occipital and temporal cortex that are thought to be involved in the perception of objects and faces, and the number increases as more studies are done (see Tsao, Moeller, & Freiwald, 2008; Tsao, Schweers, Moeller, & Freiwald, 2008). These have been defined either because they give a larger response in fMRI to objects than to the components of objects, or because they give a large response to faces (Reddy & Kanwisher, 2006). One is the occipital face area (OFA), located near V5/MT+. Another is the fusiform face area (FFA) in the fusiform gyrus, which tends to be more prominent in the right hemisphere than the left. Then there is an area activated by visual processing of body parts, the extrastriate body area (EBA); an area called the parahippocampal place area (PPA) that deals with places and scenes; and an area near the left fusiform gyrus that deals with words and strings of letters (see Baker et al., 2007). These areas are all defined by a larger activation by the stimuli that give them their names, but they are by no means activated exclusively by these stimuli.

LATERAL OCCIPITAL CORTEX

fMRI experiments comparing the responses to objects with the responses to textures and gratings (Malach et al., 1995) were the first to define the lateral occipital area as an area dealing with objects and faces. The stimuli were pictures of famous people; common recognizable objects such as tools, toys, clothing, animals, and plants; unfamiliar abstract sculptures; and various kinds of filtered pictures, textures, and noise. This area, as well as posterior parts of the fusiform and inferior temporal gyri, responds better to meaningful shapes than to scrambled contours (Gerlach et al., 2002; Fig. 7–27). There is very little response to surfaces or edges (Vinberg & Grill-Spector, 2008). The fusiform and temporal gyri were more activated by familiar than unfamiliar objects, showing that memory and learning contribute to neuronal selectivity in these regions.

Given that cells in V1 and V2 respond to contours defined by different cues (see earlier), it is not surprising that LOC responds to shapes defined by different cues (Grill-Spector et al., 1998), and that the response in more anterior parts may be enhanced if more than one cue is used (Self & Zeki, 2005). Again, given results in V1 and V2, it is not surprising that the lateral occipital cortex responds to occluded objects appropriate for amodal completion (Hegde, Fang, & Murray, 2008).

Lateral occipital cortex is not a uniform area. Close to it, and sometimes overlapping it, is an area specific for body parts—the extrastriate body area (Downing,

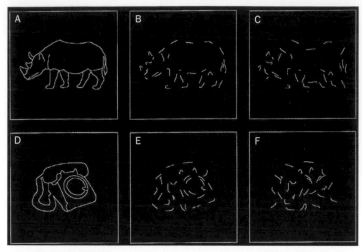

FIGURE 7–27. Shapes designed to test the response in lateral occipital cortex - the outlines of a rhinocerus (A) and a telephone (D). Full outlines (A and D); dashed outlines (B and E); and scrambled outlines (C and F). (Reprinted from Gerlach et al., with kind permission of Elsevier.)

Jiang, Shuman, & Kanwisher, 2001). The body area responds to hands, feet, and whole bodies, but much less to faces, very little to objects, and intermediately to face parts and pictures of mammals (Fig. 7–28). There is also a particular section for faces: the occipital face area (OFA), which is concerned more with the perception of face parts, and with identity as a face, rather than recognition as a particular face (see Kanwisher & Yovel, 2006). So far there is little evidence that other parts of LOC have specificity for particular classes of objects, but this may change as more experiments are done.

FUSIFORM FACE AREA

The fusiform face area was first named by Kanwisher et al. (1997) based on the observation that it is significantly more activated by faces than by other common objects. It also responded more to intact faces than scrambled faces; to frontal views of faces more than to frontal views of houses; and to photos of three-quarter view faces than to photos of human hands. Previous authors had also noted that this area is activated by faces, particularly on the right, and that the collection of areas activated by faces is different from those activated by other objects (see Sergent, Ohta, & MacDonald, 1992).

There has been some argument about whether the right FFA is specifically a face area. There is no doubt that FFA is activated by stimuli other than faces, such as houses, animals, and human-made objects, and that areas besides FFA respond to faces (Haxby et al., 2001; Kanwisher, 2004). There is also some evidence that experience increases the response in FFA to non-face stimuli (Gauthier, Skudlarski, Gore, & Anderson, 2000), such as cars and birds, even when these are

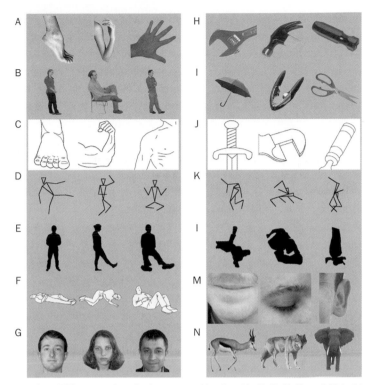

FIGURE 7-28. Area EBA responds to body parts and bodies (*A*, *B*, *C*, *D*, *E*, and *F*) but less to faces (*G*), face parts (*M*), and animals (*N*), and not to implements (*H*, *I*, and *J*), stick figures (*K*), or silhouettes (*L*). (Reprinted from Downing et al., 2001, with kind permission of AAAS.)

presented in side view so as not to be face-like (Xu, 2005). However, the response to faces in FFA is larger than the response to other objects, even after experience, and, as we will see in the next section, human lesions including the right FFA lead to specific deficits in face perception.

LESIONS IN HUMANS

The inability to recognize faces, known as prosopagnosia, has been studied for a long time (see Damasio, Damasio, & Van Hoesen, 1982). In most cases the prosopagnosia is accompanied by other visual deficits because the lesion is not confined to the face area. However, occasional lesions affecting perception of objects and faces have shown double dissociation: that is, there are a few patients who can detect objects but not faces, and, even rarer, other patients who can detect faces but not objects.

One of the former was a man who became a farmer after his accident (McNeil & Warrington, 1993). He failed numerous tests of face perception, but he learned to recognize his sheep more easily than people, even though he had had no experience of sheep before his accident. Another was asked to discriminate fruits and vegetables, and brands and models of cars (Henke et al., 1998). His performance on the objects was significantly better than the faces. Another was a Japanese man who could not recognize his own face, nor faces of family members, but could recognize animals and places (Wada & Yamamoto, 2001). When shown a picture of a famous Sumo wrestler standing in front of a famous shrine, he recognized the shrine but not the wrestler. This last case was particularly interesting, because the lesion was localized to the right fusiform and lateral occipital gyri, with no involvement of the left hemisphere.

The main example of a man who could recognize faces but not objects is patient CK (Moscovitch, Winocur, & Behrmann, 1997). He could recognize famous people, including pictures of them as children. He did well with cartoons and caricatures, and with faces seen from different viewpoints, and could learn new faces. However, he could not distinguish airplanes or soldiers from a pair of collections that he had accumulated as a child. He could not choose his food in a cafeteria by sight, and he did not pick up a cup of coffee that was offered to him because he could not distinguish it from other objects on the desk. When shown Arcimboldo paintings (Fig. 7–13), he saw the faces much more easily than the objects that made up the internal features of the face. Unfortunately the anatomy of his deficit has not yet been reported.

This double dissociation pretty much settles the argument as to whether there are particular face areas, and the case of the Japanese man confirms that some are in the right hemisphere in the fusiform and lateral occipital gyri, in agreement with fMRI recordings from normal people.

Prosopagnosia can also be a congenital or developmental problem, not associated with a particular lesion in the cortex (Duchaine & Nakayama, 2006). The perceptual deficits in developmental prosopagnosia are close to those seen in acquired prosopagnosia. There is very little literature on when it develops. Although there is no evidence of a specific lesion, the anterior fusiform gyrus does appear to be smaller in individuals with prosopagnosia (Behrmann, Avidan, Gao, & Black, 2007). There is also some evidence that developmental prosopagnosics can distinguish expressions on faces better than acquired prosopagnosics (Humphreys, Avidan, & Behrmann, 2007).

References

Baker, C. I., Liu, J., Wald, L. L., Kwong, K. K., Benner, T., & Kanwisher, N. (2007). Visual word processing and experiential origins of functional selectivity in human extrastriate cortex. *Proceedings of the National Academy of Sciences USA, 104,* 9087–9092.

Bakin, J. S., Nakayama, K., & Gilbert, C. D. (2000). Visual responses in monkey areas V1 and V2 to three-dimensional surface configurations. *Journal of Neuroscience, 20,* 8188–8198.

Barlow, H. B. (1972). Single units and sensation: a neuron doctrine for perceptual psychology? *Perception, 1,* 371–394.

Behrmann, M., Avidan, G., Gao, F., & Black, S. (2007). Structural imaging reveals anatomical alterations in inferotemporal cortex in congenital prosopagnosia. *Cerebral Cortex, 17*, 2354–2363.

Bredfeldt, C. E., & Cumming, B. G. (2006). A simple account of cyclopean edge responses in macaque V2. *Journal of Neuroscience, 26*, 7581–7596.

Bulthoff, H. H., & Bulthoff, I. (2003). Image-based recognition of biological motion, scenes, and objects. In M. A. Peterson & G. Rhodes (Eds.), *Perception of faces, objects, and scenes* (pp. 146–176). New York: Oxford University Press.

Carey, S., & Diamond, R. (1977). From piecemeal to configurational representation of faces. *Science, 195*, 312–314.

Damasio, A. R., Damasio, H., & Van Hoesen, G. W. (1982). Prosopagnosia: Anatomic basis and behavioral mechanisms. *Neurology, 32*, 331–341.

David, S. V., Hayden, B. Y., & Gallant, J. L. (2006). Spectral receptive field properties explain shape selectivity in area V4. *Journal of Neurophysiology, 96*, 3492–3505.

Delis, D. C., Robertson, L. C., & Efron, R. (1986). Hemispheric specialization of memory for visual hierarchical stimuli. *Neuropsychologia, 24*, 205–214.

Desimone, R., Albright, T. D., Gross, C. G., & Bruce, C. (1984). Stimulus-selective properties of inferior temporal neurons in the macaque. *Journal of Neuroscience, 4*, 2051–2062.

Diamond, R., & Carey, S. (1986). Why faces are and are not special: An effect of expertise. *Journal of Experimental Psychology: General, 115*, 107–117.

Downing, P. E., Jiang, Y., Shuman, M., & Kanwisher, N. (2001). A cortical area selective for visual processing of the human body. *Science, 293*, 2470–2473.

Duchaine, B. C., & Nakayama, K. (2006). Developmental prosopagnosia: A window to content-specific face processing. *Current Opinion in Neurobiology, 16*, 166–173.

Farivar, R. (2009). Dorsal-ventral integration in object recognition. *Brain Research Review, 61*, 144–153.

Friedman, H. S., Zhou, H., & von der Heydt, R. (2003). The coding of uniform colour figures in monkey visual cortex. *Journal of Physiology, 548*, 593–613.

Fujita, I., Tanaka, K., Ito, M., & Cheng, K. (1992). Columns for visual features of objects in monkey inferotemporal cortex. *Nature, 360*, 343–346.

Gallant, J. L., Braun, J., & Van Essen, D. C. (1993). Selectivity for polar, hyperbolic, and Cartesian gratings in macaque visual cortex. *Science, 259*, 100–103.

Gauthier, I., Skudlarski, P., Gore, J. C., & Anderson, A. W. (2000). Expertise for cars and birds recruits brain areas involved in face recognition. *Nature Neuroscience, 3*, 191–197.

Gerlach, C., Aaside, C. T., Humphreys, G. W., Gade, A., Paulson, O. B., & Law, I. (2002). Brain activity related to integrative processes in visual object recognition: Bottom-up integration and the modulatory influence of stored knowledge. *Neuropsychologia, 40*, 1254–1267.

Grill-Spector, K., Kushnir, T., Edelman, S., Itzchak, Y., & Malach, R. (1998). Cue-invariant activation in object-related areas of the human occipital lobe. *Neuron, 21*, 191–202.

Gross, C. G., Rocha-Miranda, C. E., & Bender, D. B. (1972). Visual properties of neurons in inferotemporal cortex of the Macaque. *Journal of Neurophysiology, 35*, 96–111.

Hanazawa, A., & Komatsu, H. (2001). Influence of the direction of elemental luminance gradients on the responses of V4 cells to textured surfaces. *Journal of Neuroscience, 21*, 4490–4497.

Haxby, J. V., Gobbini, M. I., Furey, M. L., Ishai, A., Schouten, J. L., & Pietrini, P. (2001). Distributed and overlapping representations of faces and objects in ventral temporal cortex. *Science, 293,* 2425–2430.

Hegde, J., Fang, F., & Murray, S. O. (2008). Preferential response to occluded objects in the human visual cortex. *Journal of Vision, 8,* 1–16.

Henke, K., Schweinberger, S. R., Grigo, A., Klos, T., & Sommer, W. (1998). Specificity of face recognition: Recognition of exemplars of non-face objects in prosopagnosia. *Cortex, 34,* 289–296.

Hosie, J. A., Ellis, H. D., & Haig, N. D. (1988). The effect of feature displacement on the perception of well-known faces. *Perception, 17,* 461–474.

Howe, C. Q., & Purves, D. (2005). *Perceiving geometry.* New York: Springer.

Hubel, D. H., & Wiesel, T. N. (1968). Receptive fields and functional architecture of monkey striate cortex. *Journal of Physiology, 195,* 215–243.

Hulten, I., & Pontus, K. (1924). *The Arcimboldo effect.* New York: Abbeville Press.

Humphreys, K., Avidan, G., & Behrmann, M. (2007). A detailed investigation of facial expression processing in congenital prosopagnosia as compared to acquired prosopagnosia. *Experimental Brain Research, 176,* 356–373.

Ito, M., Tamura, H., Fujita, I., & Tanaka, K. (1995). Size and position invariance of neuronal responses in monkey inferotemporal cortex. *Journal of Neurophysiology, 73,* 218–226.

Janssen, P., Vogels, R., Liu, Y., & Orban, G. A. (2001). Macaque inferior temporal neurons are selective for three-dimensional boundaries and surfaces. *Journal of Neuroscience, 21,* 9419–9429.

Kanisza, G. (1979). *Organization in vision.* New York: Praeger.

Kanwisher, N. (2004). The ventral visual object pathway in humans: Evidence from fMRI. In L. M. Chalupa & J. S. Werner (Eds.), *The visual neurosciences* (pp. 1179–1190). Cambridge, MA: MIT Press.

Kanwisher, N., McDermott, J., & Chun, M. M. (1997). The fusiform face area: A module in human extrastriate cortex specialized for face perception. *Journal of Neuroscience, 17,* 4302–4311.

Kanwisher, N., & Yovel, G. (2006). The fusiform face area: A cortical region specialized for the perception of faces. *Philosophical Transactions of the Royal Society of London B: Biolgical Sciences, 361,* 2109–2128.

Kastner, S., De Weerd, P., & Ungerleider, L. G. (2000). Texture segregation in the human visual cortex: A functional MRI study. *Journal of Neurophysiology, 83,* 2453–2457.

Kimchi, R. (2003). Relative dominance of holistic and component properties in the perceptual organization of visual objects. In M. A. Peterson & G. Rhodes (Eds.), *Perception of faces, objects, and scenes* (pp. 235–268). New York: Oxford University Press.

Kobatake, E., & Tanaka, K. (1994). Neuronal selectivities to complex object features in the ventral visual pathway of the macaque cerebral cortex. *Journal of Neurophysiology, 71,* 856–867.

Kohler, W. (1940). *Dynamics in psychology.* New York: Liveright.

Lamme, V. A. (1995). The neurophysiology of figure-ground segregation in primary visual cortex. *Journal of Neuroscience, 15,* 1605–1615.

Landy, M. S., & Graham, N. (2004). Visual perception of texture. In L. M. Chalupa & J. S. Werner (Eds.), *The visual neurosciences* (pp. 1106–1118). Cambridge, MA: MIT Press.

Lee, T. S., & Nguyen, M. (2001). Dynamics of subjective contour formation in the early visual cortex. *Proceedings of the National Academy of Sciences USA, 98,* 1907–1911.

Lehky, S. R., & Sereno, A. B. (2007). Comparison of shape encoding in primate dorsal and ventral visual pathways. *Journal of Neurophysiology, 97,* 307–319.

Leventhal, A. G., Wang, Y., Schmolesky, M. T., & Zhou, Y. (1998). Neural correlates of boundary perception. *The visual neurosciences, 15,* 1107–1118.

Li, W., Piech, V., & Gilbert, C. D. (2006). Contour saliency in primary visual cortex. *Neuron, 50,* 951–962.

Li, W., Piech, V., & Gilbert, C. D. (2008). Learning to link visual contours. *Neuron, 57,* 442–451.

Logothetis, N. K., Pauls, J., Bulthoff, H. H., & Poggio, T. (1994). View-dependent object recognition by monkeys. *Current Biology, 4,* 401–414.

Logothetis, N. K., Pauls, J., & Poggio, T. (1995). Shape representation in the inferior temporal cortex of monkeys. *Current Biology, 5,* 552–563.

Malach, R., Reppas, J. B., Benson, R. R., Kwong, K. K., Jiang, H., Kennedy, W. A., … Tootell, R. B. (1995). Object-related activity revealed by functional magnetic resonance imaging in human occipital cortex. *Proceedings of the National Academy of Sciences USA, 92,* 8135–8139.

Marcar, V. L., Raiguel, S. E., Xiao, D., & Orban, G. A. (2000). Processing of kinetically defined boundaries in areas V1 and V2 of the macaque monkey. *Journal of Neurophysiology, 84,* 2786–2798.

McCleery, J. P., Zhang, L., Ge, L., Wang, Z., Christiansen, E. M., Lee, K., & Cottrell, G. W. (2008). The roles of visual expertise and visual input in the face inversion effect: Behavioral and neurocomputational evidence. *Vision Research, 48,* 703–715.

McNeil, J. E., & Warrington, E. K. (1993). Prosopagnosia: A face-specific disorder. *Quarterly Journal of Experimental Psychology A, 46,* 1–10.

Mendola, J. D., Dale, A. M., Fischl, B., Liu, A. K., & Tootell, R. B. (1999). The representation of illusory and real contours in human cortical visual areas revealed by functional magnetic resonance imaging. *Journal of Neuroscience, 19,* 8560–8572.

Moscovitch, M., Winocur, G., & Behrmann, M. (1997). What is special about face recognition? Nineteen experiments on a person with visual object agnosia and dyslexia but normal face recognition. *Journal of Cognitive Neuroscience, 9,* 555–604.

Mysore, S. G., Vogels, R., Raiguel, S. E., & Orban, G. A. (2006). Processing of kinetic boundaries in macaque V4. *Journal of Neurophysiology, 95,* 1864–1880.

Nakayama, K., Shimojo, S., & Silverman, G. (1989). Stereoscopic depth: its relation to image segmentation, grouping, and the recognition of occluded objects. *Perception, 18,* 55–68.

Navon, D. (1977). Forest before trees: The precedence of global features in visual perception. *Cognitive Psychology, 9,* 353–383.

Palmer, S. E. (2004). *Vision science.* Cambridge, MA: MIT Press.

Pascalis, O., de Haan, M., & Nelson, C. A. (2002). Is face processing species specific during the first year of life? *Science, 296,* 1321–1323.

Pasupathy, A., & Connor, C. E. (2001). Shape representation in area V4: Position-specific tuning for boundary conformation. *Journal of Neurophysiology, 86,* 2505–2519.

Perrett, D. I., Rolls, E. T., & Caan, W. (1982). Visual neurones responsive to faces in the monkey temporal cortex. *Experimental Brain Research, 47,* 329–342.

Perrett, D. I., Smith, P. A., Potter, D. D., Mistlin, A. J., Head, A. S., Milner, A. D., & Jeeves, M. A. (1985). Visual cells in the temporal cortex sensitive to face view and gaze direction. *Proceedings of the Royal Society of London B: Biological Sciences, 223,* 293–317.

Peterson, M. A. (2003). Overlapping partial configurations in object memory: an alternative solution to classical problems in perception and recognition. In M. A. Peterson & G. Rhodes (Eds.), *Perception of faces, objects and scenes* (pp. 269–294). New York: Oxford University Press.

Peterson, M. A., & Rhodes, G. (2003). *Perception of faces, objects, and scenes.* New York: Oxford University Press.

Pinsk, M. A., Arcaro, M., Weiner, K. S., Kalkus, J. F., Inati, S. J., Gross, C. G., & Kastner, S. (2009). Neural representations of faces and body parts in macaque and human cortex: A comparative FMRI study. *Journal of Neurophysiology, 101,* 2581–2600.

Reddy, L., & Kanwisher, N. (2006). Coding of visual objects in the ventral stream. *Current Opinion in Neurobiology, 16,* 408–414.

Ringach, D. L., & Shapley, R. (1996). Spatial and temporal properties of illusory contours and amodal boundary completion. *Vision Research, 36,* 3037–3050.

Rock, I. (1974). The perception of disoriented figures. *Scientific American, 230,* 78–85.

Rolls, E. T. (2004). Invariant object and face recognition. In L. M. Chalupa & J. S. Werner (Eds.), *The visual neurosciences* (pp. 1151–1164). Cambridge, MA: MT Press.

Rolls, E. T., & Tovee, M. J. (1995). The responses of single neurons in the temporal visual cortical areas of the macaque when more than one stimulus is present in the receptive field. *Experimental Brain Research, 103,* 409–420.

Rubin, E. (1921). *Visuell Wahrgenomenne Figuren.* Copenhagen, Denmark: Gyldendalske.

Russell, R., Duchaine, B. C., & Nakayama, K. (2009). Super-recognizers: People with extraordinary face recognition. *Psychonomic Bulletin and Review, 16,* 252–257.

Sary, G., Vogels, R., & Orban, G. A. (1993). Cue-invariant shape selectivity of macaque inferior temporal neurons. *Science, 260,* 995–997.

Self, M. W., & Zeki, S. (2005). The integration of colour and motion by the human visual brain. *Cerebral Cortex, 15,* 1270–1279.

Sergent, J., Ohta, S., & MacDonald, B. (1992). Functional neuroanatomy of face and object processing. A positron emission tomography study. *Brain, 115*(Pt. 1), 15–36.

Sripati, A. P., & Olson, C. R. (2009). Representing the forest before the trees: A global advantage effect in monkey inferotemporal cortex. *Journal of Neuroscience, 29,* 7788–7796.

Sugase, Y., Yamane, S., Ueno, S., & Kawano, K. (1999). Global and fine information coded by single neurons in the temporal visual cortex. *Nature, 400,* 869–873.

Sugita, Y. (1999). Grouping of image fragments in primary visual cortex. *Nature, 401,* 269–272.

Tanaka, J. W., & Farah, M. H. (2003). The holistic representation of faces. In M. A. Peterson & G. Rhodes (Eds.), *Perception of faces, objects, and scenes* (pp. 53–74). New York: Oxford University Press.

Tanaka, K. (2004). Inferotemporal response properties. In L. M. Chalupa & J. S. Werner (Eds.), *The visual neurosciences* (pp. 1151–1164). Cambridge MA: MIT Press.

Tanifuji, M., Kaas, J. H., & Collins, C. E. (2004). The functional organization of monkey inferotemporal cortex. In J. H. Kaas & C. E. Collins (Eds.), *The primate visual system* (pp. 345–363). New York: CRC Press.

Tarr, M. J. (2003). Visual object recognition: Can a single mechanism suffice? In *Perception of faces, objects, and scenes* (pp. 177–211). New York: Oxford University Press.

Thompson, P. (1980). Margaret Thatcher: A new illusion. *Perception, 9,* 483–484.

Tsao, D. Y., Moeller, S., & Freiwald, W. A. (2008). Comparing face patch systems in macaques and humans. *Proceedings of the National Academy of Sciences USA, 105,* 19514–19519.

Tsao, D. Y., Schweers, N., Moeller, S., & Freiwald, W. A. (2008). Patches of face-selective cortex in the macaque frontal lobe. *Nature Neuroscience, 11,* 877–879.

Tsunoda, K., Yamane, Y., Nishizaki, M., & Tanifuji, M. (2001). Complex objects are represented in macaque inferotemporal cortex by the combination of feature columns. *Nature Neuroscience, 4,* 832–838.

Vinberg, J., & Grill-Spector, K. (2008). Representation of shapes, edges, and surfaces across multiple cues in the human visual cortex. *Journal of Neurophysiology, 99,* 1380–1393.

Vogels, R. (1999). Categorization of complex visual images by rhesus monkeys. Part 2: Single-cell study. *European Journal of Neuroscience, 11,* 1239–1255.

von der Heydt, R., Peterhans, E., & Baumgartner, G. (1984). Illusory contours and cortical neuron responses. *Science, 224,* 1260–1262.

von der Heydt, R., Zhou, H., & Friedman, H. S. (2000). Representation of stereoscopic edges in monkey visual cortex. *Vision Research, 40,* 1955–1967.

Wada, Y., & Yamamoto, T. (2001). Selective impairment of facial recognition due to a haematoma restricted to the right fusiform and lateral occipital region. *Journal of Neurology Neurosurgery and Psychiatry, 71,* 254–257.

Wang, G., Tanaka, K., & Tanifuji, M. (1996). Optical imaging of functional organization in the monkey inferotemporal cortex. *Science, 272,* 1665–1668.

Wertheimer, M. (1923/1938). Laws of organization in perceptual forms. In W. D. Ellis (Ed.), *A source book of Gestalt psychology* (pp. 71–88). Norwich, CT: Jarrold & Sons.

Xu, Y. (2005). Revisiting the role of the fusiform face area in visual expertise. *Cerebral Cortex, 15,* 1234–1242.

Yin, R. K. (1969). Looking at upside-down faces. *Journal of Experimental Psychology, 81,* 141–145.

Young, A. W., Hellawell, D., & Hay, D. C. (1987). Configurational information in face perception. *Perception, 16,* 747–759.

Zhou, H., Friedman, H. S., & von der Heydt, R. (2000). Coding of border ownership in monkey visual cortex. *Journal of Neuroscience, 20,* 6594–6611.

8

Control of Eye Movements

As discussed in Chapter 1, the main purpose of eye movements is to place objects of interest onto the fovea and to keep them there until a new object of interest appears. Thus, there are two general types of eye movement: those for directing the eyes to an object, and those for holding fixation on the object.

The first type includes the following:

- ¤ Saccades: rapid jumps from one point in the field of view to another
- ¤ Vergence: adjustments for looking at different depths

The second type includes the following:

- ¤ Fixation: gazing steadily in one direction
- ¤ Smooth pursuit: essentially fixation on a moving object
- ¤ Optokinetic movements: generated when the scene revolves around us, and we have to periodically move the eyes back to the center of the head in the absence of head movements
- ¤ Vestibular movements: when the head is rotating and the eyes rotate in the reverse direction to hold fixation

Both optokinetic and vestibular movements involve following the scene in one direction, then flicking the eyes back to center in a saccade-like movement. These alternating slow and fast phases are known as nystagmus. With the exception of vergence movements, all these eye movements involve movement of the two eyes in the same direction. For vergence, the eyes move in opposite directions.

We cannot move the eyes smoothly in the absence of a moving object to fixate on. This can be seen by asking a friend to hold up two arms and then try to move his or her eyes smoothly from the fingers of one hand to the fingers of the other. Watch your friend's eyes and you will see that they move with a series of jerks (saccades). This is also true when reading—we think that our eyes move smoothly along the line of text, but in fact they move with three or four saccades for each line (Dodge, 1900). Then ask your friend to fixate on a finger of one hand while moving the finger toward his/her other hand. The eye movement in this case is a smooth one.

Saccades

Saccades are ballistic eye movements: once started, they generally cannot be corrected or stopped until finished. In most cases, if a correction is required, another saccade must be programmed, after a gap of about 200 msec. Saccades are started by an initial pulse of force in the contracting muscles with complete relaxation in the opponent muscles, with a latency of 120–180 msec (Westheimer, 1954a). The eyes then move rapidly to their target, are braked there, and then are held by a new level of force appropriate to the new position. The movement can be very fast, amounting to several hundred degrees per second, with faster velocities for larger saccades.

The first step in generating a saccade is to identify a target that the subject wishes his/her eyes to move to. In the natural world, a person scanning a scene will execute a series of saccades from one object to another, choosing items of interest such as the eyes and lips in a picture of a face (Yarbus, 1967). The grouping of saccades is influenced by the instructions given to the observer (Fig. 8–1). When executing a task, such as making a cup of tea (Fig. 8–2A) or sight-reading a piece of music (Fig. 8–2B), there is a series of saccades corresponding to the various steps in the task. Selecting the target for the next saccade is obviously a very complicated business, depending on numerous factors. Some of these will be dealt with in Chapter 10, but in general the tasks used in experimental situations are simple compared to what we deal with in the natural world. The decision as to which target to move the

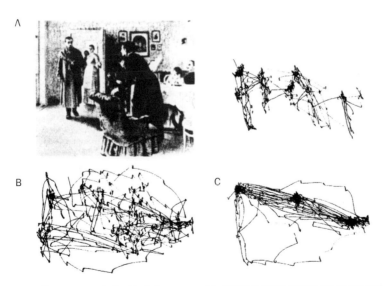

FIGURE 8–1. Eye movements looking at a scene with different instructions: (*A*) to remember the clothes worn by the people; (*B*) to remember the positions of the people and objects; and (*C*) to estimate how long the unexpected visitor had been away. (Reprinted from Yarbus, 1967, with kind permission of Plenum Press.)

eyes to can be made in as little as 30–50 msec; the rest of the time until the saccade is made is taken up by motor preparation (Stanford et al., 2010).

In ball games, a player can anticipate where a target is going and therefore can make a saccade to a position close to its destination (Land, 2004). Tennis, table tennis, and cricket players will direct their gaze to a point above the bounce of the ball some time before the ball actually makes the bounce. Baseball players may saccade to the estimated point of contact with the bat, or may use smooth pursuit for the initial part of the trajectory. Driving is another complicated task, requiring saccades to road signs, other vehicles, pedestrians and cyclists, and the curves in the road ahead.

During a saccade, vision is suppressed. This is not just the result of the image of the object on the retina being blurred. A brief stimulus flashed fast enough that it is not blurred during a saccade has to be brighter than a stimulus flashed before or after the saccade by a factor of 2–3 in order to be seen, although the factor depends very much on the stimulus used (low frequency or high frequency; color or black/white; moving or not; Burr & Morrone, 2004). Part of the reason is that the outer segments of the photoreceptors are sheared sideways during a saccade, and thus become less efficient at absorbing light (the Stiles-Crawford effect: see Westheimer, 2008), but there are other suppressive factors at work as well. Firing in the lateral geniculate nucleus is reduced during a saccade both in the presence and in the absence of a visual stimulus, showing that this suppression occurs independently of visual input (Casagrande & Royal, 2004). In any case, the perception of the scene remains clear in spite of the saccade.

The world does not appear to move during a saccade, even though there is a jump in the retinal image. Objects appear to be in the same position afterward as they had before. Helmholtz (1875/1962) suggested that there is an "efference copy" of the signal to the eye muscles that is copied to the sensory system and plays a role in this; he pointed out that if the eye is moved manually without any effort of the eye muscles, the scene does appear to move (Wurtz, 2011). Mislocalization of stimuli flashed before, during, and after a saccade shows that the timing of this efference copy mechanism does not correspond precisely to the timing of the saccade (Bischof & Kramer, 1968; Burr & Morrone, 2011; Matin, 1972). However, in spite of this mislocalization—seen in a variety of experimental situations (see Hunt & Cavanagh, 2009; Ostendorf, Fischer, Gaymard, & Ploner, 2006)—the world is stable in normal conditions through the entire time course of the saccade; there is no perception of movement of the scene in any direction. Remapping of stimuli is found within the receptive fields of cells in the visual system—more and more at successively higher levels of the system (Melcher & Colby, 2008)—which may account for the perception of stability. Lateral inhibition and masking within the sensory pathways may play a role in this remapping (e.g., Campbell & Wurtz, 1978) and so may mechanisms of visual storage (see Bays & Husain, 2007), as well as efference copy and proprioceptive signals (Tong, Lien, Cisarik, & Bedell, 2008). Most important, all these mechanisms combine to

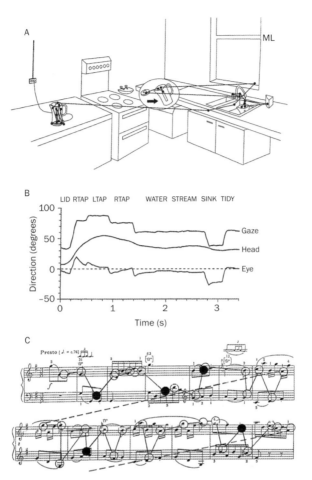

FIGURE 8–2. (*A*) Sequence of fixations in making a cup of tea, and (*B*) eye, head, and gaze movements performed. (*C*) Fixations made by an expert pianist, including glances down to the keyboard shown by the dark circles. (Reprinted from Land & Tatler, 2009, with kind permission of Oxford University Press.)

ensure that motor actions such as hammering are accurate while eye movements are made, as well as perception of the scene (Hansen & Skavenski, 1977).

When we look at a scene, the images we see between the saccades are integrated into a representation of the scene that is complete as well as stationary. Nevertheless, if a change in an object occurs during a saccade, it may not be noticed. This fascinating phenomenon is called change blindness or, more generally, change detection. For example, if the hats of two men who are standing side by side are interchanged during a saccade (Fig. 8–3), nearly all observers do not notice the switch (Grimes, 1996). Changes are noticed more frequently when making a small saccade toward or away from the object that has changed (Henderson & Hollingworth, 1999). Change blindness may also occur without a

FIGURE 8–3. During a saccade, the hats of two men standing side by side are switched. Almost nobody notices the change. (Reprinted from Grimes, 1996, with kind permission of Oxford University Press.)

saccade when an object is obscured (Simons, 2000). For example, a person can be replaced while men carrying a door pass in front of him; this is not noticed by 50% of the observers. No wonder there are so many mistakes made in identification during criminal scenes! Change blindness occurs because we notice only the most salient features of a scene, which presumably simplifies the process that needs to happen for remapping between saccades (Melcher & Colby, 2008).

Saccades can adapt to take account of changes during development. Adaptation can also be prompted by problems in the eye muscles that require a different exertion of force to provide an accurate saccade. There is a short-term mechanism of adaptation, occurring over a day or so, and also a long-term mechanism, occurring over 2 or 3 weeks (Robinson, Soetedjo, & Noto, 2006). The short-term mechanism can be reversed rapidly, whereas the long-term mechanism lasts a long time. These mechanisms are crucial for maintaining the accuracy of saccades.

Vergence

Simple horizontal vergence movements involve changing the view from an object straight ahead to another object also straight ahead, but nearer or further away. These movements may be convergent, where the eyes both move inward to look closer, or divergent, where they both move outward to look at an object further away. These movements tend to be much slower than saccades, up to 10°–20°/sec, as noted by Dodge (1903).

In the real world, however, it is much more common to look from an object straight ahead to another object at a different distance to one side or the other. In this situation, where the cues of disparity, blur, and change in size all combine to produce the movement, it is much faster, up to 100°/sec (Erkelens, Van der Steen, Steinman, & Collewijn, 1989a). Essentially, the vergence movement is combined with a saccade, and as a result the saccades in the two eyes are not equal (Erkelens, Steinman, & Collewijn, 1989b; Fig. 8–4). This is contrary to the suggestion that the two eyes always move by equal amounts, which would require the saccade to be made separately from the vergence movement (Yarbus, 1967). The saccade in the dominant eye may occur faster than the saccade in the nondominant eye, bringing the dominant eye to fixate the object first (Zee, Fitzgibbon, & Optican, 1992).

Vergence movements may be in a vertical direction or involve a rotation of the eyes, as well as being horizontal to take account of objects at different depths. All three types of vergence movement may have a very short latency, 60 msec for macaque and 85 msec for man, in response to movement of a large field stimulus, where the whole background is rotated, translated, or moved in depth (Miles, 1998). The signals for this go through the cortex but do not involve the decision making required for a saccade, where the system has to pick out one object from the rest of the scene before changing the direction of gaze and fixating on it.

Vergence movements may be elicited by the perception of depth in the absence of an actual object at a different distance. For example, the eyes will converge for the kinetic depth effect when shown a stimulus in front of the screen, and diverge for a stimulus that appears behind the screen (Ringach, Hawken, & Shapley, 1996). However, if the depth cues conflict with the perception, vergence will follow the depth cues rather than the perception (Wismeijer, van Ee, & Erkelens, 2008).

Convergence is linked to accommodation and the pupillary reflex in what is known as the near triad. When the eyes converge to look at a nearby object, the focus of the eyes changes and the pupils contract. Thus, changes in focus lead to convergence, and convergence leads to changes in focus, showing the close link between the two systems.

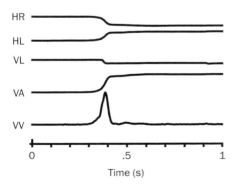

FIGURE 8–4. Unequal saccades, when a saccade is combined with vergence. HL, horizontal left eye position; HR, horizontal right eye position; VA, vergence angle, which is HL-HR; VL, vertical left eye position; VV, vergence velocity. Note that there is no sign of separate saccade and vergence movements: they are combined into a single movement in each eye. (Reprinted from Mays, 2004, with kind permission of MIT Press.)

Fixation

The nature of eye movements when we are fixating is a matter of controversy. While it has been known for centuries that the eyes are never completely at rest (see Rolfs, 2009), the significance of this point was not established until the 1950s, when three groups studied what happens with an image stabilized on the retina: it disappears (Ditchburn & Ginsborg, 1952; Riggs & Ratliff, 1952; Yarbus, 1967). This had been shown 150 years earlier for an image falling on the periphery of the retina, where the acuity is much worse and the stabilization requirements are less strict (Troxler, 1804; Fig. 8–5), and is also true for an image at the fovea if stabilization is good enough. Further study of eye movements made while the head is restrained showed that the eyes make small saccades during fixation, called microsaccades, followed by slow drifts, and that there is also a tremor. The microsacccades become less frequent during a fine task, such as threading a needle, as the thread approaches the needle (Ko, Poletti, & Rucci, 2010). These fixational movements also improve our acuity (Rucci, Iovin, Poletti, & Santini, 2007). The hypothesis is that the microsaccades prevent vision from disappearing by moving the image over the retina every second or so.

A series of papers by Steinman and colleagues (see Steinman, 2004) showed that microsaccades are much less frequent if the head is not restrained. These papers downgraded the importance of microsaccades, but nevertheless some kind of movement of the image across the retina during fixation is required to prevent the image from fading. Small saccades are related to an increase in firing in V1 of macaque (Martinez-Conde, Macknik, & Hubel, 2000), and also to the fading found in the Troxler effect (Martinez-Conde, Macknik, Tronoso, & Dyar, 2006). Thus, when they occur, they are related to the maintenance of vision. When they do not occur, the slow drift or the tremor or larger saccades must move the image across the retina sufficiently to avoid disappearance of the image.

FIGURE 8–5. The Troxler effect. Stare at the dot in the center, and the blurred circle will disappear, because it is effectively stationary on the retina. (Reprinted from Disappearing Doughnut on http://www.viperlib.com, with kind permission of Peter Thompson.)

Smooth Pursuit

The term *smooth pursuit* is generally used to describe visually following a small object that moves across the field of view against a background or in the dark. There is a latency of 80–130 msec, and the eyes can keep up with the stimulus up to about 30°/sec (see Lisberger, Morris, & Tychsen, 1987). A stimulus often used in laboratory investigations is the step-ramp, where the stimulus jumps to one side, say left, then moves at a constant speed in the opposite direction (Rashbass, 1961; Fig. 8–6). The eyes do not make a saccade to the left followed by smooth pursuit to the right; instead, they start moving smoothly to the right before the latency period for a saccade is over, and they may make a small saccade to bring the target to the fovea after the smooth pursuit movement has started.

The response to the step-ramp stimulus shows that velocity across the retina, rather than position, is the primary cue for the smooth pursuit movement. It also shows that the system has some predictive capability. The predictive capability shows up in a number of other situations. For example, faced with a stimulus moving sinusoidally from left to right, the eyes will initially lag behind the movement of the stimulus, but after a few cycles, they will start following the movement precisely (Westheimer, 1954b). Moreover, they will also follow a moving object that is illuminated periodically with a flash of light so brief that the object does not move across the retina during the time that it is illuminated, appearing to be a series of flashes rather than a moving object. However, the tracking of the object is not very good in this circumstance (Westheimer, 1954b).

When an object disappears, the eyes will stop moving after a period of about 200 msec (Becker & Fuchs, 1985). However, if the object goes behind another object and then reappears, the eyes will continue to follow it, provided the period of disappearance is not too long (Churchland, Chou, & Lisberger, 2003). The object will be followed more accurately when it is occluded, passing behind another object, than when it is turned off for the same period of time (Fig. 8–7). However, blinks of the eyelids do not interrupt a smooth pursuit eye movement. There may also be some input from the eye blink system to the eye movement system (Rambold, El Baz, & Helmchen, 2005). These observations reinforce the ability of the smooth pursuit system to predict the movement of the stimulus,

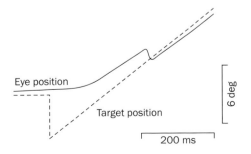

FIGURE 8–6. Macaque eye movement in response to a step-ramp stimulus. The target moves to one side in a step, then in the opposite direction with a constant velocity. The eyes start to match the velocity of the target with a smooth pursuit eye movement, then saccade to correct the position. (Photograph courtesy of Mati Joshua and Steve Lisberger.)

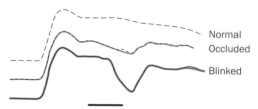

FIGURE 8–7. Eye movement in macaque in response to a step-ramp stimulus in normal conditions, with the stimulus occluded during the period of the horizontal black line, and turned off (blinked) for the same period of time. (Reprinted from Churchland et al., 2003, with kind permission of the American Physiological Society.)

seen in a number of situations where the eyes follow perceived motion rather than actual motion (Steinbach, 1976).

Sometimes a large part of the field of view moves, rather than an object within the field of view. In this case, the eyes will follow the movement of the whole field of view in what is known as ocular following (see Heinen & Keller, 2004). This is a short latency eye movement, like the vergence movements discussed earlier (Miles, 1998), and involves different cells and pathways within the visual system (see discussion of motion perception in Chapter 5).

While smooth pursuit and saccadic eye movements have been studied separately and are controlled by somewhat separate subareas in the brain, as we will see later, they often occur together to follow a stimulus. This can be seen in the response to the step-ramp stimulus, where the eyes move in the direction of the ramp, then make small saccades to bring the stimulus to the fovea. While position of the target is the primary cue for saccades, and velocity is the primary cue for smooth pursuit movements, velocity is involved in saccades to a moving target, and position in smooth pursuit of a target away from the fovea (Orban de Xivry & Lefevre, 2007). Figures quoted earlier for latencies of the two types of movement may be different when the paradigms are not arranged to isolate one type of movement from the other (Erkelens, 2006). Once a target is selected, both smooth pursuit and saccades will be directed toward it, but the smooth pursuit will occur faster than the saccade (Case & Ferrera, 2007).

Just as a decision has to be made about which object to direct attention to next, a decision may have to be made about which of several moving objects to follow. The system may pursue an average of two trajectories until saccading to one of them, or follow one if biased by a signature such as the color of the object (Lisberger & Ferrera, 1997).

Optokinetic and Vestibular Eye Movements

When the head moves in space, the eyes move in the opposite direction to maintain on the fovea whatever object is being fixated. This is controlled by both visual and vestibular inputs to the eye movement system. In the laboratory, the two components can be separated, but in the real world they almost always occur together.

If a subject sits in a chair inside a drum with vertical stripes painted on it, and the chair is rotated (Fig. 8–8), the eyes will follow the stripe that is being looked at with an ocular following movement and then, when the eyes have rotated far enough, they will flick back to the center of the head in a saccadic movement. These alternating slow and fast movements are known as nystagmus (Fig. 8–9).

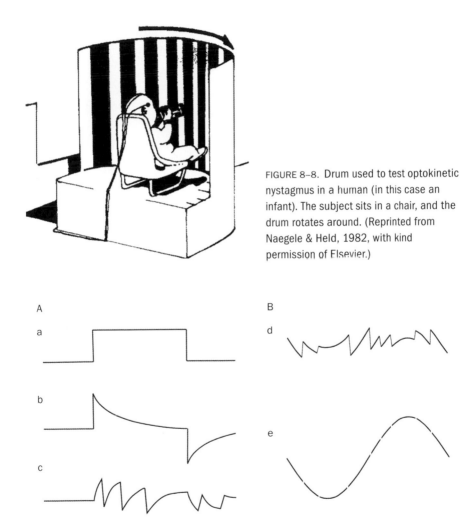

FIGURE 8–8. Drum used to test optokinetic nystagmus in a human (in this case an infant). The subject sits in a chair, and the drum rotates around. (Reprinted from Naegele & Held, 1982, with kind permission of Elsevier.)

FIGURE 8–9. (*A*) Vestibular nystagmus during turns of the head: (*a*) Velocity of the head during a constant velocity turn; (*b*) deflection of the cupula in the semicircular canals in the vestibular system; and (*c*) following and flick back movements of the eyes. (*B*) Eye movements in response to sinusoidal rotations of the head: (*d*) Following movements of the eyes, interspersed with flick backs, and (*e*) sinusoidal movements of the eyes seen by eliminating the flick backs.

The vestibular component, called vestibular nystagmus, can be isolated by turning off the lights so that the subject no longer sees the drum. The visual input can be isolated by rotating the drum instead of the subject and is called optokinetic nystagmus (OKN).

The visual component of the response is accurate but slow. The vestibular component of the response is much faster, because the vestibular ocular reflex (VOR) is a three-neuron arc from the inner ear to the vestibular nucleus, then to the oculomotor nuclei. The signal is delayed neither by the slow response of the photoreceptors nor by having to go through the cortex. This can be demonstrated by holding out your finger at arm's length and moving it from side to side while following it with your eyes, then holding your finger still while rotating your head from side to side. The improvement in clarity is striking. The VOR clearly improves performance for moderate to high frequencies.

Coordination of Head and Eye Movements

The coordination of head and eye movements is a complicated business (see Freedman, Stanford, & Sparks, 1996). In the laboratory it depends very much on the paradigm used and the instructions given to the subject. Only recently has apparatus been developed that allows the measurement of both head and eye movements while both are free to move. In one task, subjects were asked to tap a sequence of objects arranged on a table in front of them (Herst, Epelboim, & Steinman, 2001). Sometimes the head moved first, sometimes the eyes, and sometimes both simultaneously. Instructions from the cerebral cortex are clearly reaching the oculomotor nuclei and spinal cord at much the same time. After the head starts moving, the VOR helps to stabilize the eyes on the target with a very short latency.

Pupillary Response

The pupil contracts most notably to an increase in brightness, but responses have been found also to color, movement, and changes in patterns and random dot stereograms (see Li & Sun, 2005). Constriction of the pupil leads to improved acuity and depth of focus. It is also affected by emotional state, and it is part of the near triad response, together with convergence and change in focus of the lens activated by looking at a closer object. The pupillary response is the only part of the visual system that needs perception of the absolute level of illumination, as opposed to contrast with other objects in the field of view. Thus, it is served by a separate class of ganglion cells in the retina that project directly from the retina to nuclei in the brainstem controlling the pupil (see Appendix).

Areas of the Brain Involved in Eye Movements

Several areas of the brain area are involved in eye movements (Fig. 8–10). The occipital cortex projects to parietal cortex, which plays a major role in deciding the goal of the next eye movement, so activity in parietal cortex is affected by attention toward this goal. The movement areas, MT and MST, detect the movement of a stimulus in relation to the fovea, giving a signal for smooth pursuit movements. Occipital cortex, parietal cortex, and the movement areas all project to frontal cortex, which sends signals to control saccades, smooth pursuit, and vergence movements. The primary area involved here is the frontal eye field (FEF), with separate areas for these three classes of movement. There is also the supplementary eye field (SEF), which leads other areas in the upcoming choice of target.

Frontal cortex, parietal cortex, and occipital cortex all project to the superior colliculus. The rostral part of this structure is concerned with fixation, smooth pursuit, vergence, and small saccades; the caudal part is concerned with larger saccades. It has a sensory map of the visual field in its upper layers, and in its lower layers a corresponding motor map of the position in the field to which the eyes will move. It projects to the brainstem, where the two-dimensional direction of a saccade is parceled into horizontal and vertical movements. The superior colliculus is a central area in the transmission of signals from cortex to the more specific control of movements.

There are two areas in brainstem concerned with eye movements. These can be summarized as brainstem premotor nuclei (PMN) and precerebellar pontine

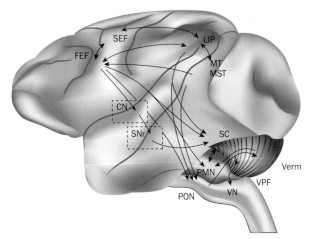

FIGURE 8–10. Areas in the primate brain involved in eye movements. CN, caudate nucleus; FEF, frontal eye fields; LIP, lateral intraparietal area; MST, medial superior temporal area; MT medial temporal area; PMN, brainstem premotor nuclei; PON, precerebellar pontine oculomotor nuclei; SC, superior colliculus; SEF, supplementary eye fields; SNr, substantia nigra pars reticulata; Verm, vermis of the cerebellum; VN, vestibular nuclei; and VPF, ventral paraflocculus of the cerebellum.

oculomotor nuclei (PON). The brainstem premotor nuclei include the paramedian pontine reticular formation (PPRF), which deals with horizontal movements, and the mesencephalic reticular formation (MRF), which deals with vertical eye movements. These areas receive input from both superior colliculus and frontal eye fields, and they distribute output to the oculomotor nuclei, which control the eye muscles.

The precerebellar pontine oculomotor nuclei receive input from multiple areas of cortex and send output to the cerebellum, which in turn sends output to the brainstem premotor nuclei. The cerebellum is important in controlling the accuracy of eye movements and in adjusting the magnitude of these movements to adapt to changing circumstances.

Finally, the basal ganglia act to release the eye muscles from a holding position when a saccade occurs. The substantia nigra inhibits the superior colliculus, the caudate nucleus inhibits the substantia nigra, and the caudate nucleus in turn is activated by the frontal eye fields. The release from inhibition enables a saccade to proceed.

This is obviously an incredibly complicated system, and it is hard to appreciate. I hope that the details given in the following sections will make it easier. It used to be thought that pathways for saccades and smooth pursuit were separate, going back to Ferrier's observation (1880) that stimulation of parietal cortex affects smooth pursuit, whereas stimulation of frontal cortex affects saccades. More recent work has shown that both types of eye movement are represented in all the areas involved, although sometimes by separate neurons and sometimes in separate subareas. Moreover, saccades and smooth pursuit are coordinated in the real world, and new experimental paradigms designed to probe this coordination are increasingly bringing this out (Krauzlis, 2004).

Occipital Cortex

The occipital cortex, of course, is the source of all visual signals projecting to parietal and frontal cortex that guide eye movements, with the exception of those fed up from the superior colliculus. While the parietal cortex is the prime area in the selection of targets for a saccade, the process starts in the occipital cortex, where the response of neurons is affected by attention. For example, the sensitivity of neurons in V4 increases just before a saccade is made to a target in the receptive field of the neuron (Schafer, Krumeich, & Moore, 2008). This will be dealt with further in Chapter 10.

Motion Areas

The motion areas of visual cortex, MT and MST, have neurons that respond to slow motion, appropriate for controlling eye movements. Early workers, recording from single cells on the anterior bank of the caudal superior temporal sulcus (STS)—which in spite of its name is generally regarded as being in posterior parietal cortex—found a number of them, which they called visual tracking neurons (Sakata, Shibutani, & Kawano, 1983). The activity of these neurons was related to the motion of a stimulus that the eyes were following, in both light and dark, if the lights were turned off for a while during the motion. These neurons were probably in MST.

Some neurons in MST are related to vergence movements as well as smooth pursuit (Akao et al., 2005). These authors found 61% related to smooth pursuit, 18% related to vergence, and 21% related to both. This is very like responses found in frontal eye fields, to be discussed later, but the responses in MST lead those in frontal eye fields, so the main influence is feedforward rather than feedback.

The primary evidence that MT and MST affect eye movements comes from lesions. Lesions in these areas result in reduced accuracy of smooth pursuit eye movements—the speed of the eye movements is not matched to that of the target—and reduced accuracy of saccades to moving targets (Newsome, Wurtz, Dursteler, & Mikami, 1985). Accuracy of saccades to stationary targets is not affected. The reduced accuracy of saccades to moving targets occurs for targets that give a response in the area of MT or MST where the lesion is, and it is independent of the direction of movement of the target (the deficit is said to be retinotopic). The inability to match speed of the eye movement to speed of the target occurs for lesions in the regions of MT and MST dealing with central vision, and it occurs for pursuit toward the side of the brain with the lesion (the deficit is directional). The difference in deficits between lesions of MT and lesions of MST is comparatively minor (Dursteler & Wurtz, 1988). Both MT and MST project to frontal eye fields and pontine oculomotor nuclei, which control these eye movements. The fact that lesions of MST have much the same effect as lesions of MT shows that the direct projection from MT to higher areas is not enough to sustain the accuracy of the eye movement.

Parietal Cortex

The parietal cortex was first investigated as an area of sensory convergence. It is involved with attention (What objects are we concerned with?) and intention (What body parts are we going to move to the object?) (Andersen, Snyder, Bradley, & Xing, 1997). There are areas that are primarily sensory, such as MST, located near visual cortex, with input from visual and vestibular systems; 7a, located near somatosensory cortex, with input from somatosensory, visual, and auditory systems; and the ventral intraparietal area (VIP), dealing with direction of motion and the face. Signals from the sensory areas are distributed to areas in posterior parietal cortex (PPC) dealing with eye movement (the lateral intraparietal area, LIP); reaching (the parietal reach area, PRR); and grasping (the anterior intraparietal area, AIP). The positions of these various areas are given in Figure 8–11. Thus, MST, 7A, and VIP are more on the sensory side, and LIP, PRR, and AIP more on the motor side, although the responses in all are related to both sensory input and motor output.

The first area in the more sensory part of parietal cortex to be investigated in some detail was area 7. Hyvarinen and Poranen (1974) noted that area 7 responds to visual as well as cutaneous stimuli. It was particularly important that the macaque be interested in, or reaching for, the object in the receptive field of the cell. A number of cells were for looking only, some for looking and reaching, and some for touching and looking. Shortly afterward, Mountcastle's group came out with papers on the same subject (Lynch, Mountcastle, Talbot, & Yin, 1977). The majority of cells were described as fixation cells, responding with fixation on a stationary or moving object (the activity of many of these was suppressed during a saccade); some fired when a saccade was intentional; and some were described as visual tracking neurons, with responses to the direction of the tracking. The cells mainly responded to objects within reach. Area VIP has cells responding particularly to direction of movement, and movement toward the face, combined with somatosensory input for these movements, so it is known as the parietal face area. Its function is more concerned with smooth pursuit than saccades (Colby, Duhamel, & Goldberg, 1993). The responses of cells in the more sensory part of parietal cortex, MST, have been discussed earlier.

One task to distinguish neurons related more to sensory aspects of the stimulus from those related more to the intended movement from the stimulus is the

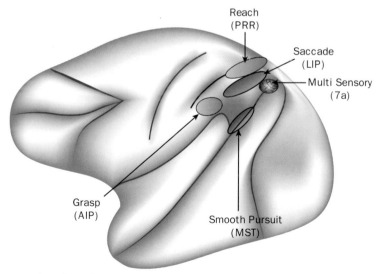

FIGURE 8–11. Locations of parietal areas concerned with eye movements and reach. AIP, anterior intraparietal area; LIP, lateral intraparietal area; MST, medial superior temporal area; PRR, parietal reach region; VIP, the ventral intraparietal area, is down in the sulcus between PRR and LIP.

memory task. Here, the animal is given a cue and trained to wait before making the movement. Neurons may respond after the cue, just before the movement, or both, and this task distinguishes which it may be (Hikosaka & Wurtz, 1983a). Another is the antisaccade task. Here, the monkey is trained to look for a cue, then make a saccade away from the cue. If the cell responds to the cue, it is sensory, and if to the saccade, it is motor. Another is a task where the monkey may either make a saccade toward the object or reach for it, which distinguishes what the movement is going to be (Andersen & Buneo, 2002). Saccades activate LIP, and reaching activates PRR. Yet more complicated tasks refine the details of the response of a neuron (Colby & Goldberg, 1999).

Since we are concerned with eye movements rather than limb movements, we will discuss LIP, rather than PRR and AIP. There are a variety of neurons within LIP with different responses, but the overall generalization is that LIP is concerned with the salience or priority of an object, which may also be described as its behavioral relevance (Colby & Goldberg, 1999). For example, a neuron will respond when a stimulus is turned on in its receptive field, either with or without an eye movement just before the stimulus is turned on, but not when the eyes move to place the object in the receptive field if it has been there all along (Fig. 8–12; Gottlieb, Kusunoki, & Goldberg, 1998). The latter is obviously a less salient stimulus. Moreover, the area is definitely concerned with the selection of the target for a saccade when more than one target, or a distracter, is present

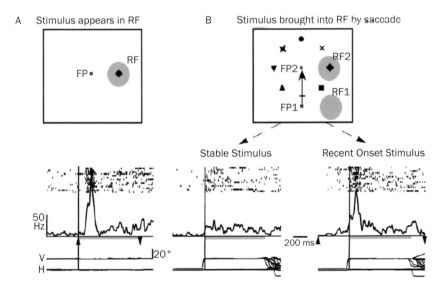

FIGURE 8–12. Response of neuron in LIP to the appearance of a stimulus in its receptive field. The neuron responds to the appearance of the stimulus with the eyes stationary (*A*), and to a stimulus turned on just before the eyes make a saccade (*B*, right), but not to a stimulus that is already there when the eyes move (*B*, left). (Reprinted from Gottlieb et al., 1998, with kind permission of MacMillan Publishers.)

(Wardak, Olivier, & Duhamel, 2002). Some of the cells also receive input about depth, presumably leading to the generation of unequal saccades that occur when a saccade is made to an object at a different depth (Gnadt & Mays, 1995). LIP does not control saccades, as frontal cortex does (Bisley & Goldberg, 2006). Microstimulation in LIP leads to an increase in the proportion of saccades toward the area represented by the site of the stimulation, and a reduced latency, but does not give saccades by itself (Hanks, Ditterich, & Shadlen, 2006). LIP is definitely on the pathway to saccade generation, but it is frontal cortex and superior colliculus that actually encode the decision to make the movement.

Recent work has also been concerned with the coordinates within which LIP neurons respond (Andersen & Buneo, 2002). The old view was that these neurons respond within an eye-centered coordinate frame, independent of whether the stimulus is visual, auditory, or somatosensory, but this has been questioned by more recent work using different techniques (Mullette-Gillman, Cohen, & Groh, 2009). Exactly how the input from various senses is combined to produce a correct saccade in different conditions thus needs more work. There also is an eye position signal, so that the eyes can compensate if a saccade to a second stimulus is planned before the saccade to the first stimulus is complete.

Parietal cortex is also an important area for remapping of the world, as well as V3A (Hall & Colby, 2011). For a saccade in any direction, LIP neurons respond as though the eyes have not moved (Heiser & Colby, 2006), so these neurons must have access to information beyond the classical receptive field of the neuron. This may have as much to do with control of the eye movements during a complicated situation, such as making two successive saccades, as with the perception of the world as being stationary (Bays & Husain, 2007).

Human parietal cortex is organized much like macaque parietal cortex. Six areas have now been identified in the intraparietal sulcus: IPS 1–5 and one in the superior parietal lobule (SPL1). There is a gradient of responses from saccades in SPL1, which is posterior and medial, to smooth pursuit in IPS1, which is anterior and lateral (Konen & Kastner, 2008). IPS1 and 2 correspond to LIP, SPL1 to 7a, and IPS5 to VIP, while the correspondence of IPS3 and 4 is not clear and may even represent functions found in human but not macaque.

Frontal Cortex

Ferrier's work (1880) on stimulation of macaque cortex suggested that there is an area in frontal cortex, known as the frontal eye fields, that is responsible for saccadic eye movements. Work since then has amply supported this point. Robinson and Fuchs (1969) stimulated in the frontal eye fields of the macaque, eliciting saccades the amplitude and direction of which varied with the position of the electrode (Fig. 8–13). The saccade was independent of the eye position before the saccade. They did not see smooth pursuit movements.

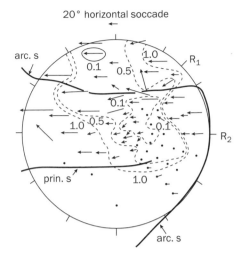

20° horizontal soccade

arc. s

prin. s

FIGURE 8–13. Drawing of the surface of the macaque frontal cortex, showing direction and amplitude of eye movements elicited by stimulation. Arrows show the direction; and length of arrows the amplitude. Thicker lines show the positions of the arcuate sulcus and the principal sulcus. Numbers represent the currents required to elicit a movement. (Reprinted from Robinson & Fuchs, 1969, with kind permission of the American Physiological Society.)

Saccade-related neurons in frontal eye fields can be divided into four types: visual, visuomotor, movement, and postsaccadic (Bruce & Goldberg, 1985). These four types can be distinguished in a task in which a cue light is turned on, there is an interval before the fixation light is turned off, as described earlier, and the monkey is trained to make a saccade to the cue (Fig. 8–14). There may be activity after the cue, before the saccade, and during the interval between cue and saccade. Figure 8–14 shows a visuomotor neuron with activity in all three periods. Figure 8–15 shows aggregate responses for a number of visual cells, visuomotor cells, and movement cells. Although the categories are separated here, there is actually more of a continuum between them. The current required to produce a saccade is lowest in the region of the movement neurons, and the saccade elicited corresponds to the response of the movement neurons recorded in the area (Bruce, Goldberg, Bushnell, & Stanton, 1985). The postsaccadic neurons, which fire after the saccade has been made, probably have to do with efference copy signals fed back to earlier areas in the visual system. The same four types of cell are found when a monkey is scanning a natural scene (Burman & Segraves, 1994; see Schall, 2002).

Although there were hints in previous papers, it was not until Lynch (1987) made bilateral lesions going deep in the arcuate sulcus that it was clearly established that the frontal eye fields play a role in smooth pursuit eye movements (SPEM). Previous authors generally did not get down there with their electrodes, nor did Ferrier's stimulation. SPEM amplitude is coded by the intensity of the stimulus, and direction of the SPEM is coded by the position in the cortex (Gottlieb, Bruce, & MacAvoy, 1993). There is also an area rostral to this where vergence movements are represented (Gamlin & Yoon, 2000) and an area for fixation movements (Izawa, Suzuki, & Shinoda, 2009). Thus, the frontal eye fields can be divided into three areas: one on the posterior curve of the arcuate gyrus

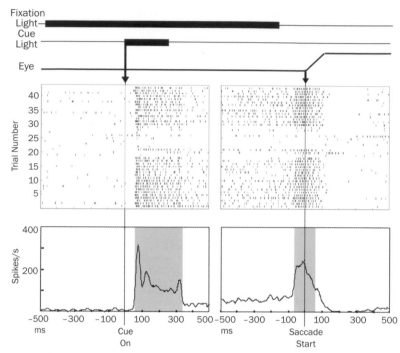

FIGURE 8.14. Response of a neuron in the frontal eye fields. The macaque is taught to move the eyes (third line) when the fixation light (first line) goes off, some time after the cue light (second line) comes on. This neuron fires at both times. (Reprinted from Bruce et al., 2004, with kind permission of MIT Press.)

dealing with saccadic eye movements; one in the depth of the arcuate sulcus and on the posterior bank dealing with smooth pursuit movements; and one anterior to the saccadic area dealing with vergence movements. Within each area there is a topography, with the direction of the movement—and in the case of saccades, also the amplitude—laid out in a map.

One might suppose that the frontal eye fields are an area where visual signals continue to be processed and projected within the area to movement neurons that send signals to the superior colliculus and brainstem to control the eye movements. Unfortunately, it is not as simple as this. Sommer and Wurtz (2001) studied the neurons that project from the frontal eye fields to the superior colliculus; they found a variety of signals represented. This includes where to make the next saccade, working memory of the target location, and spatial visual attention, as well as the location of the visual stimulus, transient visual memory, and tonic visual response. Thus, the frontal eye fields are just another step along the pathway through which visual input guides eye movements with interconnections to occipital, parietal, and temporal cortex and lower areas.

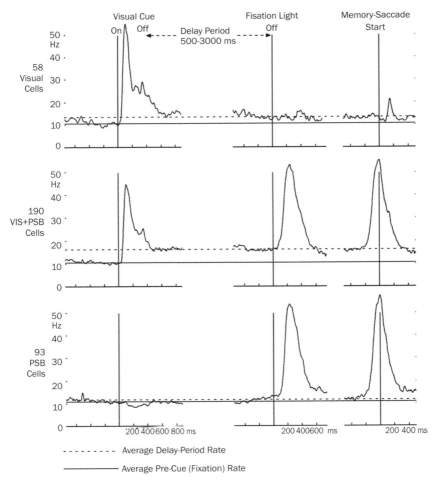

FIGURE 8–15. Three types of cell found in the frontal cortex. Visual cells fire when the visual cue goes on; presaccadic burst cells (PSB) fire just after the fixation light goes off, and before the saccade is made, and some cells, called visuomotor cells (VIS + PSD), fire on both occasions. (Reprinted from Bruce et al., 2004, with kind permission of MIT Press.)

To assess the function of the frontal eye fields, one has to consider the deficits found after lesions. A major point here is that saccades are not abolished by lesions of the frontal eye fields, or by lesions of the superior colliculus. One needs lesions of both to do the job (Schiller, True, & Conway, 1980). There is some redundancy in the system: occipital and parietal cortex project directly to the superior colliculus, and frontal cortex projects directly to areas in the brainstem. The best hypothesis seems to be that there is a progression from sensory to motor, through parietal cortex, and frontal cortex to superior colliculus, with none of these areas being totally sensory or totally motor.

Supplementary Eye Fields

The supplementary eye fields are part of an area in the midline, with hindlimbs represented caudally, eye movements rostrally, and forelimbs in between (Tehovnik et al., 2000). Cells seem to have more to do with learning than control of eye movements. Lesions of the area have little effect on saccades, and none on smooth pursuit eye movements, although smooth pursuit is represented in a small part of the area (Tian & Lynch, 1995). Stimulation moves the eyes to a particular location in space, and continued stimulation does not move the eyes further when this point is reached—in contrast to frontal eye fields, where continued stimulation will give continued saccades. Activity in supplementary eye fields tends to occur before activity in frontal eye fields. One group of cells deals with timing; another deals with location (Campos, Breznen, & Andersen, 2009). Thus, the supplementary eye fields, in a manner that is not yet fully defined, have to do with modulation of eye movements rather than direct control (see also Shichinohe et al., 2009). There are two other frontal areas concerned with eye movements—the premotor eye field and the cingulate eye field—whose function is not yet well worked out either (Amiez & Petrides, 2009).

Superior Colliculus

The superior colliculus is a layered structure. The top layer is the optic layer and receives input from the retina, with the input coming in just below it and projecting up to the optic layer in a topographical map. Below this is the superficial grey, where inputs from retina and occipital cortex converge, again in a topographical map. In the deeper layers—intermediate gray and deep gray—there are cells that have eye movement properties as well as visual properties. Many of these also receive input from auditory and somatosensory systems (Stein & Meredith, 1993; Wickelgren, 1971), again in a topographic map, so that signals from different sensory systems guide the eyes and the head to the same place in space.

Saccadic eye movements can be elicited by stimulating the deeper layers (Apter, 1946). The motor map agrees with the sensory map: the saccade elicited from a deep layer cell takes the eyes to the position of the visual receptive field of the cells above it in the superficial layers (Fig. 8–16; Robinson, 1972). The size and direction of the saccade depends on the position of the electrode in the superior colliculus, as opposed to the eye muscle nuclei, where the size depends on the intensity of the stimulation, and the direction depends on the relative firing in the different eye muscle nuclei (Schiller & Stryker, 1972), and is independent of the initial position of the eyes in the head (Robinson, 1972). The cells discharge before the saccade, and the movement field is larger than the receptive field, extending toward the fovea (Fig. 8–17; Wurtz & Goldberg, 1972). Essentially, stimulation

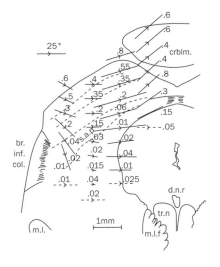

FIGURE 8–16. Vertical section through the superior colliculus, showing saccades elicited by stimulation. Length of lines shows the amplitude of the saccades, and angle shows the direction. The numbers show the current required: note that the currents are much lower in intermediate and deep layers than in superficial layers. (Reprinted from Robinson, 1972, with kind permission of Elsevier.)

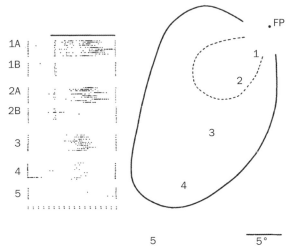

FIGURE 8–17. Receptive field and movement fields for a cell in intermediate layers of superior colliculus. On the left are responses at positions shown by the numbers in the diagram on the right. 1B and 2B are visual responses seen when no saccade was made. 1A, 2A, 3, 4, and 5 are responses obtained when a saccade was made. In the diagram on the right, the solid line outlines the movement field, and the dashed line outlines the visual receptive field. (Reprinted from Wurtz & Goldberg, 1972, with kind permission of the Association for research in Vision and Ophthalmology.)

in the deep layers allows the eyes to look at the stimulus in the part of the field of view represented there and in the layers immediately above; this process is known as foveation.

The superior colliculus has connections to frontal (FEF), parietal (LIP), and occipital cortex (see Sommer & Wurtz, 2004). These are two-way connections;

intermediate layers also project back to frontal cortex via the mediodorsal thalamus. Ablation of this pathway leads to deficits in a two-saccade task, implying that it probably carries a corollary discharge signal essential for this task (Sommer & Wurtz, 2004). The pathway also carries the corollary discharge signals that lead to shifting of the receptive field just before a saccade, which underlies the remapping of the visual world during a saccade, and perception of the world as remaining stationary (Sommer & Wurtz, 2006). Superficial layers project to occipital cortex via the pulvinar, with signals that concern attention (Petersen, Robinson, & Morris, 1987). This emphasizes again how one cannot consider the eye movement pathways as a simple sequence of steps. Even the superior colliculus is concerned with target selection as well as saccade initiation (Carello & Krauzlis, 2004; McPeek & Keller, 2004).

The movement cells in the deeper layers of superior colliculus consist of several types. There are burst cells, which fire at the time of a saccade (Fig. 8–18A; Munoz & Wurtz, 1995), and buildup cells, whose activity increases between the signal for a saccade and the saccade itself, often ending with a burst at the time of the saccade (Fig. 8–18B; Munoz & Wurtz, 1995). At the rostral end of the colliculus the cells are concerned with small deviations from the target location and fire during microsaccades (Hafed, Goffart, & Krauzlis, 2009) and smooth pursuit movements in the contraversive direction (Krauzlis, Basso, & Wurtz, 1997, 2000). Some fire particularly during fixation, which involves slow drifts as well as microsaccades, and were originally known as fixation cells. They stop firing during a

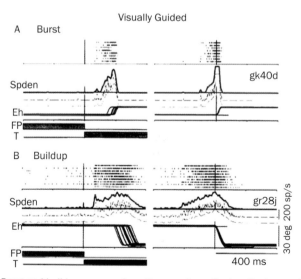

FIGURE 8–18. Burst and buildup neurons from the superior colliculus. Rasters on the left are synchronized with the target light turning on. Rasters on the right are synchronized with the saccade. Burst neurons (A) fire just before and during the saccade. Buildup neurons (B) fire in the interval between the appearance of the target and the saccade. (Reprinted from Munoz & Wurtz, 1995, with kind permission of the American Physiological Society.)

larger saccade (Munoz & Wurtz, 1993a). The burst cells are found in a layer above the buildup and fixation cells. Evidence from stimulation and inhibition of the fixation cells suggests that the cessation of their firing is related to the initiation of a saccade (Munoz & Wurtz, 1993b) through a different set of connections to neurons in the brainstem (Shinoda, Sugiuchi, Izawa, & Takahashi, 2008).

The relationship between firing of movement cells in the superior colliculus and the movement made is not an exact one-to-one relationship. A fairly wide area of colliculus fires before a saccade in a particular direction (Lee, Rohr, & Sparks, 1988). The cells in the superior colliculus have to converge onto cells in the brainstem to give the precise saccades that the system produces.

Most of the original experiments on superior colliculus were done in animals with their heads restrained. Experiments where the head is not restrained show that the colliculus controls head movements as well as eye movements (Freedman et al., 1996). What is actually produced is a signal to move the eyes to a particular point in space, done with a combination of head and eye movements—in other words, to control gaze.

Basal Ganglia

The basal ganglia provide another pathway for controlling the initiation of both saccadic and smooth pursuit eye movements. The frontal eye fields excite one part of the basal ganglia, the caudate nucleus, which inhibits another part, the substantia nigra pars reticulata, which in turn inhibits the superior colliculus. Cells in the caudate nucleus fire for an eye movement that is going to be rewarded (Lauwereyns, Watanabe, Coe, & Hikosaka, 2002). Responses in the substantia nigra are thus decreased for a stimulus of interest, which may be a visual stimulus, an auditory stimulus, the memory of a stimulus, or some cognitive input (Hikosaka & Wurtz, 1983a,b). Responses are modulated more for antisaccades (movement away from the stimulus) than prosacccades (movement toward the stimulus), presumably because antisaccades require more effort of attention (Yoshida & Tanaka, 2009a). The substantia nigra cells provide a tonic inhibition to the superior colliculus, and when it ceases, the disinhibition allows a saccade to proceed (Hikosaka & Wurtz, 1983c). The suggestion is that the basal ganglia also provide a permissive disinhibition signal for smooth pursuit in a similar, but not identical, manner to the signal it conveys for saccades (Basso, Pokorny, & Liu, 2005), although the pathway may not be precisely the same (Yoshida & Tanaka, 2009b).

Cerebellum

In the cerebellum, the cerebellar cortex and the deep nuclei are both concerned with eye movements (Robinson & Fuchs, 2001; Zee & Walker, 2004). Generally speaking, they control the accuracy of eye movements in the short term and also any adaptation that may be required over the long term to make sure that this accuracy is maintained. This is true for saccadic, smooth pursuit, and vergence eye movements, and also for the vestibulo-ocular reflex. In a landmark paper, Westheimer and Blair (1973) showed that complete ablation of the cerebellum leads to the inability to maintain gaze in an eccentric direction, absence of all smooth pursuit movements, and a deficit in convergence. The deficits in saccadic movements are not as serious. The larger deficit in smooth pursuit movements is due to the long pathway for these movements, which goes from the cerebral cortex through the dorsolateral pontine nuclei and cerebellum before joining with saccadic signals in other parts of the pons.

Brainstem Nuclei

Between the eye muscle nuclei and all the higher structures discussed so far lie the various areas of the brainstem (Fig. 8–19). These are responsible for several functions. First, this is where the signals for the various types of eye movement are combined. Whereas parietal cortex, frontal cortex, cerebellum, and superior colliculus are all concerned with saccades, smooth pursuit, vergence, and fixation, these tend to be dealt with in separate parts and separate cells within those areas. It is only in the brainstem that they are finally brought together, projecting to single cells in the eye muscle nuclei.

Second, signals about the size and direction of eye movements are split into horizontal and vertical components. Horizontal movements are dealt with in an area called the paramedian pontine reticular formation (PPRF), located near the abducens, the nucleus for one of the muscles that drives the eyes in a horizontal direction. Vertical movements are dealt with in an area called the mesencephalic reticular formation (MRF), located near the oculomotor nucleus, the nucleus for three of the muscles that drive the eyes in a vertical direction.

Third, the signals in higher centers (where firing of a neuron represents an eye movement of a particular size in a particular direction) have to be converted to signals for the muscles (with larger movements coded by greater firing) and direction of movement by the relative firing in different eye muscles. This is known as the spatial-temporal transform and as conversion from a place code to a rate code. It is not clear in detail exactly how this is done.

Fourth, an integration is performed (see Robinson, 1987). This is seen most clearly in the vestibulo-ocular reflex, where the semicircular canals in the vestibular system respond to head velocity, and the signals required for the compensatory rotation of the eyes is a signal about eye position rather than eye velocity. Integrations are also performed for saccades (integration of the burst driving the saccade for the force to hold the eyes in their new position) and for smooth

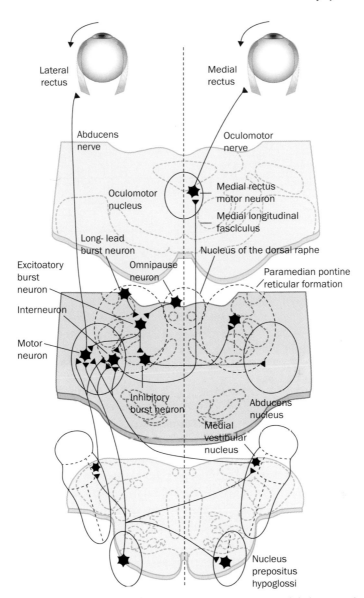

FIGURE 8–19. Nuclei in the brainstem for horizontal eye movements and their connections. Abducens nucleus controls lateral horizontal movements, and oculomotor nucleus controls the muscle for medial horizontal movements, as well as three of the vertical eye movement muscles. Mesencephalic reticular formation, which is concerned with vertical movements, is not shown.

pursuit eye movements (again, integration to provide a position signal). The same integrator may be used for all three functions. This integrator consists of a feedback circuit, but it is still not quite clear where the feedback circuit resides, and there may be more than one.

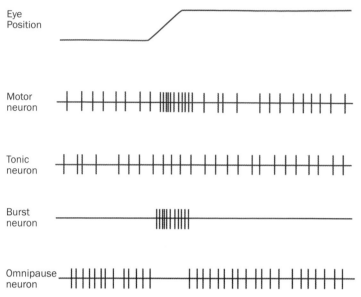

FIGURE 8–20. Firing patterns of cells in the brainstem for saccades. The motor neuron fires a burst to initiate the saccade, with maintained firing afterward to hold the eyes in their new position. In the brainstem, there are neurons that fire tonically, neurons that fire in a burst associated with the saccade, and omnipause neurons that cease firing during the saccade.

The first recordings to be made from the brainstem outside the eye muscle nuclei showed four types of responses in the neurons (Keller, 1974; Luschei & Fuchs, 1972). There were burst neurons, which fire in a burst just before a saccade; tonic neurons, which fire tonically; burst-tonic neurons, which fire with a burst followed by tonic firing, and reflect what is seen in the eye muscle nuclei; and pause neurons, which fire continually, except just before a saccade (Fig. 8–20). To a certain extent, these patterns of firing reflect what is seen at higher levels, such as the superior colliculus. The categories have been subdivided (long-lead, short-lead, excitatory, and inhibitory), but basically the same four categories are still found in recent investigations. The firing rate in burst neurons is related to the velocity of a saccade, and the number of spikes in the burst to the amplitude of the saccade; the tonic neurons are related to holding the eye in a particular position; the burst-tonic neurons are related to making a saccade and then holding the eyes in a new position, and the pause neurons are related to allowing a saccade to proceed, although they also play a role in smooth pursuit (Missal & Keller, 2002). There are numerous additional points to be made, found in more specialized reviews (Scudder, Kaneko, & Fuchs, 2002; Sparks, 2002).

There are also nuclei in the brainstem that receive signals from various areas of cortex and project to the cerebellum. These are collectively known as the pontine oculomotor nuclei (PON) and include the dorsolateral pontine nucleus (DLPN) and the nucleus reticularis tegmenti pontis (NRTP) (Ono, Das, & Mustari, 2004). Originally thought to deal only with smooth pursuit movements, they are now known to deal with saccades as well (Dicke, Barash, Ilg, & Thier, 2004; Kaneko & Fuchs, 2006). The function of the pontine oculomotor nuclei may be simply to collect signals from frontal, parietal, and occipital cortex for transmission to the cerebellum. The cerebellum then projects back to the brainstem to the premotor nuclei to be combined with signals from the superior colliculus.

References

Akao, T., Mustari, M. J., Fukushima, J., Kurkin, S., & Fukushima, K. (2005). Discharge characteristics of pursuit neurons in MST during vergence eye movements. *Journal of Neurophysiology, 93*, 2415–2434.

Amiez, C., & Petrides, M. (2009). Anatomical organization of the eye fields in the human and non-human primate frontal cortex. *Progress in Neurobiology, 89*, 220–230.

Andersen, R. A., & Buneo, C. A. (2002). Intentional maps in posterior parietal cortex. *Annual Review of Neuroscience, 25*, 189–220.

Andersen, R. A., Snyder, L. H., Bradley, D. C., & Xing, J. (1997). Multimodal representation of space in the posterior parietal cortex and its use in planning movements. *Annual Review of Neuroscience, 20*, 303–330.

Apter, J. T. (1946). Eye movements following strychninization of the superior colliculus of the cat. *Journal of Neurophysiology, 9*, 73–86.

Basso, M. A., Pokorny, J. J., & Liu, P. (2005). Activity of substantia nigra pars reticulata neurons during smooth pursuit eye movements in monkeys. *European Journal of Neuroscience, 22*, 448–464.

Bays, P. M., & Husain, M. (2007). Spatial remapping of the visual world across saccades. *Neuroreport, 18*, 1207–1213.

Becker, W., & Fuchs, A. F. (1985). Prediction in the oculomotor system: Smooth pursuit during transient disappearance of a visual target. *Experimental Brain Research, 57*, 562–575.

Bischof, N., & Kramer, E. (1968). [Investigations and considerations of directional perception during voluntary saccadic eye movements]. *Psychologische Forschung, 32*, 185–218.

Bisley, J. W., & Goldberg, M. E. (2006). Neural correlates of attention and distractibility in the lateral intraparietal area. *Journal of Neurophysiology, 95*, 1696–1717.

Bruce, C. J., & Goldberg, M. E. (1985). Primate frontal eye fields. I. Single neurons discharging before saccades. *Journal of Neurophysiology, 53*, 603–635.

Bruce, C. J., Goldberg, M. E., Bushnell, M. C., & Stanton, G. B. (1985). Primate frontal eye fields. II. Physiological and anatomical correlates of electrically evoked eye movements. *Journal of Neurophysiology, 54*, 714–734.

Burman, D. D., & Segraves, M. A. (1994). Primate frontal eye field activity during natural scanning eye movements. *Journal of Neurophysiology, 71*, 1266–1271.

Burr, D. C., & Morrone, M. C. (2004). Visual perception during saccades. In L. M. Chalupa & J. S. Werner (Eds.), *The visual neurosciences* (pp. 1391–1401). Cambridge, MA: MIT Press.

Burr, D. C., & Morrone, M. C. (2011). Spatiotopic coding and remapping in humans. *Philosophical Transactions of the Royal Society of London B: Biological Sciences, 366,* 504–515.

Campbell, F. W., & Wurtz, R. H. (1978). Saccadic omission: Why we do not see a grey-out during a saccadic eye movement. *Vision Research, 18,* 1297–1303.

Campos, M., Breznen, B., & Andersen, R. A. (2009). Separate representations of target and timing cue locations in the supplementary eye fields. *Journal of Neurophysiology, 101,* 448–459.

Carello, C. D., & Krauzlis, R. J. (2004). Manipulating intent: Evidence for a causal role of the superior colliculus in target selection. *Neuron, 43,* 575–583.

Casagrande, V. A., & Royal, D. W. (2004). Parallel visual pathways in a dynamic system. In J. H. Kaas & C. E. Collins (Eds.), *The primate visual system* (pp. 1–28). Boca Raton, FL: CRC Press.

Case, G. R., & Ferrera, V. P. (2007). Coordination of smooth pursuit and saccade target selection in monkeys. *Journal of Neurophysiology, 98,* 2206–2214.

Churchland, M. M., Chou, I. H., & Lisberger, S. G. (2003). Evidence for object permanence in the smooth-pursuit eye movements of monkeys. *Journal of Neurophysiology, 90,* 2205–2218.

Colby, C. L., Duhamel, J. R., & Goldberg, M. E. (1993). Ventral intraparietal area of the macaque: Anatomic location and visual response properties. *Journal of Neurophysiology, 69,* 902–914.

Colby, C. L., & Goldberg, M. E. (1999). Space and attention in parietal cortex. *Annual Review of Neuroscience, 22,* 319–349.

Dicke, P. W., Barash, S., Ilg, U. J., & Thier, P. (2004). Single-neuron evidence for a contribution of the dorsal pontine nuclei to both types of target-directed eye movements, saccades and smooth-pursuit. *European Journal of Neuroscience, 19,* 609–624.

Ditchburn, R. W., & Ginsborg, B. L. (1952). Vision with a stabilized retinal image. *Nature, 170,* 36–37.

Dodge, R. (1900). Visual perception during eye movement. *Psychological Review, 7,* 454–465.

Dodge, R. (1903). Five types of eye movement in the horizontal meridian plane of the field of regard. *American Journal of Physiology, 8,* 307–329.

Dursteler, M. R., & Wurtz, R. H. (1988). Pursuit and optokinetic deficits following chemical lesions of cortical areas MT and MST. *Journal of Neurophysiology, 60,* 940–965.

Erkelens, C. J. (2006). Coordination of smooth pursuit and saccades. *Vision Research, 46,* 163–170.

Erkelens, C. J., Van der Steen, J., Steinman, R. M., & Collewijn, H. (1989a). Ocular vergence under natural conditions. I. Continuous changes of target distance along the median plane. *Proceedings of the Royal Society of London B: Biological Sciences, 236,* 417–440.

Erkelens, C. J., Steinman, R. M., & Collewijn, H. (1989b). Ocular vergence under natural conditions. II. Gaze shifts between real targets differing in distance and direction. *Proceedings of the Royal Society of London B: Biological Sciences, 236,* 441–465.

Ferrier, D. (1880). *The functions of the brain.* New York: Putnam's.

Freedman, E. G., Stanford, T. R., & Sparks, D. L. (1996). Combined eye-head gaze shifts produced by electrical stimulation of the superior colliculus in rhesus monkeys. *Journal of Neurophysiology, 76,* 927–952.

Gamlin, P. D., & Yoon, K. (2000). An area for vergence eye movement in primate frontal cortex. *Nature, 407*, 1003–1007.

Gnadt, J. W., & Mays, L. E. (1995). Neurons in monkey parietal area LIP are tuned for eye-movement parameters in three-dimensional space. *Journal of Neurophysiology, 73*, 280–297.

Gottlieb, J. P., Bruce, C. J., & MacAvoy, M. G. (1993). Smooth eye movements elicited by microstimulation in the primate frontal eye field. *Journal of Neurophysiology, 69*, 786–799.

Gottlieb, J. P., Kusunoki, M., & Goldberg, M. E. (1998). The representation of visual salience in monkey parietal cortex. *Nature, 391*, 481–484.

Grimes, J. (1996). On the failure to detect changes in scenes across saccades. In K. Akins (Ed.), *Perception* (pp. 89–110). New York: Oxford University Press.

Hafed, Z. M., Goffart, L., & Krauzlis, R. J. (2009). A neural mechanism for microsaccade generation in the primate superior colliculus. *Science, 323*, 940–943.

Hall, N. J. & Colby, C. L. (2011). Remapping for visual stability. *Philosophical Transactions of the Royal Society of London, series B, Biological Sciences, 366*, 528–539.

Hanks, T. D., Ditterich, J., & Shadlen, M. N. (2006). Microstimulation of macaque area LIP affects decision-making in a motion discrimination task. *Nature Neuroscience, 9*, 682–689.

Hansen, R. M., & Skavenski, A. A. (1977). Accuracy of eye position information for motor control. *Vision Research, 17*, 919–926.

Heinen, S. J., & Keller, E. L. (2004). Smooth pursuit eye movements: recent advances. In L. M. Chalupa & J. S. Werner (Eds.), *The visual neurosciences* (pp. 1402–1414). Cambridge, MA: MIT Press.

Heiser, L. M., & Colby, C. L. (2006). Spatial updating in area LIP is independent of saccade direction. *Journal of Neurophysiology, 95*, 2751–2767.

Helmholtz, H. (1875/1962). *Treatise on physiological optics*. New York: Dover.

Henderson, J. M., & Hollingworth, A. (1999). The role in fixation position in detecting scene changes across saccades. *Psychological Science, 10*, 438–443.

Herst, A. N., Epelboim, J., & Steinman, R. M. (2001). Temporal coordination of the human head and eye during a natural sequential tapping task. *Vision Research, 41*, 3307–3319.

Hikosaka, O., & Wurtz, R. H. (1983a). Visual and oculomotor functions of monkey substantia nigra pars reticulata. III. Memory-contingent visual and saccade responses. *Journal of Neurophysiology, 49*, 1268–1284.

Hikosaka, O., & Wurtz, R. H. (1983b). Visual and oculomotor functions of monkey substantia nigra pars reticulata. I. Relation of visual and auditory responses to saccades. *Journal of Neurophysiology, 49*, 1230–1253.

Hikosaka, O., & Wurtz, R. H. (1983c). Visual and oculomotor functions of monkey substantia nigra pars reticulata. IV. Relation of substantia nigra to superior colliculus. *Journal of Neurophysiology, 49*, 1285–1301.

Hunt, A. R., & Cavanagh, P. (2009). Looking ahead: the perceived direction of gaze shifts before the eyes move. *Journal of Vision, 9*, 1 1–7.

Hyvarinen, J., & Poranen, A. (1974). Function of the parietal associative area 7 as revealed from cellular discharges in alert monkeys. *Brain, 97*, 673–692.

Izawa, Y., Suzuki, H., & Shinoda, Y. (2009). Response properties of fixation neurons and their location in the frontal eye field in the monkey. *Journal of Neurophysiology, 102*, 2410–2422.

Kaneko, C. R., & Fuchs, A. F. (2006). Effect of pharmacological inactivation of nucleus reticularis tegmenti pontis on saccadic eye movements in the monkey. *Journal of Neurophysiology, 95*, 3698–3711.

Keller, E. L. (1974). Participation of medial pontine reticular formation in eye movement generation in monkey. *Journal of Neurophysiology, 37*, 316–332.

Ko, H. K., Poletti, M., & Rucci, M. (2010). Microsaccades precisely relocate gaze in a high visual acuity task. *Nature Neuroscience, 13*, 1549–1553.

Konen, C. S., & Kastner, S. (2008). Representation of eye movements and stimulus motion in topographically organized areas of human posterior parietal cortex. *Journal of Neuroscience, 28*, 8361–8375.

Krauzlis, R. J. (2004). Recasting the smooth pursuit eye movement system. *Journal of Neurophysiology, 91*, 591–603.

Krauzlis, R. J., Basso, M. A., & Wurtz, R. H. (1997). Shared motor error for multiple eye movements. *Science, 276*, 1693–1695.

Krauzlis, R. J., Basso, M. A., & Wurtz, R. H. (2000). Discharge properties of neurons in the rostral superior colliculus of the monkey during smooth-pursuit eye movements. *Journal of Neurophysiology, 84*, 876–891.

Land, M. F. (2004). Eye movements in daily life. In L. M. Chalupa & J. S. Werner (Eds.), *The visual neurosciences* (pp. 1357–1368). Cambridge, MA: MIT Press.

Land, M. F., & Tatler, B. W. (2009). *Looking and seeing.* New York: Oxford University Press.

Lauwereyns, J., Watanabe, K., Coe, B., & Hikosaka, O. (2002). A neural correlate of response bias in monkey caudate nucleus. *Nature, 418*, 413–417.

Lee, C., Rohrer, W. H., & Sparks, D. L. (1988). Population coding of saccadic eye movements by neurons in the superior colliculus. *Nature, 332*, 357–360.

Li, Z., & Sun, F. (2005). Pupillary response induced by stereoscopic stimuli. *Experimental Brain Research, 160*, 394–397.

Lisberger, S. G., & Ferrera, V. P. (1997). Vector averaging for smooth pursuit eye movements initiated by two moving targets in monkeys. *Journal of Neuroscience, 17*, 7490–7502.

Lisberger, S. G., Morris, E. J., & Tychsen, L. (1987). Visual motion processing and sensory-motor integration for smooth pursuit eye movements. *Annual Review of Neuroscience, 10*, 97–129.

Luschei, E. S., & Fuchs, A. F. (1972). Activity of brain stem neurons during eye movements of alert monkeys. *Journal of Neurophysiology, 35*, 445–461.

Lynch, J. C. (1987). Frontal eye field lesions in monkeys disrupt visual pursuit. *Experimental Brain Research, 68*, 437–441.

Lynch, J. C., Mountcastle, V. B., Talbot, W. H., & Yin, T. C. (1977). Parietal lobe mechanisms for directed visual attention. *Journal of Neurophysiology, 40*, 362–389.

Martinez-Conde, S., Macknik, S. L., & Hubel, D. H. (2000). Microsaccadic eye movements and firing of single cells in the striate cortex of macaque monkeys. *Nature Neuroscience, 3*, 251–258.

Martinez-Conde, S., Macknik, S. L., Troncoso, X. G., & Dyar, T. A. (2006). Microsaccades counteract visual fading during fixation. *Neuron, 49*, 297–305.

Matin, L. (1972). Eye movements and perceived visual direction. In D. Jameson & L. M. Hurvich (Eds.), *Handbook of sensory physiology* (pp. 331–380). Berlin: Springer-Verlag.

Mays, L. E. (2004). Neural control of vergence eye movements. In L. M. Chalupa & J. S. Werner (Eds.), *The visual neurosciences* (pp. 1415–1427). Cambridge MA: MIT Press.

McPeek, R. M., & Keller, E. L. (2004). Deficits in saccade target selection after inactivation of superior colliculus. *Nature Neuroscience, 7,* 757–763.

Melcher, D., & Colby, C. L. (2008). Trans-saccadic perception. *Trends in Cognitive Science, 12,* 466–473.

Miles, F. A. (1998). Visual stabilization of the eyes in primates. *Current Opinion in Neurobiology, 7,* 867–871.

Missal, M., & Keller, E. L. (2002). Common inhibitory mechanism for saccades and smooth-pursuit eye movements. *Journal of Neurophysiology, 88,* 1880–1892.

Mullette-Gillman, O. A., Cohen, Y. E., & Groh, J. M. (2009). Motor-related signals in the intraparietal cortex encode locations in a hybrid, rather than eye-centered reference frame. *Cereb Cortex, 19,* 1761–1775.

Munoz, D. P., & Wurtz, R. H. (1993a). Fixation cells in monkey superior colliculus. I. Characteristics of cell discharge. *Journal of Neurophysiology, 70,* 559–575.

Munoz, D. P., & Wurtz, R. H. (1993b). Fixation cells in monkey superior colliculus. II. Reversible activation and deactivation. *Journal of Neurophysiology, 70,* 576–589.

Munoz, D. P., & Wurtz, R. H. (1995). Saccade-related activity in monkey superior colliculus. I. Characteristics of burst and buildup cells. *Journal of Neurophysiology, 73,* 2313–2333.

Naegele, J. R., & Held, R. (1982). The postnatal development of monocular optokinetic nystagmus in infants. *Vision Research, 22,* 341–346.

Newsome, W. T., Wurtz, R. H., Dursteler, M. R., & Mikami, A. (1985). Deficits in visual motion processing following ibotenic acid lesions of the middle temporal visual area of the macaque monkey. *Journal of Neuroscience, 5,* 825–840.

Ono, S., Das, V. E., & Mustari, M. J. (2004). Gaze-related response properties of DLPN and NRTP neurons in the rhesus macaque. *Journal of Neurophysiology, 91,* 2484–2500.

Orban de Xivry, J. J., & Lefevre, P. (2007). Saccades and pursuit: two outcomes of a single sensorimotor process. *Journal of Physiology, 584,* 11–23.

Ostendorf, F., Fischer, C., Gaymard, B., & Ploner, C. J. (2006). Perisaccadic mislocalization without saccadic eye movements. *Neuroscience, 137,* 737–745.

Petersen, S. E., Robinson, D. L., & Morris, J. D. (1987). Contributions of the pulvinar to visual spatial attention. *Neuropsychologia, 25,* 97–105.

Rambold, H., El Baz, I., & Helmchen, C. (2005). Blink effects on ongoing smooth pursuit eye movements in humans. *Experimental Brain Research, 161,* 11–26.

Rashbass, C. (1961). The relationship between saccadic and smooth tracking eye movements. *Journal of Physiology, 159,* 326–338.

Riggs, L. A., & Ratliff, F. (1952). The effects of counteracting the normal movements of the eye. *Proceedings of the National Academy of Sciences USA, 42,* 872–873.

Ringach, D. L., Hawken, M. J., & Shapley, R. (1996). Binocular eye movements caused by the perception of three-dimensional structure from motion. *Vision Research, 36,* 1479–1492.

Robinson, D. A. (1972). Eye movements evoked by collicular stimulation in the alert monkey. *Vision Research, 12,* 1795–1808.

Robinson, D. A. (1987). The windfalls of technology in the oculomotor system. Proctor lecture. *Investigative Ophthalmology and Visual Science, 28,* 1912–1924.

Robinson, D. A., & Fuchs, A. F. (1969). Eye movements evoked by stimulation of frontal eye fields. *Journal of Neurophysiology, 32,* 637–648.

Robinson, F. R., & Fuchs, A. F. (2001). The role of the cerebellum in voluntary eye movements. *Annual Review of Neuroscience, 24,* 981–1004.

Robinson, F. R., Soetedjo, R., & Noto, C. (2006). Distinct short-term and long-term adaptation to reduce saccade size in monkey. *Journal of Neurophysiology, 96,* 1030–1041.

Rolfs, M. (2009). Microsaccades: small steps on a long way. *Vision Research, 49,* 2415–2441.

Rucci, M., Iovin, R., Poletti, M., & Santini, F. (2007). Miniature eye movements enhance fine spatial detail. *Nature, 447,* 851–854.

Sakata, H., Shibutani, H., & Kawano, K. (1983). Functional properties of visual tracking neurons in posterior parietal association cortex of the monkey. *Journal of Neurophysiology, 49,* 1364–1380.

Schafer, R. J., Krumeich, E. A., & Moore, T. (2008). Dynamic sensitivity of area V4 neurons during saccade preparation. *Society for Neuroscience - Abstracts,* 165.124.

Schall, J. D. (2002). The neural selection and control of saccades by the frontal eye field. *Philosophical Transactions of the Royal Society of London B: Biological Sciences, 357,* 1073–1082.

Schiller, P. H., & Stryker, M. (1972). Single-unit recording and stimulation in superior colliculus of the alert rhesus monkey. *Journal of Neurophysiology, 35,* 915–924.

Schiller, P. H., True, S. D., & Conway, J. L. (1980). Deficits in eye movements following frontal eye-field and superior colliculus ablations. *Journal of Neurophysiology, 44,* 1175–1189.

Scudder, C. A., Kaneko, C. S., & Fuchs, A. F. (2002). The brainstem burst generator for saccadic eye movements: A modern synthesis. *Experimental Brain Research, 142,* 439–462.

Shichinohe, N., Akao, T., Kurkin, S., Fukushima, J., Kaneko, C. R., & Fukushima, K. (2009). Memory and decision making in the frontal cortex during visual motion processing for smooth pursuit eye movements. *Neuron, 62,* 717–732.

Shinoda, Y., Sugiuchi, Y., Izawa, Y., & Takahashi, M. (2008). Neural circuits for triggering saccades in the brainstem. *Progress in Brain Research, 171,* 79–85.

Simons, D. J. (2000). Current approaches to change blindness. *Visual Cognition, 7,* 1–15.

Sommer, M. A., & Wurtz, R. H. (2001). Frontal eye field sends delay activity related to movement, memory, and vision to the superior colliculus. *Journal of Neurophysiology, 85,* 1673–1685.

Sommer, M. A., & Wurtz, R. H. (2004). The dialog between cerebral cortex and superior colliculus: Implications for saccadic target selection and corollary discharge. In L. M. Chalupa & J. S. Werner (Eds.), *The visual neurosciences* (pp. 1466–1484). Cambridge, MA: MIT Press.

Sommer, M. A., & Wurtz, R. H. (2006). Influence of the thalamus on spatial visual processing in frontal cortex. *Nature, 444,* 374–377.

Sparks, D. L. (2002). The brainstem control of eye movements. *Nature Reviews Neuroscience, 3,* 952–964.

Stanford, T. R., Shankar, S., Massoglia, D. P., Costello, M. G., & Salinas, E. (2010). Perceptual decision making in less than 30 milliseconds. *Nature Neuroscience, 13,* 379–385.

Stein, B. E., & Meredith, M. A. (1993). *The merging of the senses.* Cambridge, MA: MIT Press.

Steinbach, M. J. (1976). Pursuing the perceptual rather than the retinal stimulus. *Vision Research, 16,* 1371–1376.

Steinman, R. M. (2004). Gaze control under natural conditions. In L. M. Chalupa & J. S. Werner (Eds.), *The visual neurosciences* (pp. 1339–1356). Cambridge, MA: MIT Press.

Tehovnik, E. J., Sommer, M. A., Chou, I. H., Slocum, W. M., & Schiller, P. H. (2000). Eye fields in the frontal lobes of primates. *Brain Research Reviews, 32,* 413–448.

Tian, J. R., & Lynch, J. C. (1995). Slow and saccadic eye movements evoked by microstimulation in the supplementary eye field of the cebus monkey. *Journal of Neurophysiology, 74,* 2204–2210.

Tong, J., Lien, T. C., Cisarik, P. M., & Bedell, H. E. (2008). Motion sensitivity during fixation in straight-ahead and lateral eccentric gaze. *Experimental Brain Research, 190,* 189–200.

Troxler, D. (1804). *Ophthalmologische Bibliothek*. Jena, Germany: Springer.

Wardak, C., Olivier, E., & Duhamel, J. R. (2002). Saccadic target selection deficits after lateral intraparietal area inactivation in monkeys. *Journal of Neuroscience, 22,* 9877–9884.

Westheimer, G. (1954a). Mechanism of saccadic eye movements. *Archives of Ophthalmology, 52,* 710–724.

Westheimer, G. (1954b). Eye movement responses to a horizontally moving visual stimulus. *Archives of Ophthalmology, 52,* 932–941.

Westheimer, G. (2008). Directional sensitivity of the retina: 75 years of Stiles-Crawford effect. *Proceedings of the Royal Society of London B: Biological Sciences, 275,* 2777–2786.

Westheimer, G., & Blair, S. M. (1973). Oculomotor defects in cerebellectomized monkeys. *Investigative Ophthalmology, 12,* 618–621.

Wickelgren, B. G. (1971). Superior colliculus: some receptive field properties of bimodally responsive cells. *Science, 173,* 69–72.

Wismeijer, D. A., van Ee, R., & Erkelens, C. J. (2008). Depth cues, rather than perceived depth, govern vergence. *Experimental Brain Research, 184,* 61–70.

Wurtz, R. H., Joiner, W. M., & Berman, R. A. (2011). Neuronal mechanisms for visual stability: progress and problems. *Philosophical Transactions of the Royal Society, London, B: Biological Sciences, 366,* 492–503.

Wurtz, R. H., & Goldberg, M. E. (1972). The primate superior colliculus and the shift of visual attention. *Investigative Ophthalmology, 11,* 441–450.

Yarbus, A. L. (1967). *Eye movements and vision*. New York: Plenum.

Yoshida, A., & Tanaka, M. (2009a). Enhanced modulation of neuronal activity during antisaccades in the primate globus pallidus. *Cerebral Cortex, 19,* 206–217.

Yoshida, A., & Tanaka, M. (2009b). Neuronal activity in the primate globus pallidus during smooth pursuit eye movements. *Neuroreport, 20,* 121–125.

Zee, D. S., Fitzgibbon, E. J., & Optican, L. M. (1992). Saccade-vergence interactions in humans. *Journal of Neurophysiology, 68,* 1624–1641.

Zee, D. S., & Walker, M. F. (2004). Cerebellar control of eye movements. In L. M. Chalupa & J. S. Werner (Eds.), *The visual neurosciences* (pp 1485–1498). Cambridge, MA: MIT Press.

9

Adaptation and Aftereffects

All aspects of vision adapt. The simplest form of visual adaptation is light and dark adaptation, which enables the system to respond over a range of 10 billion in overall level of intensity of illumination, when the difference between a white and a black at any particular level of illumination is only 100. Then there are a series of aftereffects, such as the waterfall illusion, where looking at a waterfall for several seconds, and then switching one's attention to the bank beside the waterfall, makes the bank appear to move upward. There are also various visuomotor adaptations. For example, when throwing a dart at a dartboard while looking through a prism, initially one misses in one direction but adapts to hit the dartboard after a few seconds; when the prism is removed, the throw will initially be inaccurate in the opposite direction. Finally, there are situations where the whole world can be reversed, left to right, up to down, or both, by wearing optical devices. In this case, at the end of several days, there are visuomotor adaptations, but not complete visual adaptations. There are a variety of mechanisms involved, and surprisingly many of them are known.

Light and Dark Adaptation

Light and dark adaptation is measured from the threshold required to see a spot of light. When we walk from a dark room into daylight, or when a bright background is turned on, it takes a few seconds to see clearly. To be seen, the intensity of the spot of light has to be increased by an amount that is linearly related to the intensity of the background, a relationship first described by Weber in 1834. This is light adaptation (Fig. 9–1A). When we walk back into the dark room, it takes some time before the dim objects there can be seen, because they are below threshold. After being in a very bright light, complete dark adaptation may take 45 minutes.

Light and dark adaptation in animals such as humans, who possess both rods and cones, occurs in two stages. In dark adaptation over the first 10–15 minutes, the cones adapt comparatively rapidly because the reactions within them are faster. After the curve reaches a steady state, the rods adapt more slowly over the next 30 minutes (Fig. 9–1B). In complete dark adaptation, a rod will be activated by a single quantum of light, and 5–7 rods activated over an area will give a visual response (Hecht, Haig, & Chase, 1937).

Within the photoreceptors, the visual pigment (rhodopsin in rods, cone opsin in cones), is converted from the 11-cis configuration to the all-trans configuration by the absorption of light. This is known as bleaching, because rhodopsin is purple in the 11-cis configuration but colorless in the all-trans configuration. The transition, after some intermediates, activates cyclic guanosine monophosphate (cGMP), which closes channels in the membranes of the photoreceptors and hyperpolarizes

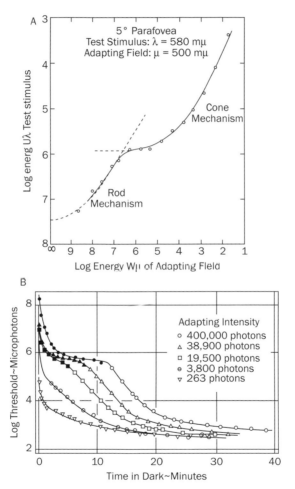

FIGURE 9–1. Light and dark adaptation. In light adaptation (*A*), the threshold for seeing a spot of light increases with the intensity of the background. In dark adaptation (*B*), after bleaching the pigment in the photoreceptors, threshold drops over a period of up to 40 minutes, depending on the intensity of the bleach. In both cases, the part of the curve representing the rods is more sensitive than the part of the curve representing the cones. (Reprinted from Stiles, 1932, with kind permission of Springer-Verlag, and from Hecht et al., 1937, with kind permission of Rockefeller University Press.)

the cell, leading to a reduction in the release of transmitter onto the next cells in the retina, with activation of some and inhibition of others. The logarithm of the threshold for seeing is linearly related to the fraction of rhodopsin bleached (Dowling, 1960; Rushton, 1961; Fig. 9–2). Rods will saturate when only about 10% of their rhodopsin is bleached, due to inability of the channels to respond anymore.

Many years ago, Stiles and Crawford (1932) proposed that bleached pigment acts like an "equivalent background"—now described as a "dark light"—to increase threshold for seeing. We now know that as long as the pigment remains bleached, it continues to activate cGMP, for a variety of reasons (see Luo, Xue, & Yau, 2008). A model for the kinetics of these reactions accurately predicts the time course and extent of dark adaptation (Lamb & Pugh, 2006). The all-trans part of the pigment has to migrate to the pigment epithelium cells to be turned back into the 11-cis configuration, and this takes time (longer in rods than in cones), resulting in the slow time course of dark adaptation (see Dowling, 1987).

Light adaptation is due to calcium, which accumulates in the outer segments of the photoreceptors during adaptation (see Fain, 2001). Calcium affects the enzymes creating and degrading cGMP, particularly the synthetic enzyme, and it brings the concentration of cGMP back to a level where light around the level of adaptation will again activate the photoreceptor.

The threshold for detection of a spot is also affected by illumination of the surrounding area. However, this is not really adaptation, because it occurs very rapidly. It is simply an example of the response of the visual system to contrast, rather than luminance (Chapter 3). Nevertheless, it is a most important part of

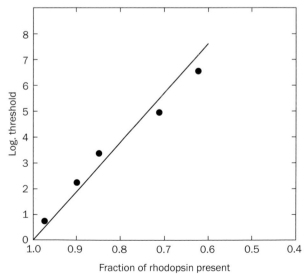

FIGURE 9–2. Relationship between log threshold and fraction of rhodopsin bleached, from a human with no cone pigment. (Reprinted from Rushton, 1961, with kind permission of the Physiological Society.)

how we see as we look around a scene from brightly lit parts to the shadows, and from one set of shadows to a deeper set of shadows (see Rieke & Rudd, 2009).

Colored Afterimages

There is also a well-known adaptation of color known as successive color contrast, already illustrated. Stare at the cross in the center at the top of Figure 4–2 for a minute or so, then transfer your gaze to the cross in the center at the bottom of the figure. The complementary colors will be seen. The phenomenon is explained by adaptation in the red-, green-, and blue-absorbing cones. After one of these is activated, its output is reduced, so that white light produces a larger signal from the other two.

Contrast Adaptation

The system also adapts to contrast (Blakemore & Campbell, 1969). This can be seen using Figure 9–3. First observe 9–3B, and draw a rough trace of the curve where the lines disappear. Then look at Figure 9–3A, moving your eyes along the small horizontal rectangle to avoid afterimages, for a minute or more. Look back at Figure 9–3B and you will notice that the low-contrast lines of the same periodicity as those in 9–3A are less visible for 10–30 seconds. Then look at Figure 9–3C for a few minutes, followed by Figure 9–3B, and notice that the effect does not occur. The effect is a reduction in visibility of a low-contrast grating after looking at a high-contrast grating for a period of time, and it is specific for orientation and spatial frequency (see also Adapt from http://viperlib.york.ac.uk/).

The effect is also noticeable in recordings from cat visual cortex (Maffei, Fiorentini, & Bisti, 1973). One can construct a contrast-response curve (Fig. 9–4), plotting the number of spikes recorded against log contrast (Ohzawa, Sclar, & Freeman, 1982). Contrast adaptation moves the curve horizontally to the right. It is due to hyperpolarization of the cells in the visual cortex (Carandini & Ferster, 1997) as a result of accumulation of sodium and calcium in the cell, which activates potassium currents (Sanchez-Vives, Nowak, & McCormick, 2000). A smaller effect may be seen in the retina, where the mechanism is different (Manookin & Demb, 2006) and is, of course, not specific for orientation.

Motion Aftereffects

The waterfall illusion is the most famous example of a motion aftereffect. It was described by Addams (1834) from a visit to a waterfall in Scotland, and it was mentioned by Aristotle 1400 years before (see Falls at http://viperlib.york.ac.uk/—set it

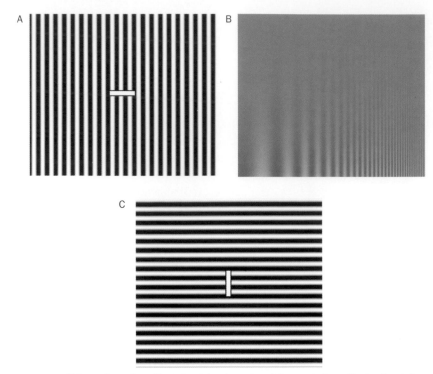

FIGURE 9–3. Orientation aftereffect. Look backward and forward along the horizontal rectangle in the middle of the top display (*A*). Then observe the display in the middle (*B*). Lines of the same spatial frequency as the top display will be less visible. Note that the aftereffect is not seen after looking at the perpendicular lines in the bottom display (*C*). (Reprinted from Kohn, 2007, with kind permission of the American Physiological Society.)

to Loop, under View in QuickTime Player). Another example is the spiral aftereffect, where one stares at the center of a rotating spiral for a minute or so (see Spiral Motion After-effect on http://michaelbach.de/ot/). When the rotation is stopped, the spiral appears to rotate in the opposite direction for a number of seconds. Also, after sitting in a train looking backward for a while, the view out of the window appears to move in the other direction when the train stops.

Addams suggested that the phenomenon is due to movement of the eyes. However, it occurs when the eyes are not moving, and Barlow and Hill (1963), recording from direction-selective cells in the rabbit retina, showed that stimulation with a pattern of dots moving in the preferred direction leads to an aftereffect of reduced firing, while stimulation with a pattern of dots moving in the null direction does not lead to an aftereffect. Thus, the phenomenon can be explained by the relative firing of cells specific for movement in the direction of the stimulus, compared to the firing of cells specific for movement in the opposite direction. As expected, aftereffects are seen using functional magnetic resonance imaging

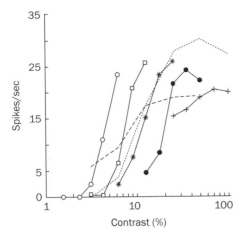

FIGURE 9–4. Contrast-response curves for gratings drifting across the receptive field of a simple cell in the cat visual cortex. Vertical axis gives responses in spikes per second. Horizontal axis gives contrast in percentage modulation of the average luminance. Adaptation to successively higher levels of contrast is shown by solid curves, going from left to right. (Reprinted from Ohzawa et al., with kind permission of MacMillan Publishers.)

(fMRI) in various parts of the brain that contain direction-selective cells, with the largest effect seen in MT (Tootell et al., 1995).

Orientation Aftereffects

Orientation aftereffects were first noted by Wundt in 1898, and then investigated by Gibson (1933). He was looking through a prism, following up on the experiments of Stratton (see later), and noticed that straight lines looked curved, but that the curvature was reduced over time, and when he took the prisms off, straight lines appeared curved in the opposite direction. The effect could also be produced by looking for a period at an array of curved lines, followed by an array of straight lines (Fig. 9–5). He followed this up with a demonstration of the tilt aftereffect, where one looks for a period at an array of tilted lines, after which vertical lines appear to be tilted in the opposite direction. These effects can be obtained after looking for a minute, are confined to the part of the field of view used, and are long-lasting after wearing prisms for a day or more. They transfer from one eye to the other and can easily be explained as an adaptation of orientation-selective cells in primary visual cortex with binocular input. More specific shape-dependent effects have correlates in V4 (Muller, Wilke, & Leopold, 2009), as might be expected from the properties of the cells there (see Chapter 7).

Stereo Aftereffects

Depth perception also adapts. Early on, the question was confused by the use of line figures, with confounding cues based on the slant of lines and curvature. However, there is no doubt that stereo adapts when random dot stereograms are used, avoiding any confounding cues (Blakemore & Julesz, 1971). The

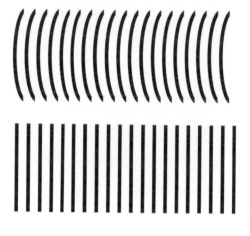

FIGURE 9–5. Curvature aftereffect. Look along the array of curved lines (*top*) for a minute or so, then transfer your attention to the straight lines below. They will appear to be curved in the opposite direction for a while.

A

B

FIGURE 9–6. Adaptation of random dot stereograms. Cross your eyes to fuse the top pair of stereograms (*A*). They should appear flat. Now transfer your attention to the bottom pair of stereograms (*B*). They should appear concave. After looking at the bottom pair for a minute or so, look again at the top pair. They should now appear convex. (Reprinted from Domini et al., 2001, with kind permission of Elsevier.)

phenomenon can be seen by looking at Figure 9–6. Cross your eyes to provide a fused image and observe the upper half of the figure. It should appear flat. Then cover the upper half and cross your eyes to look at the lower half. It should appear concave. Now uncover the upper half and look at it, keeping your eyes crossed. It should now appear convex.

Contingent Aftereffects

All the aftereffects described so far exist in one aspect or dimension of visual perception—lightness, color, motion, orientation, curvature, spatial frequency, or depth. There are also aftereffects that depend on two, or even three, aspects of vision. The first to be described was the McCullough effect (1965), where color of the aftereffect depends on orientation. In Figure 9–7, look alternately at the orange and black vertical stripes and the blue and black horizontal stripes in the top half of the figure for a minute or more, shifting your gaze every few seconds. Then look at the black and white vertical stripes, and the black and white horizontal stripes in the bottom

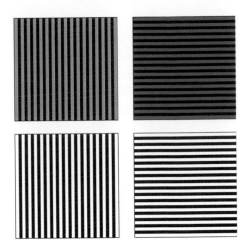

FIGURE 9–7. McCullough effect. Look at the top two displays, transferring your attention from left to right every second or so, for a minute or more. Then look at the bottom two displays. The horizontal lines should appear warm colored, and the vertical lines cool colored. This is a long-lasting aftereffect, if one looks at it for long enough initially. (Reprinted from McCullough, 1965, with kind permission of AAAS.)

half of the picture. The vertical stripes should appear cool colored, and the horizontal stripes warm colored. The suggestion is that there are cells specific for both orientation and color, and the output of these is reduced after prolonged stimulation.

Almost every combination of two aspects of vision can be used to produce a contingent aftereffect, and many of them have been tried. These contingent aftereffects last longer than aftereffects in a single aspect of vision. Looking for several minutes can give an aftereffect that lasts several hours, even to the next day. There appear to be two stages to the aftereffect—a short lasting one, with a time constant of 30 sec, and a long-lasting one, which may be almost permanent (Vul, Krizay, & MacLeod, 2008).

Location of Aftereffects

The common explanation for aftereffects is that there are channels within the visual system for different quantitative values of an aspect of vision. The most obvious example is color, where there are red-absorbing, green-absorbing, and blue-absorbing cones. Activation of red-absorbing cones makes them less sensitive, after which the output from the green- and blue-absorbing cones from white light is larger than the output of the red-absorbing cones, giving the perception of cyan. Similarly, cells for different spatial frequencies are found in the visual cortex, so that activation of fine-tuned cells makes them less sensitive compared to coarse-tuned cells, accounting for the spatial frequency aftereffect. Similar arguments go for orientation, disparity, and direction of motion.

In general, the location of an aftereffect is assumed to be the area where cells responding to the stimulus are found (e.g., MT for motion aftereffects), and fMRI experiments generally bear this out (Tootell et al., 1995). If the aftereffect transfers from one eye to the other, which direction aftereffects (Barlow & Brindley, 1963) and orientation aftereffects (Gibson & Radner, 1937) do, but the McCullough effect does not, then the location is assumed to be at a level after the signals from the two eyes have converged. However, if the left eye sees a disc rotating to the left, and the right eye sees a disc rotating to the right, the aftereffect is that a stationary disc is seen to be rotating right by the left eye, and left by the right eye, implying a peripheral component as well as a central component (Anstis & Moulden, 1970).

Adaptation of Faces

One also adapts to faces (Webster & MacLin, 1999). Looking at a contracted face followed by a normal face makes the normal face appear expanded, and vice versa (Fig. 9–8).

This is true of upside-down faces as well as right-side-up faces, although adaptation to an upside-down face does not transfer to a right-side-up face. Looking at a face from one direction affects the perception of the face as seen from another direction (Fang & He, 2006). Moreover, adapting to a face of one size affects the perception of faces of different sizes (Zhao & Chubb, 2001). Thus, this adaptation may well represent the adaptation of cells in the face-selective areas, not simply adaptations of the components of faces represented at lower levels of the system.

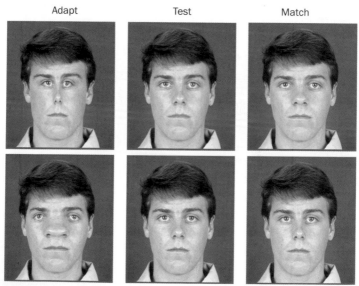

FIGURE 9–8. Aftereffect of faces. Faces may be contracted (*top left*) or expanded (*bottom left*). The aftereffect of a contracted face is that a normal face appears expanded (*top right*), and the aftereffect of an expanded face is that a normal face appears contracted (*bottom right*). (Reprinted from Webster & MacLin, 1999, with kind permission of the Psychonomic Society.)

Visuomotor Adaptations

Visuomotor adaptations have been known since Helmholtz. He discussed prism adaptation, later studied by Held and colleagues (Held, 1965). A subject with accurate pointing is studied (Fig. 9–9A). If the subject looks through a prism with base to the left, the image is displaced to the right, and he points initially to the right of the image (Fig. 9–9B). After a period in which the hand can be observed, moving it toward various objects, it will start to point straight again (Fig. 9–9C). Removal of the prism gives an aftereffect, in which the hand points to the left of the object (Fig. 9–9D). This is an adaptation of the felt position of the hand, because it transfers to auditory signals, irrespective of which muscles are used to get there, but not to the other hand (Harris, 1963).

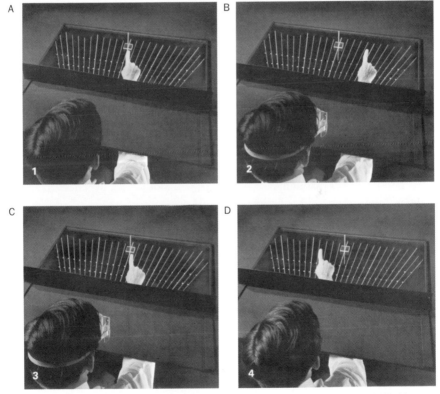

FIGURE 9–9. The subject lifts his hand accurately to touch a marker straight ahead (*A*). After putting on prisms that displace the image to the right, the subject points to the right (*B*). The subject then moves his hand around, continuing to view it through the prisms for a while. He then points accurately at the marker again (*C*). Immediately after taking the prisms off, his aim is inaccurate to the left (*D*). (Reprinted from Harris, 1980, with kind permission of Taylor & Francis Group.)

Mechanisms

All the visual adaptations discussed can be explained in terms of activation of a cell, or cells, which are specific for the features adapted. In the case of contingent aftereffects, it is easiest to make the argument in terms of cells that are specific for a conjunction of features, but this is not theoretically necessary. After the cells are activated, their responses are reduced. As pointed out for motion aftereffects, this explanation agrees with the fact that fMRI shows the largest aftereffects in those areas with cells specific for the features involved. The cellular mechanisms involved are really only worked out for light and dark adaptation, colored afterimages, and contrast adaptation. The mechanism for contrast adaptation—hyperpolarization of the cell due to an accumulation of sodium and calcium, which activates potassium currents—may well apply to a number of other adaptations, since this mechanism is common to all nerve cells.

As might be expected, visuomotor adaptations are due to changes in the cerebellum (Martin, Keating, Goodkin, Bastian, & Thach, 1965), since lesions of the cerebellum, inferior olive, and infarcts of the inferior cerebellar artery all affect them. They are also affected by lesions of the left parietal cortex, but not the right parietal cortex (Mutha, Sainberg, & Haaland, 2011).

Adaptations to Changes in the Complete Field of View

The first person to investigate complete reversal of the field of view was George Stratton (1897). He wore a telescope in front of one eye (it was too difficult to coordinate the views through telescopes in front of both eyes), which reversed the image both up-down and left-right. He could see approximately 45° of the field of view. In an initial experiment, he wore them for 21 hours over 3 days, and in a later one for several weeks. He noticed that the felt position of limbs seen in the central field of view after a while agreed with the seen position of limbs, but this was not true of limbs outside the field of view.

This was followed up in the 1940s by a series of experiments by Erismann and his colleague Ivo Kohler, translated into English some time later (Kohler, 1964). They used mirrors or prisms to reverse the field of view in one dimension, either left-right or up-down. Their report on this is fascinating reading. Visuomotor adaptation was obtained after a week or two. Subjects with left-right reversing goggles could ride a bicycle, and subjects with up-down reversals could go skiing. There was some visual adaptation, but it depended on the circumstances. For example, a subject with up-down reversals looked at a candle and said that it was upside down, but when it was lit said that it now looked right side up. A subject with left-right reversals looked at a car driving from left to right down the street and said that it was driving from left to right, but that the letters on the license plate were reversed. Similar semi-adaptations were seen in up-down reversals—one subject, shown snow falling on trees, said that he saw snow falling downward, but that the trees were upside down. Another, presented with two faces, one upside down and the other right side up, said that he saw two faces, both of which were upright, but pointing in different directions.

Like the prism adaptations of Held, these results were interpreted by some as being primarily an adaptation in the felt position of limbs, and secondarily as an adaptation within the visual system (Harris, 1980). However, experiments with single-unit recordings in the macaque show changes in the receptive fields of cells in V1 (Sugita, 1996), and experiments with fMRI in humans support this point (Miyauchi et al., 2004). There are clearly both visuomotor and visual adaptations. Movies of subjects undergoing these experiments may be seen at http://www-karc.nict.go.jp/brain/t20040000/.

A second series of experiments by Kohler describes what he calls situational adaptations. In one, he fitted subjects with two-colored goggles, yellow in the right half and blue in the left, with a vertical line between them (Fig. 9–10). After a while, objects in both halves on the field of view appeared to be normally colored, independent of where the eyes were looking. Thus, the area in the central part of the field of view, around the fovea, learned to adapt to two different sets of colors, depending on the position of the eyes. One can even have aftereffects of depth and color develop independently of each other over the same period of time (Nieman, Hayashi, Andersen, & Shimojo, 2005).

Adaptation to Spectacles

These situational adaptations have a most important application in the wearing of spectacles. Indeed, this was one of Kohler's first concerns in his description of his results. He employed goggles that were a prism in the lower half of the field, and plain in the upper. Subjects could learn to adapt so that they could tell what was straight ahead when looking through either half of the goggles. However, looking directly at the boundary was confusing, and they tended to avoid that. Kohler's half prisms have obvious relevance to the wearing of bifocal lenses.

FIGURE 9–10. Two-colored goggles for situational adaptation. The world initially appeared yellow when looking to the right, and blue when looking to the left. After a while, it appeared normally colored when looking in either direction, and the subject could transfer his attention from one side to the other without noticing the difference.

Adaptation to spectacles has obviously been known for a long time to anybody who wears them. Burian (1943) discussed one situation—the wearing of cylindrical lenses. This leads to distortions of shape and depth, which wear off over a few days. There is also an aftereffect when the lenses are taken off. Other adaptations are well known in the offices of eye care practitioners, but not discussed extensively in the scientific literature.

References

Addams, R. (1834). An account of a peculiar optical phenomenon seen after having looked at a moving body, etc. *London and Edinburgh Philosophical Magazine Journal of Science, 5*, 373–374.

Anstis, S. M., & Moulden, B. P. (1970). After effect of seen movement: Evidence for peripheral and central components. *Quarterly Journal of Experimental Psychology, 22*, 222–229.

Barlow, H. B., & Brindley, G. S. (1963). Inter-ocular transfer of movement after-effects during pressure blinding of the stimulated eye. *Nature, 200*, 1347.

Barlow, H. B., & Hill, R. M. (1963). Evidence for a physiological explanation of the waterfall phenomenon and figural after-effects. *Nature, 200*, 1345–1347.

Blakemore, C., & Campbell, F. W. (1969). On the existence of neurones in the human visual system selectively sensitive to the orientation and size of retinal images. *Journal of Physiology, 203*, 237–260.

Blakemore, C., & Julesz, B. (1971). Stereoscopic depth aftereffect produced without monocular cues. *Science, 171*, 286–288.

Burian, H. M. (1943). Clinical significance of aniseikonia. *Archives of Ophthalmology, 21*, 116–133.

Carandini, M., & Ferster, D. (1997). A tonic hyperpolarization underlying contrast adaptation in cat visual cortex. *Science, 276*, 949–952.

Domini, F., Adams, W., & Banks, M. S. (2001). 3D after-effects are due to shape and not disparity adaptation. *Vision Research, 41*, 2733–2739.

Dowling, J. E. (1960). Chemistry of visual adaptation in the rat. *Nature, 188*, 114–118.

Dowling, J. E. (1987). *The retina*. Cambridge, MA: Harvard University Press.

Fain, G. L. (2001). Dark adaptation. *Progress in Brain Research, 131*, 383–394.

Fang, F., & He, S. (2005). Viewer-centered object representation in the human visual system revealed by viewpoint aftereffects. *Neuron, 45*, 793–800.

Gibson, J. J. (1933). Adaptation: after-effect and contrast in the perception of curved lines. *Journal of Experimental Psychology, 16*, 1–31.

Gibson, J. J., & Radner, M. (1937). Adaptation, after-effect, and contrast in the perception of tilted lines I. Quantitative studies. *Journal of Experimental Psychology, 20*, 453–467.

Harris, C. S. (1963). Adaptation to displaced vision: visual, motor, or proprioceptive change? *Science, 140*, 812–813.

Harris, C. S. (1965). Perceptual adaptation to inverted, reversed, and displaced vision. *Psychological Review, 72*, 419–444.

Harris, C. S. (1980). Insight or out of sight? Two examples of perceptual plasticity in the human adult. In C. S. Harris (Ed.), *Visual coding and adaptability* (pp. 95–149). Hillsdale, NJ: Erlbaum.

Hecht, S., Haig, C., & Chase, A. M. (1937). The influence of light adaptation on subsequent dark adaptation of the eye. *Journal of General Physiology, 20,* 831–850.

Held, R. (1965). Plasticity in sensory-motor systems. *Scientific American, 213,* 84–94.

Kohler, I. (1964). The formation and transformation of the perceptual world. (H. Fiss, Trans.). *Psychological Issues, 12.*

Kohn, A. (2007). Visual adaptation: Physiology, mechanisms, and functional benefits. *Journal of Neurophysiology, 97,* 3155–3164.

Lamb, T. D., & Pugh, E. N., Jr. (2006). Phototransduction, dark adaptation, and rhodopsin regeneration: the Proctor Lecture. *Investigative Ophthalmology and Visual Sciences, 47,* 5137–5152.

Luo, D. G., Xue, T., & Yau, K. W. (2008). How vision begins: an odyssey. *Proceedings of the National Academy of Sciences USA, 105,* 9855–9862.

Maffei, L., Fiorentini, A., & Bisti, S. (1973). Neural correlate of perceptual adaptation to gratings. *Science, 182,* 1036–1038.

Manookin, M. B., & Demb, J. B. (2006). Presynaptic mechanism for slow contrast adaptation in mammalian retinal ganglion cells. *Neuron, 50,* 453–464.

Martin, T. A., Keating, J. G., Goodkin, H. P., Bastian, A. J., & Thach, W. T. (1996). Throwing while looking through prisms. I. Focal olivocerebellar lesions impair adaptation. *Brain, 119*(Pt. 4), 1183–1198.

McCullough, C. (1965). Color-adaptation of edge detectors in the human visual system. *Science, 149,* 1115.

Miyauchi, S., Egusa, H., Amagase, M., Sekiyama, K., Imaruoka, T., & Tashiro, T. (2004). Adaptation to left-right reversed vision rapidly activates ipsilateral visual cortex in humans. *Journal of Physiology Paris, 98,* 207–219.

Muller, K. M., Wilke, M., & Leopold, D. A. (2009). Visual adaptation to convexity in macaque area V4. *Neuroscience, 161,* 655–662.

Mutha, P. K., Sainburg, R. L., Haaland K. Y. (2011). Left parietal regions are critical for adaptive visuomotor control. Journal of Neuroscience, 31, 6972-6981.

Nieman, D. R., Hayashi, R., Andersen, R. A., & Shimojo, S. (2005). Gaze direction modulates visual aftereffects in depth and color. *Vision Research, 45,* 2885–2894.

Ohzawa, I., Sclar, G., & Freeman, R. D. (1982). Contrast gain control in the cat visual cortex. *Nature, 298,* 266–268.

Rieke, F., & Rudd, M. E. (2009). The challenges natural images pose for visual adaptation. *Neuron, 64,* 605–616.

Rushton, W. A. (1961). Rhodopsin measurement and dark-adaptation in a subject deficient in cone vision. *Journal of Physiology, 156,* 193–205.

Sanchez-Vives, M. V., Nowak, L. G., & McCormick, D. A. (2000). Cellular mechanisms of long-lasting adaptation in visual cortical neurons in vitro. *Journal of Neuroscience, 20,* 4286–4299.

Stiles, W. S. (1949). Increment thresholds and the mechanisms of colour vision. *Documenta Ophthalmologica, 3,* 138–165.

Stiles, W. S., & Crawford, B. H. (1932). Equivalent adaptation levels on localized retinal areas. In W. S. Stiles (Ed.), *Report of a joint discussion on vision* (pp. 194–211). London: Physical Society.

Stratton, G. M. (1897). Vision without inversion of the retinal image. *Psychological Review, 4*, 241–360.

Sugita, Y. (1996). Global plasticity in adult visual cortex following reversal of visual input. *Nature, 380*, 523–526.

Tootell, R. B., Reppas, J. B., Dale, A. M., Look, R. B., Sereno, M. I., Malach, R., ... Rosen, B. R. (1995). Visual motion aftereffect in human cortical area MT revealed by functional magnetic resonance imaging. *Nature, 375*, 139–141.

Vul, E., Krizay, E., & MacLeod, D. I. (2008). The McCollough effect reflects permanent and transient adaptation in early visual cortex. *Journal of Vision, 8*, 4 1–12.

Weber, E. H. (1834). *De pulsu, resorptione, auditu et tactu annotiones anatomicae et phsyiologicae*. Leipzig, Germany: Koehler.

Webster, M. A., & MacLin, O. H. (1999). Figural aftereffects in the perception of faces. *Psychological Bulletin Review, 6*, 647–653.

Zhao, L., & Chubb, C. (2001). The size-tuning of the face-distortion after-effect. *Vision Research, 41*, 2979–2994.

10

Attention

The scene in front of us contains millions of pixels of information. How do we analyze it to focus on the items of interest and to put the details together into a representation of the whole picture? As we look around the scene with a series of saccadic eye movements, how do we retain features of interest and ignore the rest? Some selection has to take place; otherwise the visual system would be overwhelmed with more information than it could hold (Hayhoe, 2000). This is the subject of attention.

We have already discussed the patterns of saccadic eye movements made as one looks around a scene (Chapter 8), noting how the eyes dwell on objects of interest such as the lips, nose, and eyes in a famous face (Fig. 10–1; Yarbus, 1967). The object for the next fixation obviously has to be selected by observing items in the peripheral part of the field of view, away from the fovea, so the whole field of view has to be evaluated in some manner after each saccade. As discussed, the process can be influenced considerably by the instructions given to the observer (see Fig. 8–1 in Chapter 8) and by the requirements of the task being performed (see Fig. 8–2 in Chapter 8). Attention determines what is noticed in this process, and what is not noticed and is ignored.

What Is Noticed?

The sudden appearance of an object is one factor that will help to make it noticed, as described by Titchener (1908) a century ago. This can be evaluated with a pattern of letters (E, H, P, S, and U) made up from line segments (Yantis & Jonides, 1984). A letter may have an abrupt onset, or appear by the removal of a line segment. The abrupt onset letter is noticed faster. However, if attention is already directed to the location where the letter is to appear, there is no advantage to an abrupt onset.

In the absence of sudden appearance, the noticeability of an object depends very much on the other objects that it is embedded in, and on the similarity between the object and others around it. For example, the boundary between tilted Ts and upright Ts is more noticeable than the boundary between upright Ts

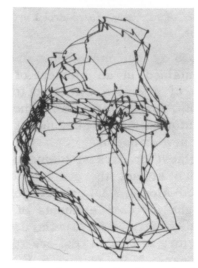

FIGURE 10.1 When looking at the outline of a famous face, the eyes dwell on the most salient features: the eyes, nose, lips, chin, and ear. (Reprinted from Yarbus, 1967, with kind permission of Plenum Press.)

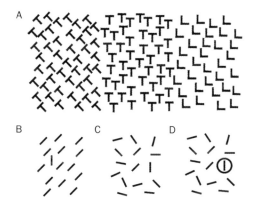

FIGURE 10.2 The boundary between the upright T's and the slanted T's is much more apparent than the boundary between the upright T's and the upright L's (A). The upright line is apparent in (B), but not very apparent in (C), unless outlined with a circle as in (D). (Panel A reprinted from Kimchi, 2003, with kind permission of Oxford University Press.)

and upright Ls (Fig. 10–2A; Kimchi, 2003). Moreover, a slanted line embedded in a number of vertical lines is more apparent than a slanted line embedded in lines of all orientations (Figs. 10–2B and 10–2D). In some cases the object pops out, and in other cases it does not.

An object pops out most easily if it differs from the surrounding objects in a single attribute. For example, an X will easily pop out in the middle of a sea of O's, or a green X in a sea of red X's (Fig. 10–3). However, a red X in the middle of green X's and red O's will not be seen as easily (Treisman & Gelade, 1980). The task becomes even harder if misleading cues are introduced. For example, words that are in different colors can be read almost as quickly as the same word in black, but the colors of the word are named significantly more slowly than the same color

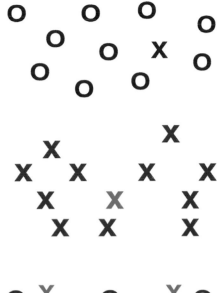

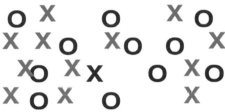

FIGURE 10.3 An X in the middle of O's is easily seen, as is a green X in the middle of red X's. The red X in the middle of green X's and red O's is more difficult.

seen in a swatch without the interference of the conflicting word (Fig. 10–4; Stroop, 1935). This phenomenon has a correlate in recordings from human visual cortex (Scalf & Beck, 2010).

The task also depends on any directions given. One can present subjects with a series of five figures such as those in Figure 10–5, with instructions to rate the red figures (or, alternatively, the green figures) on a scale of 1 to 5 for how pleasing they are (Rock & Gutman, 1981), then show the subjects 15 outlines in black and white: five like the red ones previously seen, five like the green ones, and five new. If they were previously asked to rate the red ones, then the corresponding set of five will be picked out, and if previously asked to rate the green ones, that set of five will be picked out. The ones that were not rated are not recognized. There may even be an unconscious bias so that repetition in the presentation of the stimulus in the same location leads to a faster recognition, without any directions being given (Fecteau, Korjoufov, & Roelfsema, 2009).

A major question in how objects are noticed concerns whether this is done by looking at one object after another (serial mode) or viewing them all at the same time to extract the relevant one (parallel mode). The answer, as in many biological questions, is not one or the other, but both. The point has been well illustrated by Wolfe (2005) in a figure with a variety of colored symbols (Fig. 10–6). If you

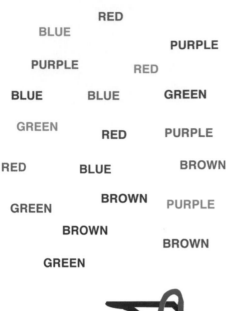

RED
BLUE
PURPLE
PURPLE   RED
BLUE   **BLUE**   **GREEN**
GREEN
RED   **PURPLE**
RED   **BLUE**   **BROWN**
GREEN   **BROWN**   PURPLE
BROWN
BROWN
GREEN

FIGURE 10.4 The Stroop effect. The words can be read almost as quickly as the same word in black. However, the colors of each word are named significantly more slowly than the same color printed in squares.

FIGURE 10.5 Subjects are asked to rate the red figures on a scale of 1 to 5 for how pleasing they are. After looking at five displays like this, they can pick out black and white figures like the red ones, from a display of 15 figures, five shaped like the red ones, five shaped like the green ones, and five new. They do not remember any of the green ones.

look for the blue diamond, all the blue symbols come out; similarly, if you look for the yellow square, all the yellow symbols come out. This clearly implies some sort of parallel processing. Now look for the crosses with a red vertical bar. More detailed search with more eye movements is required, and you may not immediately notice that there are two of them. This implies serial processing. When double conjunctions are searched for (color x form, color x orientation, and color x size) and compared to triple conjunctions, the triple conjunctions are found faster, also implying a parallel process (Wolfe, Cave, & Franzel, 1989).

What Is Not Noticed?

Just as important as what is noticed is what is not noticed or ignored. This was illustrated in a test of "head up" displays, where a display of various flight parameters is superimposed on the view through the windshield of an airplane cockpit. Using these displays in a flight simulator, a significant number

FIGURE 10.6 Look for the blue diamond, and all the blue objects will come to your attention (parallel processing). Similarly, look for the yellow square, and all the yellow objects will come to your attention. Now look for the crosses where the vertical bar is red. There is a tendency to look at them one by one (serial processing). (Reprinted from Wolfe, 2005, with kind permission of AAAS.)

of pilots did not notice another airplane appearing on the runway in front of them (Haines, 1991). The importance can be readily appreciated by anybody who flies, as pilot or passenger!

A similar situation was investigated by Neisser and Becklen (1975). They had observers view two superimposed scenes at the same time. In one, teams were playing handball. In the other, two people were playing a hand-slapping game. Observers could follow one scene or the other, but not both at the same time. If, for example, they were following the hand-slapping game, they would not notice if men in the handball-playing team were replaced by women, or if the ball went out of the court. If they were following the handball game, they would not notice if the hands did not move in the hand-slapping game. Presumably the pilots who did not notice the plane on the runway were concentrating on the fight parameter display to the exclusion of what they could see out of the windscreen.

Instructions, which affect the direction of attention, will affect the situation. There is a dramatic demonstration in which two teams of three people each are playing handball (Simons & Chabris, 1999; see http://www.dansimons.com/videos.html). One team is dressed in white, and the other in black. Observers are given the task of counting the number of passes for one team or the other. During the game, another person, dressed as a gorilla in black, walks through the game. Only 8% of observers who are counting passes for the white team notice the gorilla, while 67% of observers who are counting passes for the black team notice. Observers who view the demonstration again after being told what happened are incredulous, because the gorilla is so obvious when attention is not directed. However, now that you are primed, the gorilla will probably be apparent in the Web site demonstration to you. Try it on a friend who has not seen the demonstration before, and do not prompt him or her about the answer.

There are several other situations where changes in a scene are not noticed, going under the heading of change blindness. How this occurs during a saccade was mentioned in Chapter 8. A dramatic example occurs during reading of a text in AlTeRnAtInG case (McConkie & Zola, 1979). If the case is changed during a saccade, so that upper case becomes lower and vice versa, the reader just keeps on reading and does not notice the case change.

Inconsistent changes are noticed more easily than consistent changes (Hollingworth & Henderson, 2000). For example, if a chair in an indoor scene is replaced by a fire hydrant, or a fire hydrant in an outdoor scene is replaced by a chair, this will be noticed more easily than the reverse changes.

One fails to notice changes in the periphery more frequently than changes in areas that one looks at directly, but even changes in areas viewed directly may not be noticed (O'Regan, Deubel, Clark, & Rensink, 2000). It seems that one explores a scene with an aim in mind, and factors that do not fit in with that aim may be neglected. One tends to attend to what is relevant to the immediate task. For example, in making a peanut butter and jelly sandwich and pouring a cola, other objects in the scene will be ignored (Hayhoe, 2000).

Even though a change may not be explicitly noticed in change blindness, some aspects of the change may be retained in a subconscious memory. Where an undergraduate was talking to a basketball player, and a crowd of other undergraduates passed between them and either gave the player a ball or took a ball away from him, most undergraduates did not notice the change (Simons, Chabris, Schnur, & Levin, 2002). However, when prompted with leading questions about the color of the stripe on the ball, some remembered something.

As already mentioned, changes are not noticed during saccades (see Fig. 8–3 in Chapter 8) or if the scene is interrupted by people passing in front of it. Change blindness also occurs if there is an interval between the presentation of one scene and presentation of the next. This is called the attentional blink. Information presented between 180 ms and 450 ms after the recognition of a letter may not be seen, while information presented after shorter or longer intervals is seen (Raymond, Shapiro, & Arnell, 1992). There is improvement in recognition if the subject is given a verbal cue, or if the changed element is an important one (Rensink, O'Regan, & Clark, 1997).

All these examples of change blindness show that the visual system does not keep everything in memory. Most of the representation of one scene is wiped out when the next scene comes along. Only the most salient features are retained. Which features are salient depends on the task being undertaken and on the instructions given to the observer.

Overt Attention and Covert Attention

Attention to an object in a scene which leads to a saccadic eye movement to look at the object is known as overt attention. It is also possible to keep one's eyes fixated on the current location, yet to notice and pay attention to objects elsewhere.

This is known as covert attention. Even more important, one can train macaque monkeys to do this, which enables one to distinguish which parts of the brain deal with eye movements and which deal with attention.

Location of Attention in the Brain

Attention affects the response of cells in all parts of the brain dealing with vision and eye movements. This includes the lateral geniculate nucleus (McAlonan, Cavanaugh, & Wurtz, 2008), primary visual cortex (Motter, 1993), V4 (Moran & Desimone, 1985), MT (Treue & Maunsell, 1996), occipito-temporal cortex (O'Craven, Downing, & Kanwisher, 1999), pulvinar (Robinson & Petersen, 1992), parietal cortex (LIP; Bisley & Goldberg, 2006), frontal cortex (FEF; Moore & Fallah, 2001), and superior colliculus (Cavanaugh & Wurtz, 2004). The response of cells in the thalamic reticular nucleus, called the perigeniculate, around the lateral geniculate in the visual system goes down rather than up with attention (McAlonan et al., 2008), and the perigeniculate inhibits the lateral geniculate, so the thalamic reticular nucleus could well provide a place where attention feeds back to the system, in accordance with the thalamic searchlight hypothesis put forward by Crick (1984).

The point that areas concerned with eye movements and areas concerned with attention are the same led to the premotor theory of attention, in which attention is regarded as a factor leading up to a saccadic eye movement (Rizzolatti, Riggio, Dascola, & Umilta, 1987). The use of attention here helps particularly in eye movements across the horizontal and vertical meridians. The congruence of the areas involved in covert attention and eye movement tasks is supported by fMRI measurements in humans (Corbetta et al., 1998). Attention to the target of a saccade, compared to attention to a target elsewhere, makes the saccade more accurate and go faster (Kowler, Anderson, Dosher, & Blaser, 1995). However, as pointed out previously, there are visual cells, motor cells, and visuomotor cells in the frontal eye fields (see Chapter 8). The visual cells are affected by attention, but not by saccades (Fig. 10–7; Thompson, Biscoe, & Sato, 2005). Thus, the same areas may be involved in attention and eye movements, but not necessarily the same cells within those areas.

The effects of attention in sensory areas amount to an increase in the response of a cell when a stimulus that activates it is attended (Fig. 10–8; Moran & Desimone, 1985). In humans, this may mean that the stimulus appears to have a greater contrast (Stormer, McDonald, & Hillyard, 2009). Comparing LGN, V1, V2, and V4, the amount by which the response is increased goes up as one moves higher in the system: about 10% in lower areas, up to 40% in V4 (Motter, 1993). The response is increased more for a stimulus within the receptive field of the cell than for a stimulus outside it (Chelazzi, Miller, Duncan, & Desimone, 2001; also review Moran & Desimone, 1985), and attention to a stimulus within the receptive field of the cell may change the shape of the receptive field toward

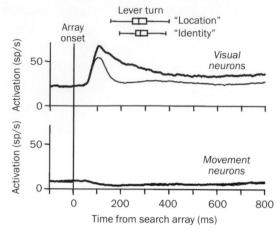

FIGURE 10–7. Two macaques were trained to turn a lever, in response to a stimulus, without moving their eyes. One had a location task (stimulus left or right), and one an identity task (a Landolt C, with the gap either to the left or the right). Turning the lever in the correct direction was rewarded. The visual neurons in the frontal eye fields responded to this covert attention task, but the movement neurons did not. (Reprinted from Thompson et al., 2005, with kind permission of the Society for Neuroscience.)

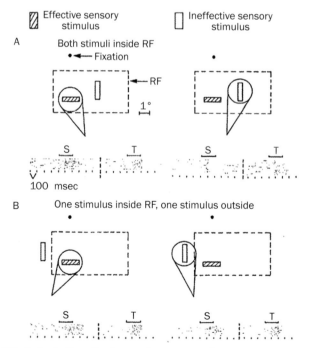

FIGURE 10–8. Effect of selective attention on the response of a neuron in V4. The cell responded when the macaque attended to an effective stimulus, but not when it attended to an ineffective stimulus, when both stimuli were inside the receptive field (A), and also when one stimulus was outside the receptive field (B). (Reprinted from Moran & Desimone, 1985, with kind permission of AAAS.)

the attended location (Womelsdorf, Anton-Erxleben, Pieper, & Treue, 2006). In cells specific for the orientation of a stimulus, the overall response is affected, but not the orientation specificity (Fig. 10–9; McAdams & Maunsell, 1999). However, where neurons are specific for both color and orientation, as in V4, attention to one of these attributes may affect that attribute specifically (Mirabella et al., 2007). Moreover, attention to faces, houses, and motion specifically affects fusiform gyrus, parahippocampal gyrus, and MT respectively, as might be expected (O'Craven, Downing, & Kanwisher, 1999).

The visuomotor areas, LIP, FEF, and SC, are affected by eye movements resulting from attention, and also by covert attention when eye movements are not made. When FEFs are inactivated, a macaque will neither make saccades nor respond to tasks involving covert attention with no eye movements (Wardak, Ibos, Duhamel, & Olivier, 2006). Application of a cause-and-effect technique, called Grainger causality, suggests that FEF exerts a top-down effect on sensory visual areas, and probably also on parietal cortex (Bressler et al., 2008), and parietal cortex in turn exerts a top-down influence on occipital cortex (Lauritzen, D'Esposito, Heeger, & Silver, 2009), although there are also direct influences of FEF on occipital cortex. Within extrastriate cortex there are also competitive and suppressive interactions, which help to focus attention toward a particular area rather than areas around it (Kastner, De Weerd, Desimone, & Ungerleider, 1998). Thus there are both top-down and bottom-up effects influencing attention.

Interestingly, stimulation of the superior colliculus antagonizes change blindness at the site stimulated (Cavanaugh & Wurtz, 2004). Stimulation also enhances visual performance at the site stimulated in a covert attention task (Muller, Philiastides, & Newsome, 2005), and inactivation of the superior colliculus can affect covert attention to a stimulus when distractors are present (Lovejoy & Krauzlis, 2010).

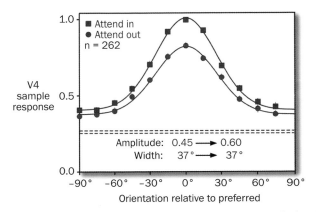

FIGURE 10–9. Tuning curves for a population of neurons that were measured when the macaque was attending (solid squares) and also when the macaque was not attending (open circles). Attention increases the response at all orientations. (Reprinted from McAdams & Maunsell, 1999, with kind permission of the Society for Neuroscience.)

It is not known whether these effects on the superior colliculus act on the rest of the system through the feedback projections to the frontal cortex recently discovered, or through projections to occipital cortex through the pulvinar. Both of these pathways were discussed in Chapter 8. However, it is most interesting that an area considered to be late in visuomotor processing, such as the superior colliculus, should have an effect on a higher level function such as attention.

Oscillations and Drugs

When paying attention to an object in a particular part of the field of view, cells in occipital cortex and in frontal cortex that have receptive fields for this location will oscillate together at gamma frequencies (35–90 Hz; Gregoriou, Gotts, Zhou, & Desimone, 2009). The exact role of these oscillations is a matter of speculation at the moment, but they may play some role in the top-down influence of frontal cortex on attention.

Application of the drug acetylcholine increases the attentional modulation of cells in V1, and application of the acetylcholine antagonist scopolamine reduces it (Herrero et al., 2008). Acetylcholine is the neurotransmitter for a group of cells in the basal forebrain that send their endings all over the cerebral cortex. Dopamine also affects attention through its action on neurons in the prefrontal cortex (Noudoust & Moore, 2011). Very likely attention will also be shown to be modulated by other groups of cells that project all over the cortex and use serotonin and noradrenaline as neurotransmitters.

Neglect

The opposite of attention is neglect. As might be expected, lesions in humans in almost any part of the visual and visuomotor systems will produce some kind of failure to notice objects, or neglect. Lesions in sensory areas will also produce a blind spot, known as a scotoma, and lesions in visuomotor areas will also produce a failure to make eye movements. It is lesions of the area in between that produce pure neglect.

Neglect is usually on one side of the brain. Patients with neglect, when asked to draw a man, will draw one half and leave the other half blank (Fig. 10–10). They may also explore less in the neglected hemifield. A patient asked to circle all the A's in a pattern of letters will not circle the A's on one side of the pattern, although free to look anywhere he wants (Fig. 10–11). When given a tray of food, the patient may just not eat the food on one side of the tray. The patient may be aware of the other half of the field of view, but not at a conscious level. For example, a patient with left hemifield neglect, if presented with two pictures of houses in this hemifield, one with flames coming out and one with no flames, the patient will say that there is no difference, but if asked which one she prefers, she will say she prefers

FIGURE 10–10. (*A*) Drawing by a patient who had neglect of the left hemifield, when asked to reproduce a picture of a woman. (*B*) Drawings of composite animals. Patients would recognize the right half, but not the left. (*C*) Eye movements of a patient looking at a composite face of a woman on the left, and a man on the right. The left side was inspected, but not reported. (Reprinted from Mattingley & Walker, 2003, with kind permission of Oxford University Press.)

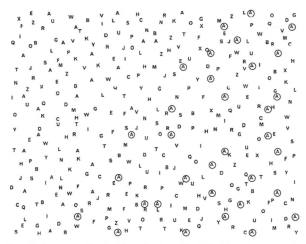

FIGURE 10–11. Results from a patient with neglect on the left side, who was asked to circle all the A's in the display. Only the ones on the right side were circled, even though the patient was free to look all over the display. (Reprinted from Mesulam, 1999, with kind permission of the Royal Society.)

the one without the flames. It is a defect of remembered objects as well as those seen: patients who knew Milan, when asked to visualize the main square facing the cathedral, mentioned buildings on the right but not the left; when asked to face away from the cathedral, the reverse was true (Bisiach & Luzzatti, 1978). These different aspects of neglect—sensory-representational, motor-exploratory, and limbic-motivational (Mesulam, 1999)—depend on which part of the brain is lesioned.

There is an asymmetry in the seriousness of neglect in humans. A lesion in the left hemisphere affects primarily attention on the right side of the field of view. A lesion in the right hemisphere affects attention in both halves of the field of view, although more on the left. Some people have suggested that this asymmetry of attention, larger in the right hemisphere, parallels the development of language in the left hemisphere.

Pure neglect might be expected to occur primarily from lesions in the parietal cortex, since this is neither sensory nor motor. In the literature, pure neglect is also known as parietal neglect. However, a study of 49 patients with neglect, 24 of whom had cortical lesions not including the basal ganglia or thalamus, showed that the cortical area most frequently involved was the superior temporal gyrus (Karnath, Ferber, & Himmelbach, 2001). Neglect can also occur from lesions of subcortical structures such as the pulvinar (see Karnath, Himmelbach, & Rorden, 2002).

There are also patients who can only recognize one object in the field of view, when several objects are present—a phenomenon known as simultanagnosia (Heilman, Watson, & Valenstein, 2003). These patients have lesions that include the occipital cortex as well as the parietal cortex. Simultanagnosia is an important component of Balint syndrome.

References

Bisiach, E., & Luzzatti, C. (1978). Unilateral neglect of representational space. *Cortex*, *14*, 129–133.

Bisley, J. W., & Goldberg, M. E. (2006). Neural correlates of attention and distractibility in the lateral intraparietal area. *Journal of Neurophysiology*, *95*, 1696–1717.

Bressler, S. L., Tang, W., Sylvester, C. M., & Shulman, G. L., & Corbetta, M. (2008). Top-down control of human visual cortex by frontal and parietal cortex in anticipatory visual spatial attention. *Journal of Neuroscience*, *28*, 10056–10061.

Cavanaugh, J., & Wurtz, R. H. (2004). Subcortical modulation of attention counters change blindness. *Journal of Neuroscience 24*, 11236–11243.

Chelazzi, L., Miller, E. K., Duncan, J., & Desimone, R. (2001). Responses of neurons in macaque area V4 during memory-guided visual search. *Cerebral Cortex*, *11*, 761–772.

Corbetta, M., Akbudak, E., Conturo, T. E., Snyder, A. Z., Ollinger, J. M., Drury, H. A., Linenweber, M. R., Petersen, S. E., Raichle, M. E., Van Essen, D. C., Shulman, G. L. (1998). A common network of functional areas for attention and eye movements. *Neuron*, *21*, 761–773.

Crick, F. (1984). Function of the thalamic reticular complex: the searchlight hypothesis. *Proceedings of the National Academy Science USA*, *81*, 4586–4590.

Fecteau, J. H., Korjoukov, I., & Roelfsema, P. R. (2009). Location and color biases have different influences on selective attention. *Vision Research*, *49*, 996–1005.

Gregoriou, G. G., Gotts, S. J., Zhou, H., & Desimone, R. (2009). High-frequency, long-range coupling between prefrontal and visual cortex during attention. *Science*, *324*, 1207–1210.

Haines, R. F. (1991). A breakdown in simultaneous information processing. In G. Obrecht & L. W. Stark (Eds.), *Presbyopia research* (pp. 171–175). New York: Plenum.

Hayhoe, M. (2000). Vision using routines: A functional account of vision. *Visual Cognition, 7,* 43–64.

Heilman, K. M., Watson, R. T., & Valenstein, E. (2003). Neglect and related disorders. In K. M. Heilman (Ed.), *Clinical neuropsychology* (pp. 296–346). New York: Oxford University Press.

Herrero, J. L., Roberts, M. J., Delicato, L. S., Gieselmann, M. A., Dayan, P., & Thiele, A. (2008). Acetylcholine contributes through muscarinic receptors to attentional modulation in V1. *Nature, 454,* 1110–1114.

Hollingworth, A., & Henderson, J. M. (2000). Semantic informativeness mediates the detection of changes in natural scenes. *Visual Cognition, 7,* 213–235.

Karnath, H. O., Ferber, S., & Himmelbach, M. (2001). Spatial awareness is a function of the temporal not the posterior parietal lobe. *Nature, 411,* 950–953.

Karnath, H. O., Himmelbach, M., & Rorden, C. (2002). The subcortical anatomy of human spatial neglect: putamen, caudate nucleus and pulvinar. *Brain, 125,* 350–360.

Kastner, S., De Weerd, P., Desimone, R., & Ungerleider, L. G. (1998). Mechanisms of directed attention in the human extrastriate cortex as revealed by functional MRI. *Science, 282,* 108–111.

Kimchi, R. (2003). Relative dominance of holistic and component properties in the perceptual organization of visual objects. In M. A. Peterson & G. Rhodes (Eds.), *Perception of faces, objects, and scenes* (pp. 235–268). New York: Oxford University Press.

Kowler, E., Anderson, E., Dosher, B., & Blaser, E. (1995). The role of attention in the programming of saccades. *Vision Research, 35,* 1897–1916.

Lauritzen, T. Z., D'Esposito, M., Heeger, D. J., & Silver, M. A. (2009). Top-down flow of visual spatial attention signals from parietal to occipital cortex. *Journal of Vision, 9,* 18 11–14.

Lovejoy, L. P., & Krauzlis, R. J. (2010). Inactivation of primate superior colliculus impairs covert selection of signals for perceptual judgments. *Nature Neuroscience, 13,* 261–266.

Mattingley, J. B., & Walker, R. (2003). The blind leading the mind. In L. Pessoa & P. de Weerd (Eds.), Filling in (pp. 207–227). New York: Oxford University Press.

McAdams, C. J., & Maunsell, J. H. (1999). Effects of attention on orientation-tuning functions of single neurons in macaque cortical area V4. *Journal of Neuroscience, 19,* 431–441.

McAlonan, K., Cavanaugh, J., & Wurtz, R. H. (2008). Guarding the gateway to cortex with attention in visual thalamus. *Nature, 456,* 391–394.

McConkie, G. W., & Zola, D. (1979). Is visual information integrated across successive fixations in reading? *Perception and Psychophysics, 25,* 221–224.

Mesulam, M. M. (1999). Spatial attention and neglect: Parietal, frontal and cingulate contributions to the mental representation and attentional targeting of salient extrapersonal events. *Philosophical Transactions of the Royal Society of London B: Biological Sciences, 354,* 1325–1346.

Mirabella, G., Bertini, G., Samengo, I., Kilavik, B. E., Frilli, D., Della Libera, C., & Chelazzi, L. (2007). Neurons in area V4 of the macaque translate attended visual features into behaviorally relevant categories. *Neuron, 54,* 303–318.

Moore, T., & Fallah, M. (2001). Control of eye movements and spatial attention. *Proceedings of the National Academy of Sciences USA, 98*, 1273–1276.

Moran, J., & Desimone, R. (1985). Selective attention gates visual processing in the extrastriate cortex. *Science, 229*, 782–784.

Motter, B. C. (1993). Focal attention produces spatially selective processing in visual cortical areas V1, V2, and V4 in the presence of competing stimuli. *Journal of Neurophysiology, 70*, 909–919.

Muller, J. R., Philiastides, M. G., & Newsome, W. T. (2005). Microstimulation of the superior colliculus focuses attention without moving the eyes. *Proceedings of the National Academy of Sciences USA, 102*, 524–529.

Neisser, U., & Becklen, R. (1975). Selective looking: attending to visually specified events. *Cognitive Psychology, 7*, 480–494.

Noudoost, B., Moore, T. (2011) Control of visual cortical signals by prefrontal dopamine. *Nature, 474*, 372-375.

O'Craven, K. M., Downing, P. E., & Kanwisher, N. (1999). fMRI evidence for objects as the units of attentional selection. *Nature, 401*, 584–587.

O'Regan, J. K., Deubel, H., Clark, J. J., & Rensink, R. A. (2000). Picture changes during blinks: Looking without seeing and seeing without looking. *Visual Cognition, 7*, 191–211.

Raymond, J. E., Shapiro, K. L., & Arnell, K. M. (1992). Temporary suppression of visual processing in an RSVP task: An attentional blink? *Journal of Experimental Psychology: Human Perception and Performance, 18*, 849–860.

Rensink, R. A., O'Regan, J. K., & Clark, J. J. (1997). The need for attention to perceive changes in scenes. *Psychological Science, 8*, 368–375.

Rizzolatti, G., Riggio, L., Dascola, I., & Umilta, C. (1987). Reorienting attention across the horizontal and vertical meridians: Evidence in favor of a premotor theory of attention. *Neuropsychologia, 25*, 31–40.

Robinson, D. L., & Petersen, S. E. (1992). The pulvinar and visual salience. *Trends in Neuroscience, 15*, 127–132.

Rock, I., & Gutman, D. (1981). The effect of inattention on form perception. *Journal of Experimental Psychology: Human Perception and Performance, 7*, 275–285.

Scalf, P. E., & Beck, D. M. (2010). Competition in visual cortex impedes attention to multiple items. *Journal of Neuroscience, 30*, 161–169.

Simons, D. J., & Chabris, C. F. (1999). Gorillas in our midst: Sustained inattentional blindness for dynamic events. *Perception, 28*, 1059–1074.

Simons, D. J., Chabris, C. F., Schnur, T., & Levin, D. T. (2002). Evidence for preserved representations in change blindness. *Consciousness and Cognition, 11*, 78–97.

Stormer, V. S., McDonald, J. J., & Hillyard, S. A. (2009). Cross-modal cueing of attention alters appearance and early cortical processing of visual stimuli. *Proceedings of the National Academy of Sciences USA, 106*, 22456–22461.

Stroop, J. R. (1935). Interference in serial verbal reactions. *Journal of Experimental Psychology, 18*, 643–662.

Thompson, K. G., Biscoe, K. L., & Sato, T. R. (2005). Neuronal basis of covert spatial attention in the frontal eye field. *Journal of Neuroscience, 25*, 9479–9487.

Titchener, E. B. (1908). *Lectures on the elementary psychology of feeling and attention.* New York: MacMillan.

Treisman, A. M., & Gelade, G. (1980). A feature-integration theory of attention. *Cognitive Psychology, 12*, 97–136.

Treue, S., & Maunsell, J. H. (1996). Attentional modulation of visual motion processing in cortical areas MT and MST. *Nature, 382*, 539–541.

Wardak, C., Ibos, G., Duhamel, J. R., & Olivier, E. (2006). Contribution of the monkey frontal eye field to covert visual attention. *Journal of Neuroscience, 26*, 4228–4235.

Wolfe, J. M. (2005). Neuroscience. Watching single cells pay attention. *Science, 308*, 503–504.

Wolfe, J. M., Cave, K. R., & Franzel, S. L. (1989). Guided search: An alternative to the feature integration model for visual search. *Journal of Experimental Psychology: Human Perception and Performance, 15*, 419–433.

Womelsdorf, T., Anton-Erxleben, K., Pieper, F., & Treue, S. (2006). Dynamic shifts of visual receptive fields in cortical area MT by spatial attention. *Nature Neuroscience, 9*, 1156–1160.

Yantis, S., & Jonides, J. (1984). Abrupt visual onsets and selective attention: Evidence from visual search. *Journal of Experimental Psychology: Human Perception and Performance, 10*, 601–621.

Yarbus, A. L. (1967). *Eye movements and vision*. New York: Plenum.

11

Visual Memory

There are many different aspects to visual memory. What most of us mean by memory is the recall of events that happened some time ago—visual long-term memory. If this is a recall that we are aware of, it is known as declarative memory. However, we also store habits and procedures without being aware that we have stored them—nondeclarative memory. Moreover, what we store over the first half second (visual sensory memory) is more than what we store over the first few seconds (visual short-term memory), which is different from what is stored for a long period of time. These differences are now known to be related to neural processes in different parts of the brain.

Visual Sensory Memory

Visual sensory memory occurs simply because the response of cells in the visual system outlasts the stimulus. Thus, the response of ganglion cells in the retina lasts 50–70 msec, even if the stimulus was a flash of light lasting 1 msec (Levick & Zacks, 1970). This is the reason that movies and TV sets, which are flickering at a rate of 60 frames per second, appear to be continuous. It can also be illustrated by flashing one pattern of dots followed by another, which may be recognized as letters if the flashes occur less than 100 msec apart, but not if separated by more than that (Fig. 11–1; Eriksen & Collins, 1967). Moreover, the left and right eye components of a random dot stereogram are seen in depth if the two displays are presented within 80 msec of each other, but not if the delay is more than that.

Visual Short-Term Memory

The average number of items that can be retained in short-term memory is four. However, if a cue is given, more short-term memory is available in the first second (Sperling, 1960). Subjects in Sperling's experiments were shown an array of 12 letters in three rows. They could remember 4–5 after 1 sec. During the first few hundred milliseconds, if prompted by a tone about the line to be remembered (high for the top line, medium for the middle line, and low for the bottom line),

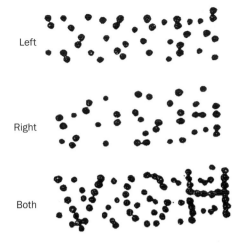

Left

Right

Both

FIGURE 11–1. Two patterns of dots (Left and Right) are presented to the two eyes. If seen rather less than 100 msec apart, the letters V, O and H appear (Both). If seen rather more than 100 msec apart, they are seen as a jumble of dots. (Reprinted from Eriksen & Collins, 1967, with kind permission of the American Psychological Association.)

they could remember up to 9 out of the 12, but this number decayed to approximately 4 after 1 sec.

The number of items retained is more than four if there are objects with more than one feature, such as objects that vary in color, orientation, size, and the presence of a gap in the line, with up to four possibilities for each feature (Luck & Vogel, 1997). The experiment is to present up to 12 items, wait 900 msec, then present the array again, either the same or with one item changed. The task is to say whether the array was changed or not. The performance depends on the number of objects presented, rather than the total number of features, which would be 16 if all features were considered separately (4 colors x 4 orientations—Fig. 11–2a, or 2 colors × 2 orientations × 2 sizes × gap or no gap—Fig. 11–2b).

In most of these experiments, there is a blank interval between the presentation of the stimulus to be remembered and the presentation of the test. If some other stimulus intervenes, it may disrupt the memory. In a simple form, this is known as masking (Averbach & Coriell, 1961). An array of 16 letters is presented, then after a variable interval, a bar marker is shown and the subject is asked to remember the letter underneath the bar marker (Fig. 11–3). If a circle is shown around a letter a little less than 100 msec after the presentation of the letters, this letter is masked or erased from memory.

This masking also occurs with a series of pictures presented sequentially. If 16 photographs are shown, and the observer is then shown one out of the sequence and asked if it was present, the answer depends very much on how fast the photographs are shown (Potter, 1976). At a rate of one per second, the recognition is very high. As the rate is increased to 3, 4, 6, or 8 per second, the performance drops precipitously. Masking finds a correlate in the temporal cortex, where the response persists for longer than the retinal response but is abolished by a subsequent image (Baylis & Rolls, 1987; Keysers, Xiao, Foldiak, & Perrett, 2005).

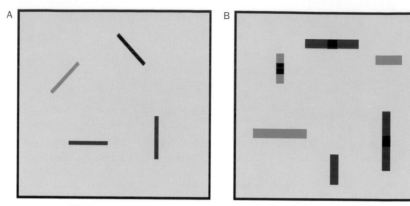

FIGURE 11–2. (*A*) Four objects with 16 possible features—one of four orientations, and one of four colors. (*B*) Six objects with 16 possible features—one of two orientations, one of two lengths, one of two colors, and gap or no gap. The task of the subject is to have such a display presented, followed by another display with one feature changed, and to say which object has changed. The performance depends on the number of objects, not the number of features. (Reprinted from Luck & Vogel, 1997, with kind permission of MacMillan Publishers.)

Memory From One Fixation to Another

The masking or erasure of the response to one stimulus by another one falling on the same part of the retina obviously plays a role in how snapshots of a scene are integrated between the fixation before a saccade and the fixation afterward. One needs to remember aspects of a scene from the first fixation in relation to the scene as seen in the second fixation, according to where they are in space rather than where they are on the retina. For this purpose, images falling on the same part of the retina need to be erased. As Irwin (1992, p.160) puts it, "Intuitively this perception (of a single stable scene as the eyes move around) would seem to require a detailed memory of the contents of the presaccadic fixation that could be combined with the postsaccadic fixation to render an integrated composite representation of the visual environment. It is possible, however, that this intuition is exactly backwards. The world may seem stable and continuous across eye movements not because integration occurs, but because very little is remembered from one fixation to the next."

After many years of research, it is still not completely clear exactly what does get remembered from one fixation to the next and what gets erased, or how the parts to be remembered are chosen. From the discussion of change blindness in Chapter 10, we know that many aspects are forgotten, and that directing one's attention can affect which ones. In the demonstration of the gorilla in the middle of a ball game, for example, the gorilla is not noticed by naïve observers but is immediately seen by observers who have viewed the demonstration before (see Chapter 10). Some overall appreciation of the scene as a whole is clearly stored, because in a task

FIGURE 11–3. Masking. The subject is presented with 16 letters and is asked to remember them, then recall the one under the bar marker. If a circle appears around a letter a little less than 100 msec after the letters are presented, then it is difficult to recall that letter.

involving making tea, for example, the sequence of saccades goes from one task in the scene to another without any mistaken saccades to other places not involved in the task (Land & Tatler, 2009; Fig. 11–4). However, not everything is remembered, as illustrated by asking a subject to describe the difference between two scenes that have one or two items altered (Irwin, 1992). The subjects look backward and forward between one scene and the other, rather than scan all over one scene and then transfer their attention to the other (Fig. 11–5). It appears that about five objects are remembered—the number stored in visual short-term memory—and that the ones most recently and most often foveated are remembered best (Irwin & Zelitsky, 2002; Pertzov, Avidan, & Zohary, 2009). However, there has to be some appreciation for objects in the periphery as well, to govern large saccades seen in the tasks that Land and Tatler describe. All one can really say is that the parietal cortex is involved, as expected from previous discussions of its role in attention and eye movements (Prime, Vesia, & Crawford, 2009).

Visual Long-Term Memory

We now come to memory as we usually think of it: the ability to recall events from the past. For example, we may remember that the last time we went to visit the village green, there was a fair going on, and we bought a book, then ate pancakes. This memory can be triggered by another visit to the village green, looking at the book that we bought, the smell of pancakes, or being reminded of it in conversation with members of the family. It is a complete memory of the whole event, with the various components of the event stored together in memory. We are aware of the event and its memory, and thus it is long-term declarative memory, in this case termed *episodic*, since it is a memory of a particular episode and is usually related to a particular date.

There is another kind of declarative memory called semantic. This is memory for general facts, such as that oranges are orange, apples are red or green, the sky is blue, and so on (Tulving, 1972). Items in episodic memory are remembered; items in semantic memory are known.

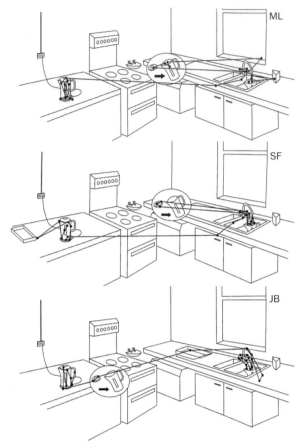

FIGURE 11–4. Fixations made by three subjects while filling a kettle prior to making a cup of tea. (Reprinted from Land & Tatler, 1999, with kind permission of Pion.)

Declarative memory can be extremely good. One study showed that subjects would recognize 60% of a set of 200 black-and-white photographs presented for 5 seconds each, even after a year (Nickerson, 1968), and in another study the results were even more surprising—86% of 10,000 photos presented for 5 seconds each were recognized (Standing, 1973). This is recognition, which means that it is not the whole scene that is remembered, just some aspect of it that enables one to recognize whether it was in the previously viewed set or not. The distinction becomes clear in an experiment from Rock and Engelstein (1959). They had subjects view a shape (shape 10 in Fig. 11–6), then some time later reproduce it, then pick out the shape that they remembered from an assortment of 10 shapes (Fig. 11–6). A group of judges evaluated whether the shape reproduced was like the original or not. Reproduction became very poor after a week or so, whereas recognition remained almost perfect for several weeks. However, in a more recent study, objects could be remembered compared to

FIGURE 11–5. Two sketches with a few small differences between them. One is not capable of taking in all of one sketch before looking at the other. To detect the differences, one has to shift one's gaze up and down between the two sketches.

the same object with a slightly different aspect (Brady, Konkle, Alvarez, & Oliva, 2008).

When an object and a background are presented together, both object and background are remembered better if they are consistent with each other (Davenport & Potter, 2004). For this experiment, the scene was presented for a short period of time—80 msec—followed by a mask. An item in the foreground was either consistent or inconsistent with the background. Subjects were then asked to name the object in the foreground in one experiment, and another set of subjects were asked to describe the nature of the background in another (Fig. 11–7). The result emphasizes the point made above that what is remembered is an overall impression of the scene rather than a lot of details. Some of these details can be filled in from the overall impression if the particular detail does not immediately come to mind.

Associations may be formed in memory. In the example given earlier, the village green, purchase of a book, eating of pancakes, and the event of a fair were all associated. Within visual memory, a priest in the foreground and church in the background are associated, which is why one remembers the priest better if the background is a church than if the background is a football field. One can also learn to associate shapes with each other over a period of training, even if there is no obvious association from previous experience. We will come back to this point in discussing where declarative memory is located in the brain.

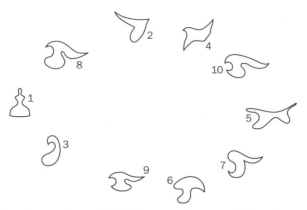

FIGURE 11–6. Ten shapes to be recalled. Subjects are shown one of them, for example, shape 10. When presented later with all 10 shapes as shown, they recognize which one they saw previously almost perfectly for several weeks. When asked to draw the shape that they first saw, their performance was not nearly as good, dropping dramatically over the first week. (Reprinted from Rock & Engelstein, 1959, with kind permission of the University of Illinois Press.)

Location of Memory

Memories are distributed all over the visual system, with components in occipital, parietal, temporal, and frontal cortices. Indeed, it seems that memories are stored in very much the same locations as those that originally gave rise to the perception, or at least in a network of neurons that includes them (see Farah, 1988; Fuster, 1997; Gaffan, 2002).

Traces of shorter term memories are found in occipital cortex. If subjects are presented with two gratings, one after the other, then with a third grating after a delay of several seconds, they can judge the orientation of the third grating in relation to the first two, and functional magnetic resonance imaging (fMRI) shows that activity in V1–V4 reflects this fact (Harrison & Tong, 2009). In another experiment, patients were shown a pattern of a few dots, followed after an interval by an arrow. They were asked to state whether the arrow pointed to one of the dots or not (Butter, Kosslyn, Mijovic-Prelec, & Riffle, 1997). Normal subjects could do this very well. Subjects with occipital lesions that made them blind in one half of the field of view were then asked to do it, with unrestricted vision of the pattern of dots in all parts of the field of view, followed by an arrow that might point to the blind half of the field of view or to the normal half. Their performance was better if the arrow pointed to the normal half. The task therefore depends on the integrity of occipital cortex as well as other areas of the visual system.

Correlates of longer term memories are found in temporal cortex (Sakai & Miyashita, 1991). Monkeys can be trained to associate 12 pairs of patterns (Fig. 11–8A). After weeks to months of training, their performance in recalling one member of a pair after the other is presented reaches more than 85%. Recordings

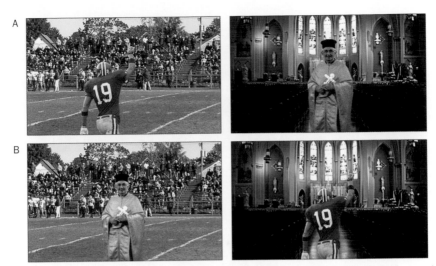

FIGURE 11–7. (*A*) In these two photographs, the foreground is consistent with the background. (*B*) In these two photographs the foregrounds have been switched, so that they are not consistent with the background. The foreground is remembered better when it is consistent, probably because one stores in memory an overall impression of the scene, rather than all the individual details. (Reprinted from Davenport & Potter, 2004, with kind permission of Sage Publications.)

then made in the temporal cortex show that there are neurons that respond to both members of a pair, but not to any members of the other pairs (Fig. 11–8B), or rather better than members of the other pairs (Fig. 11–8C). Such neurons are not found before the training starts.

While evidence that this association is found in temporal cortex is clear, memory of the association does not reside there, but is fed back from other structures (Higuchi & Miyashita, 1996). Monkeys can be trained to make the associations with one set A, and the associations show up in recordings in temporal cortex, as in the experiment mentioned earlier. Lesions are then made in entorhinal and perirhinal cortex, and the monkeys learn to make a new set of associations B and also relearn the original set A. The learning of both sets of associations is successful. However, at the end, correlates of neither set of associations are found in temporal cortex. Thus, the memory of the associations is fed back to temporal cortex from or through entorhinal and perirhinal cortices. The memory is also affected by top-down influences from frontal cortex (Tomita et al., 1999).

Neurons may learn to associate stimuli in one category with stimuli in another, even if the categories are usually dealt with in different areas of visual cortex. For example, macaques can learn to associate upward motion with an upward arrow, and downward motion with a downward arrow (Schlack & Albright, 2007; Fig. 11–9). In area MT, which is known to be specific for direction of motion, 86% of the neurons are selective for a particular direction of motion, but only 4%

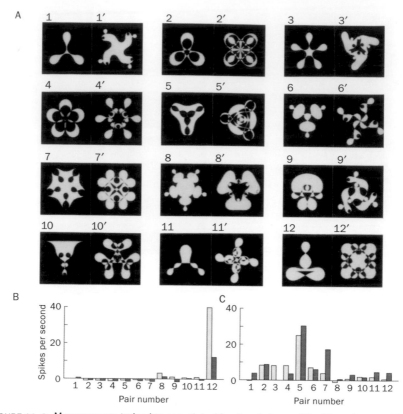

FIGURE 11–8. Macaques are trained to associate 12 pairs of shapes (*A*) with each other. After training, some cells in inferotemporal cortex fire strongly with either one of a shape pair, but not the others (*B*), and some cells fire better to one shape pair than the others (*C*). (Reprinted from Sakai & Miyashita, 1991, with kind permission of MacMillan Publishers.)

are selective for the direction of an arrow. After the macaques learned this association, the percentage of neurons selective for motion was unchanged but the percentage selective for direction of the arrow increased from 4% to 19%, and the strength of the selectivity increased. Indeed, macaques may also learn to associate motion in one direction with an arrow pointing in the opposite direction, and this is also reflected in the responses of MT neurons (Fig. 11–10).

Just as there are different perceptions dealt with in the "what" ventral pathway compared to the "where" dorsal pathway, so are there different memories dealt with in the two pathways. This is most clearly illustrated with lesions of the pathways. Levine et al. (1985) studied two patients, one with lesions in the temporal lobe, the other with lesions in the parieto-occipital area, in both cases bilateral. The first patient did not recognize faces, even his wife and doctors, and could not remember faces of famous people such as Winston Churchill and John F. Kennedy. However, he could get around Boston and Cambridge on his own, and he could describe the route from Harvard to the Massachusetts General Hospital

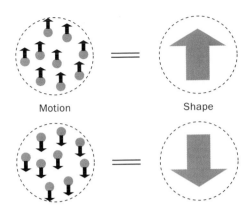

Motion   Shape

FIGURE 11–9. Neurons in MT normally respond to direction of motion (*left*). After the macaque learns to associate upward motion with an upward arrow, and downward motion with a downward arrow, these neurons start to respond to the arrow orientation as well (*right*). (Reprinted from Schlack & Albright, 2007, with kind permission of Cell Press.)

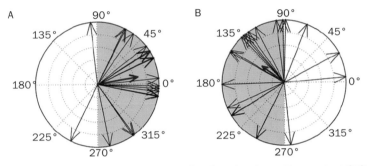

FIGURE 11–10. Macaque A learned to associate direction of motion with an arrow pointing in the same direction. (*A*) A representation of the difference in preferred direction between the moving stimuli and the stationary arrow. Each arrow gives the difference for one neuron in MT and shows an average close to 0 deg. (*B*) Macaque B learned to associate direction of motion with an arrow pointing in the opposite direction, and the difference in preferred directions for the two stimuli is close to 140 deg. (Reprinted from Schlack & Albright, 2007, with kind permission of Cell Press.)

in detail from memory. The second patient could identify faces, objects, and animals. When asked to describe these from memory, such as the features of his wife and his examiners, or a giraffe, he did quite adequately. However, he frequently got lost in his own house, and he could not describe how he used to get from his house to the corner grocery store, a trip that he had made several times a week for 5 years. The authors found a number of cases in the literature where both memory and perception of objects were deficient, but the ability to navigate in space and spatial memory were both preserved; they also found a number of cases of the reverse. All these patients had other problems, as is always true with lesions in the human brain, so the results were not always clean, but the general conclusion is clear: both perception and memory of the identity of objects involve the ventral pathway, whereas both perception and memory of where we are in space involve the dorsal pathway.

Consolidation of Memory

As pointed out earlier, the immediate perception of a scene can be erased or masked by the next stimulus. It may be remembered, but only if it is repeated or occurred in conjunction with a strong emotional response, and it depends on your state of attention. While the immediate perception is found in temporal cortex, working memory is found in prefrontal cortex. Thus, the memory trace in temporal cortex can be erased by a subsequent stimulus, but the memory trace in prefrontal cortex is not (Miller, Erickson, & Desimone, 1996). The process of turning immediate perception into working memory, then into a more permanent long-term memory, is known as consolidation.

The consolidation of memory and its anatomical location were brought out by one of the most famous subjects in neuroscience, known as HM. HM had a large part of his medial temporal lobes removed for intractable epilepsy. He could remember events that had happened a long time ago, but not events that had happened more recently—a phenomenon called amnesia (Milner, Whitty, & Zangwill, 1966). The extent of amnesia varies considerably with different patients, and with their lesions, the extreme case being a musician, Clive Wearing, who could not remember anything that happened recently, including his wife's face, for more than a minute (Sacks, 2007). The extent of amnesia also varies with the types of memory tested. However, what is clear is that the hippocampus and medial temporal lobes are involved in the formation of declarative memories, but that once a memory is formed and has been stored away for some time, many but not all types of memory remain (Corkin, 2002).

Another factor in the consolidation of memory is sleep. Abolition of rapid eye movement sleep (REM sleep) reduces the performance on a visual detection task (Fig. 11–11; Karni et al., 1994). This is nondeclarative memory (see later) rather than declarative memory, and whether the same point applies to declarative memory is ambiguous, but sleep has a positive effect on the consolidation of at least some forms of memory.

Once memories have been consolidated and stored, they can still be modified. This point has been known for a long time to lawyers and judges, and it is the reason that lawyers are not allowed to ask what are called leading questions, which are phrased in such a way as to suggest the answer. For example, a subject may be shown a movie of a car coming to an intersection with a road sign at it—either a stop sign or a yield sign (Loftus, Miller, & Burns, 1978). If asked a question with the words *stop sign* in it, then asked a week later whether the sign was a stop sign or a yield sign, they will tend to say "stop sign," and vice versa. So much for eyewitness testimony! There is also a tendency over a period of time for a memory to change in the direction of "goodness," which can mean various things, including simplification and consistency within the elements of the memory.

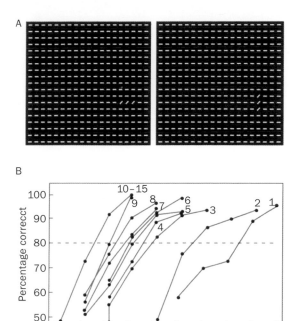

FIGURE 11–11. The subject fixates on the center of a display of horizontal lines, with three slated lines embedded (*A*). The task is to detect the orientation of the embedded lines. The task takes over 160 msec on the first day (*B*), and 50 msec on days 10–15 after practice every day. Performance on this task does not improve if the subject is deprived of sleep. (Reprinted from Karni et al., 1994, with kind permission of AAAS.)

Nondeclarative Memory

It was the study of HM that brought out the distinction between declarative and nondeclarative memory (Squire, 2009). HM was asked to trace a star, which was viewed in a mirror, keeping his pencil within the two lines that marked the boundary (Fig. 11–12a; Milner et al., 1966). At first, he made about 30 mistakes, counting the number of times that his pencil strayed outside the boundary. However, over the course of 3 days, his performance improved to fewer than 5 mistakes, and this level was retained (Fig. 11–12b). He was not aware that he had done the task before. This is a visuomotor skill, which takes everybody some time to learn (ask your dentist or dental hygienist). It was clearly not abolished by HM's lesion, and this is generally true in other people with amnesia. This experiment brought out two fundamental points: (*1*) that there is more than one kind of memory, and (*2*) that different kinds of memory are located in different places in the brain.

Another example of a visuomotor skill is the visuomotor adaptation discussed in Chapter 9, where a subject points at a target, then looks at the target through

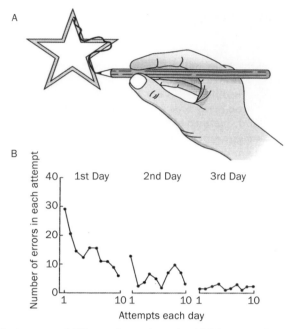

FIGURE 11–12. Performance of HM on a visuomotor task, which is to trace between the two lines forming the star, observing it through a mirror (*A*). There is distinct improvement between the first and third days (*B*). (Reprinted from Squire & Kandel, 2009, with kind permission of Roberts & Co.)

a prism that displaces the image on the retina sideways. Initially the darts are thrown to one side, but the aim becomes accurate over minutes. When the prisms are taken off, the aim is initially wrong in the reverse direction, and the adaptation goes away with the same time course (Held, 1965). So far as I know, this task has not been tried in amnesics, but the adaptation is abolished in patients with lesions of the inferior olive, which sends its projections to the cerebellum, and with lesions of various components of the posterior cerebellum (Martin, Keating, Goodkin, Bastian, & Thach, 1996).

Another form of nondeclarative memory involves learning an association by repetition, without being aware that one has learned it, sometimes known as habit learning. In one such task, subjects and patients were shown one, two, or three of a set of four cards, then asked to predict whether there was going to be rain or sunshine (Knowlton, Mangels, & Squire, 1996; Fig. 11–13). They were then told whether their answer was correct or not, accompanied by an icon of the correct response. Unknown to the subjects, the four cards were associated with rain 75%, 57%, 43%, or 25% of the time, and with sunshine 25%, 43%, 57%, and 75% of the time. For normal controls, the performance increased from 50% to 70% over 50 trials, and they were not aware of what was happening. Amnesic patients learned the task, whereas Parkinson disease patients with lesions of the neostriatum

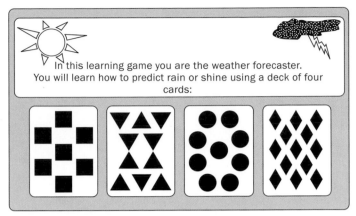

FIGURE 11–13. Weather forecasting task. Subject is shown one of the four cards, and asked whether it will be sunny or rainy. Unknown to the subject, the cards are associated with one prediction 25%, 43%, 57%, and 75% of the time, and with the other prediction the rest of the time. The probability that the subject will give the associated prediction improves with practice, although the subject is not aware of this. (Reprinted from Knowlton et al., 1996, with kind permission of AAAS.)

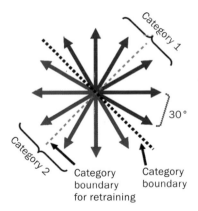

FIGURE 11–14. Macaques learn to put all the directions of motion shown in red in one category, and all the directions shown in blue in another. Neurons in LIP reflect this categorization, whereas neurons in MT do not. (Reprinted from Freedman & Assad, 2006, with kind permission of MacMillan Publishers.)

(caudate nucleus and putamen), and maybe frontal cortex, were deficient at the task but had normal declarative memory.

In some tests, the answer may be primed by previous exposure. Subjects can be presented with a list of 15 words, one every 3.5 sec, and asked to rate them on a scale of 1 to 5 according to how much they liked the meaning of the word. A little while later, they can then be presented with 20 word stems, such as GAR,

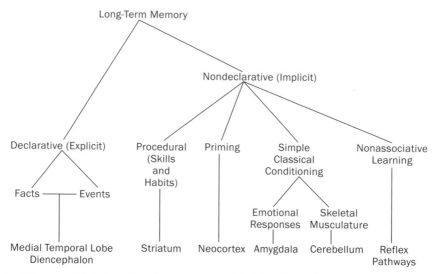

FIGURE 11–15. Categories of long-term memory and their location in the brain. (Reprinted from Squire & Knowlton, 1995, with kind permission of the National Academy of Sciences.)

of which 10 could be used to form a word and 10 could not. They are then asked to associate a word with each of the word stems. If the original list included the word GARNISH, they would tend to choose it. This type of task can be done by amnesic patients as well as normal subjects (Warrington & Weiskrantz, 1974), and in a brain scan, the task activates occipital and frontal cortex rather than the hippocampal area (Buckner et al., 1995).

Humans and primates can also learn to put stimuli into categories. For exam ple, macaques can be taught to group 12 directions of motion into two categories (Fig. 11–14). Neurons in the lateral intraparietal area (LIP) reflect this categoriza-tion, but neurons in MT (the area of temporal cortex dealing with direction of motion) do not (Freedman & Assad, 2006). Amnesic patients can perform such categorization tasks (Squire & Knowlton, 1995). Thus, this is one more example of nondeclarative memory, located this time in parietal cortex.

Another form of memory is called perceptual learning (Karni & Sagi, 1991). This was referred to earlier, as an example of how sleep helps the consolidation of memory. Subjects learn to discriminate a horizontal group of three lines from a vertical group of them in one quadrant of the field of view (Fig. 11–11). The ability to do this improves with practice, from a latency of 170 msec to a latency of 50 msec, over a period of days. The likely location for this form of memory is areas V1 and V2 in occipital cortex (Squire & Kandel, 2009, p. 183). Another example is the learning of direction of an arrow with direction of motion, referred to earlier, which is associated with activity in the visual part of the parietal cortex, LIP.

Finally, there is the emotional component to memory. Clive Wearing, men-tioned earlier, could not describe his wife's face, or even that she had been there a few minutes ago, but when he was looking directly at her, he had a definite positive emotional reaction (Sacks, 2007). As mentioned in Chapter 7, there are separate areas for the recognition and the emotional content of faces in the inferior temporal cortex. The amygdala is important for emotions, and this is spared in amnesic patients such as Clive Wearing (Squire & Kandel, 2009)

References

Averbach, E, & Coriell, A. (1961). Short-term memory in vision. *Bell Systems Technical Journal, 40,* 309–328.

Baylis, G. C., & Rolls, E. T. (1987). Responses of neurons in the inferior temporal cortex in short term and serial recognition memory tasks. *Experimental Brain Research, 65,* 614–622.

Brady, T. F., Konkle, T., Alvarez, G. A., & Oliva, A. (2008). Visual long-term memory has a massive storage capacity for object details. *Proceedings of the National Academy of Sciences USA, 105,* 14325–14329.

Buckner, R. L., Petersen, S. E., Ojemann, J. G., Miezin, F. M., Squire, L. R., & Raichle, M. E. (1995). Functional anatomical studies of explicit and implicit memory retrieval tasks. *Journal of Neuroscience, 15,* 12–29.

Butter, C. M., Kosslyn, S., Mijovic-Prelec, D., & Riffle, A. (1997). Field-specific deficits in visual imagery following hemianopia due to unilateral occipital infarcts. *Brain, 120*(Pt. 2), 217–228.

Corkin, S. (2002). What's new with the amnesic patient H.M.? *Nature Reviews Neuroscience, 3,* 1–8.

Davenport, J. L., & Potter, M. C. (2004). Scene consistency in object and background perception. *Psychological Science, 15,* 559–564.

Eriksen, C. W., & Collins, J. F. (1967). Some temporal characteristics of visual pattern perception. *Journal of Experimental Psychology, 74,* 476–484.

Farah, M. J. (1988). Is visual imagery really visual? Overlooked evidence from neuropsychology. *Psychological Review, 95,* 307–317.

Freedman, D. J., & Assad, J. A. (2006). Experience-dependent representation of visual categories in parietal cortex. *Nature, 443,* 85–88.

Fuster, J. M. (1997). Network memory. *Trends in Neuroscience, 20,* 451–459.

Gaffan, D. (2002). Against memory systems. *Philosophical Transactions of the Royal Society of London B: Biological Sciences, 357,* 1111–1121.

Harrison, S. A., & Tong, F. (2009). Decoding reveals the contents of visual working memory in early visual areas. *Nature, 458,* 632–635.

Held, R. (1965). Plasticity in sensory-motor systems. *Scientific American, 213,* 84–94.

Higuchi, S., & Miyashita, Y. (1996). Formation of mnemonic neuronal responses to visual paired associates in inferotemporal cortex is impaired by perirhinal and entorhinal lesions. *Proceedings of the National Academy of Sciences USA, 93,* 739–743.

Irwin, D. E. (1992). Visual memory within and across fixations. In K. Rayner (Ed.), *Eye movements and cognition: Perception and reading* (pp. 116–135). New York: Springer-Verlag.

Irwin, D. E., & Zelitsky, G. J. (2002). Eye movement and scene perception: Memory for things observed. *Perception and Psychophysics, 64,* 882–895.

Karni, A., & Sagi, D. (1991). Where practice makes perfect in texture discrimination: Evidence for primary visual cortex plasticity. *Proceedings of the National Academy of Sciences USA, 88,* 4966–4970.

Karni, A., Tanne, D., Rubenstein, B. S., Askenasy, J. J., & Sagi, D. (1994). Dependence on REM sleep of overnight improvement of a perceptual skill. *Science, 265,* 679–682.

Keysers, C., Xiao, D-K., Foldiak, P., & Perrett, D. I. (2005). Out of sight but not out of mind: The neuropsychology of iconic memory in the superior temporal sulcus. *Cognitive Neuropsychology, 22,* 316–332.

Knowlton, B. J., Mangels, J. A., & Squire, L. R. (1996). A neostriatal habit learning system in humans. *Science, 273,* 1399–1402.

Land, M. F., & Tatler, B. W. (2009). *Looking and seeing.* New York: Oxford University Press.

Levick, W. R., & Zacks, J. L. (1970). Responses of cat retinal ganglion cells to brief flashes of light. *Journal of Physiology, 206,* 677–700.

Levine, D. N., Warach, J., & Farah, M. (1985). Two visual systems in mental imagery: Dissociation of "what" and "where" in imagery disorders due to bilateral posterior cerebral lesions. *Neurology, 35,* 1010–1018.

Loftus, E. F., Miller, D. G., & Burns, H. J. (1978). Semantic integration of verbal information into a visual memory. *Journal of Experimental Psychology: Human Learning and Memory, 4,* 19–31.

Luck, S. J., & Vogel, E. K. (1997). The capacity of visual working memory for features and conjunctions. *Nature, 390,* 279–281.

Martin, T. A., Keating, J. G., Goodkin, H. P., Bastian, A. J., & Thach, W. T. (1996). Throwing while looking through prisms. *Brain, 119,* 1183–1198.

Miller, E. K., Erickson, C. A., & Desimone, R. (1996). Neural mechanisms of visual working memory in prefrontal cortex of the macaque. *Journal of Neuroscience, 16,* 5154–5167.

Milner, B., Whitty, C. W. M., & Zangwill, O. L. (1966). Amnesia following operation on the temporal lobes. In C. W. M. Whitty & O. L. Zangwill (Eds.), *Amnesia* (pp. 109–133). London: Butterworths.

Nickerson, S. R. (1968). A note on long-term recognition memory for pictorial material. *Psychonomic Science, 11,* 58.

Pertzov, Y., Avidan, G., & Zohary, E. (2009). Accumulation of visual information across multiple fixations. *Journal of Vision, 9*(10), 2, 1–12.

Potter, M. C. (1976). Short-term conceptual memory for pictures. *Journal of Experimental Psychology: Human Learning and Memory, 2,* 509–522.

Prime, S. L., Vesia, M., & Crawford, J. D. (2009). TMS over human frontal eye fields disrupts trans-saccadic memory of multiple objects. *Cerebral Cortex, 20,* 759–772.

Rock, I., & Engelstein, P. (1959). A study of memory for visual form. *American Journal of Psychology, 72,* 221–229.

Sacks, O. (2007, September 24). The abyss. *The New Yorker,* pp. 100–113.

Sakai, K., & Miyashita, Y. (1991). Neural organization for the long-term memory of paired associates. *Nature, 354,* 152–155.

Schlack, A., & Albright, T. D. (2007). Remembering visual motion: Neural correlates of associative plasticity and motion recall in cortical area MT. *Neuron, 53,* 881–890.

Sperling, G. (1960). The information available in brief visual presentations. *Psychological Monographs, 74,* 1–29.

Squire, L., & Kandel, E. R. (2009). *Memory from mind to molecules.* Greenwood Village, CO: Roberts & Co.

Squire, L. R. (2009). The legacy of patient H.M. for neuroscience. *Neuron, 61*, 6–9.

Squire, L. R., & Knowlton, B. J. (1995). Learning about categories in the absence of memory. *Proceedings of the National Academy of Sciences USA, 92*, 12470–12474.

Standing, I. (1973). Learning 10,000 pictures. *Quarterly Journal of Experimental Psychology, 25*, 207–222.

Tomita, H., Ohbayashi, M., Nakahara, K., Hasegawa, I., & Miyashita, Y. (1999). Top-down signal from prefrontal cortex in executive control of memory retrieval. *Nature, 401*, 699–703.

Tulving, E. (1972). Episodic and semantic memory. In E. Tulving & W. Donaldson (Eds.), *Organization of memory* (pp. 382–403). New York: Academic Press.

Warrington, E. K., & Weiskrantz, L. (1974). The effect of prior learning on subsequent retention in amnesic patients. *Neuropsychologia, 12*, 419–428.

12

Summary

In summary, the visual system is very efficiently organized to recognize objects, to pick out the ones that need attention, to decide whether they should be grasped or avoided, to remember them, and to do all of this in a brief moment of time. To accomplish this, different aspects are analyzed in different areas of the system, and in different clusters or columns within those areas.

Organization of the Visual System

Within the visual system, there are separate pathways that run parallel to each other. The "where" pathway starts in the retina with M cells, which are particularly sensitive to movement of a stimulus. These project to the M layers of the lateral geniculate nucleus, then to layers IVCα and layer IVB in V1, then to the thick stripes in V2, then to V5 (also called MT), and on to parietal cortex. Parietal cortex determines the salience of an object and passes a signal to frontal cortex to move the eyes to look at an object judged to be salient. Frontal cortex then instructs the eye muscles through the superior colliculus and brainstem.

The "what" pathway starts with the P cells in the retina, which project to the P layers in the lateral geniculate nucleus, layers IVCβ, III, and II in V1, then to the thin stripes and pale stripes in V2, then to V4, then to various areas in lateral occipital and temporal cortex. Within the "what" pathway there are two streams, one including the blobs in V1, the thin stripes in V2, and some parts of V4, which is more concerned with color; the other including the interblobs in V1, the pale stripes in V2, and other parts of V4, which is more concerned with form. These pathways are not totally separate; there are connections between them. However, there is no doubt that some lesions in the human brain affect primarily color vision, whereas others affect primarily motion perception, and psychophysical experiments support the division into parallel pathways.

Visual cortex is organized into a columnar system. In V1, there are columns for ocular dominance, orientation of the stimulus, and color versus form, and similarly in V2 with stripes rather than columns. V4 has columns for color versus form. V5 has columns for direction of movement, and separate areas deal with near and far depth.

The various areas of cortex can be arranged into a hierarchy by the anatomical nature of the connections between them, and the latencies of response. The primary projections go from lower areas to higher areas in the hierarchy, but there are also feedback projections from higher areas to lower ones. As one goes up the hierarchy, the cells respond to more specific aspects of the stimulus and receive input from a wider area of the retina. The function of the feedback connections is not fully understood, but part of it may be to bring in influences from a wider area than the direct projections.

Brightness and Contrast

The perception of the lightness of an object depends on contrast with the immediate surround and also with interactions with objects further away. In most situations, this results in a perception where lightness is closely related to the reflectance of the object, helping us to both recognize objects independent of the overall level of illumination and to recognize what other objects are placed around the primary object. If there is a shadow, or a boundary of illumination in the field, or other transparent objects floating in front, these are usually seen as such, again enabling the perception of objects.

The first step in lightness perception is that cells in the visual system respond to contrast, both contrast with the immediate surround in the retina and lateral geniculate nucleus, and with areas further away in primary visual cortex. Sharp boundaries are recognized, and slow variations of luminance or reflectance across an object may be ignored, which correlates with the response of some cells in V2. Where and how the effects of edges of illumination (shadows) and transparency are assessed, and ignored in the perception of the lightness of an object, is not yet understood.

Color Vision

Color vision in humans is trichromatic due to three types of cone photoreceptors with different spectral sensitivities. These cones feed into opponent color cells in the retina, which are either red opposed by green or yellow opposed by blue. These in turn project through the lateral geniculate nucleus to double opponent cells in primary visual cortex, which respond to contrasting colors. Color cells in primary visual cortex project to cells in V2, then to V4. It seems likely that cells in V4 give responses appropriate to color constancy. V4 and inferotemporal cortex (IT) form a large area with patches concerned with color. In all these areas in the cortex, there are columns of cells specific for color interspersed with columns of cells specific for orientation or patterns and columns specific for both. There is an area in humans which, if lesioned, makes everything look gray (achromatopsia). This corresponds to a region in macaques that includes V4 and some temporal cortex. The visual system is also capable of distinguishing boundaries of illumination from boundaries between objects, but how and where this is coded in the brain is not known.

Perception of Motion

Motion of an object is seen relative to other objects, particularly those around it, and is affected by the eye movements made as the observer looks around the scene. An object flashed in one position, followed by being flashed in another position, may be seen as moving between the two positions. In the analysis of motion by the visual system, lower areas process the motion of components of the object, and higher areas process the motion of the object as a whole. The perception of motion is also affected by the perception of depth—that is, when two objects are at the same depth, they are seen to move relative to each other, but when they are at different depths, they may be seen to move independently of each other. Particularly interesting is that a human or an animal moving with lights attached to its limbs is perceived as a human or an animal, even if only the lights are visible. The system may even detect the difference between a man and a woman in this situation.

Motion is analyzed in the dorsal pathway, particularly in areas such as MT (V5) and MST. MT brings together signals about motion and signals about depth. Cells in this area respond to differences in velocity in the two eyes and to changes in disparity, both of which are signals for motion in depth, toward or away from the observer. MST contains cells responding to optic flow, where the whole scene moves toward or away from the observer, and by combining these signals with signals from the vestibular system about movement in space, gives a perception of where the observer is headed. MT and MST also make a distinction between local motion (motion of an object in relation to objects around it, giving the perception of movement of objects) and global motion (movement of the scene as a whole, giving the perception of heading of the observer). This is dealt with by different bands of cells in MT and different areas of MST.

Depth Perception

Depth perception is a hard problem for the visual system, because it must all be reconstructed from the two-dimensional images on the two retinas. Thus, depth is extracted from the retinal images using a variety of cues, the most important of which is disparity. It is processed in a wide variety of areas of the brain. This corresponds to its involvement in the shape and contours of objects, location of objects in depth, and control of vergence eye movements. It is represented on both dorsal and ventral pathways, as expected from its function, and in eye movement areas. There are interactions between depth cues and other properties such as contours and movement, so that depth cues can help to define these other properties. Numerous psychophysical results find a parallel in the response of single units in the various areas of the visual cortex.

Investigations of physiological processes in the brain have been dominated by disparity stimuli leading to stereopsis. A few have used stimuli for motion parallax, motion in depth, structure from motion, and superposition. None have investigated the other cues—accommodation and convergence, perspective, texture gradients, and shading—because the experiments are extremely difficult. Not very many have worked on how the cues are brought together or where this occurs. Nevertheless, an enormous amount has been learned over the past 50 years, leading to a real appreciation of how the whole system works.

Objects and Faces

Objects and faces are analyzed at a series of levels within the visual system, with the cells responding to increasingly complex features of the stimulus as we move from the retina and lateral geniculate to the visual cortex to other areas within occipital cortex and areas within temporal cortex. The retina and lateral geniculate respond to spots of light; V1 and V2 respond to edges defined by depth, texture, movement, and completion as well as luminance; V4 responds to geometrical shapes and maybe other aspects of the stimulus; and temporal cortex responds to complete objects and shapes and faces. An object is represented at each level by activity in a number of cells over a number of columns within the area—distributed coding of objects, rather than grandmother cells signaling each object.

The general picture of this coding, initially established based on single-neuron recordings from animals, has been more recently replicated using modern techniques—functional magnetic resonance imaging (fMRI) recordings in humans and optical imaging in macaque monkeys. How connections within the various levels of the system converge to produce these results remains to be worked out, and it will be best tackled in the macaque with a combination of fMRI, single-unit recording, and anatomy after the homologies between macaque and human have been established (Moeller, Freiwald, & Tsao, 2008).

Control of Eye Movements

The eye movement system consists of two types of movement for placing the object to be inspected on the fovea: saccades and vergence movements. Fixation holds the object on the fovea, once it has been acquired. Smooth pursuit eye movements keep the object on the fovea when it moves in relation to the rest of the scene. The optokinetic response and the vestibular-ocular response combine to keep the image on the fovea when the whole world moves around us and when the head moves.

There is a system for deciding which object is going to be the next to be inspected. There is also a system for holding the visual image stationary so that, as the eyes make saccades around a scene, the snapshots of each section of the scene integrate into a single view.

Broadly speaking, the system to accomplish all of this can be divided into two parts. First is the part located in the occipital, parietal, and frontal cortices, and in the cerebellum and superior colliculus. All of this together determines when and whether to make a saccade, the size and direction of the saccade, when to hold the eyes fixed on an object, and how to keep the eyes fixated on a moving object for a smooth eye movement. It used to be thought that these different parts of the brain deal with different eye movements, but it is now clear that they all deal with all eye movements and there are subareas within them to deal with the different types of eye movement. Formerly it was believed that occipital cortex passes signals to parietal and frontal cortex, and these in turn project to superior colliculus and cerebellum in a hierarchical fashion. It is now known that all the areas are interconnected with some redundancy and numerous feedback pathways, so that the system is not strictly hierarchical; one can destroy one part of it to produce deficient eye movements but not a total loss.

The second part consists of the brainstem nuclei. The higher areas specify the amplitude and direction of a saccade and the velocity for a smooth pursuit movement. This gets translated in the brainstem to specific signals for specific eye muscles, which is not a simple procedure.

Adaptation and Aftereffects

The visual system adapts to a wide variety of different situations: brightness, color, contrast, motion, orientation, depth, and faces. It will also adapt to combinations of these attributes, and to changes in the coordination of vision and the position of the limbs. It is even possible to transpose the whole world on the retina—up-down, left-right, or both—and nonetheless, after a week or two, manage to navigate around. There are visuomotor components to these adaptations and also visual components. This amazing ability involves changes in the properties of the cells that code for the various properties, which are of course located in various parts of the visual and visuomotor systems.

Attention

Attention is what enables us to isolate and notice salient aspects of a scene, as we look around it with a series of saccades, and put them together into a representation of the whole scene. What gets noticed will depend on whether there is anything unusual about an object. The items also depend on our purpose in looking around the scene, and they are influenced by any instructions given to us. In the jargon of the field, there are both bottom-up and top-down influences. Inevitably, a number of items do not get noticed: if they all were, the system would be completely overloaded (hence the unreliability of eyewitness evidence).

The responses of cells at all levels of the system are increased by attention. Some of this comes from the frontal eye fields, where some cells respond to attention as it leads to an eye movement, and some respond even if an eye movement is not made (overt vs. covert attention). Even the superior colliculus is involved. (Which cells at higher levels feed top-down input to the frontal eye field neurons is not yet known.) Thus, lesions at all levels of the system also affect attention. However, those in visual cortex also affect other sensory functions, and those in eye movement cortex also affect eye movements. It is lesions of parietal or temporal cortex that give what is known as pure neglect.

Visual Memory

There are many different forms of visual memory, short term and long term. What we normally think of as memory—events that can be stored away and recalled (episodic memory), and general associations and facts that we come to know from experience (semantic memory)—are formed and consolidated through the medial temporal lobe, which includes the hippocampus and nearby areas, such as entorhinal, perirhinal, and parahippocampal cortex. They are then stored over all parts of the visual system, generally in the same areas that gave rise to the perception in the first place. There are a number of other forms of memory that we are not aware of, grouped together under the heading of nondeclarative memory. These include skills, habits, priming, perceptual learning, and emotions associated with visual images. Amnesic patients who have lesions of the medial temporal area generally have nondeclarative memories. Lesions that may affect various forms of nondeclarative memory are lesions in the striatum, cerebellum, neocortex, and amygdala.

All of this shows that the visual system is an amazing phenomenon. It can take in 100 million bits of information through the photoreceptors of the retina. It can direct the eyes to look at any object that seems to be of interest, when deciding what is of interest can be a major task. It can deduce the lightness and color of an object, ignoring the intensity and wavelengths of the illumination of the object. It can detect motion of an object, distinguishing this from motion of the body through the environment to give a percept of where one is headed. It can detect the distance of an object in relation to other objects, and in relation to the point of view of the observer. It can recognize thousands of faces, as well as thousands of other objects after practice. In some cases the perception does not correspond to the actual situation in the world, but these illusions are the exception rather than the rule and have attracted attention primarily because they are exceptional. And it can do all of this in a fraction of a second. Incredible!

Reference

Moeller, S., Freiwald, W. A., & Tsao, D. Y. (2008). Patches with links: a unified system for processing faces in the macaque temporal lobe. Science 320:1355-1359.

APPENDIX

Circadian Rhythms and Pupillary Reflex

Some important aspects of vision do not involve seeing. Because they have to do with the perception of light rather than the seeing of objects, these are called non-image-forming aspects of vision. They include circadian rhythms of various functions in the body, and the pupillary light reflex.

Circadian rhythms are rhythms that vary daily, occurring on an approximately 24-hour cycle. They include the sleep-wake cycle, activity, feeding, drinking, body temperature, effect of liver enzymes on glycogenesis, a cycle in the pineal hormone melatonin, and sex. A particularly useful circadian rhythm for the purpose of experiments is the cycle of activity in rodents (Richter, 1967). Nocturnal rodents run at night—sometimes 30 or 40 miles per night on wheels in their cages. This activity can be monitored on an activity meter. If the rat is blinded, then it continues to run on a cycle that is approximately, but not exactly, 24 hours: some rats will start running a little earlier each day, and some a little later each day, but each one will keep a regular cycle for months after blinding. If the animal is kept continually in the dark, the same result occurs, and the cycle can be reset by a pulse of light.

These results show that there is an oscillator somewhere in the brain that keeps the approximately 24-hour cycle, and it can be reset, or entrained by light. Lesions of the adrenal glands and hypophysis do not affect the cycles, nor do starvation, dehydration, hypothermia, changes of respiration or heartbeat, or application of various drugs (Richter, 1967). The rhythm is there in congenitally blind rodents and in humans. Lesions of various parts of the image-forming visual system do not affect it either: the crucial area that does is the suprachiasmatic nucleus in the hypothalamus (SCN), demonstrated by lesions of this nucleus, or of the projections from it by a lesion just behind it, which abolish the circadian rhythm (Stephan & Zucker, 1972). The point is buttressed by experiments in Syrian hamsters, where a mutant of the tau gene changes the period from 24 hours to 20 hours. An isolated cultured SCN shows an endogenous rhythm, and deletion of the SCN in normal hamsters, followed by implantation of a SCN from a tau mutant hamster, changes the period from normal to the tau period of 20 hours, and vice versa (Ralph, Foster, Davis, & Menaker, 1990). Thus, there must be an endogenous clock in the SCN.

The clock in the SCN consists of a number of genes that feed back on each other. The prime genes in the nucleus are the period genes (Per1, Per2, and Per3) and the cryptochrome genes (Cry1 and Cry2). These genes are activated by a heterodimer of two transcription factors, CLOCK and BMAL1 (Reppert & Weaver, 2002). The proteins produced by the period and cryptochrome genes eventually migrate from the cytoplasm back to the nucleus, where they inhibit the transcription by CLOCK and BMAL1 in a negative feedback loop (Fig. Appx–1). The system is complicated by a number of other genes and feedback loops, but this is the essential mechanism. There are some 20,000 cells in the SCN, and the clocks in each of them are synchronized by neurotransmitter interactions to produce a cycle for the whole nucleus. There are also clocks located in other tissues, such as the liver, that the SCN influences through neural or humoral effects. Some of them may keep cycling for 3 weeks or more in isolation, as long as the culture is maintained, but the rhythm is controlled by the SCN in the intact system (Nishide et al., 2006). There is also a circadian clock in the retina; it controls the

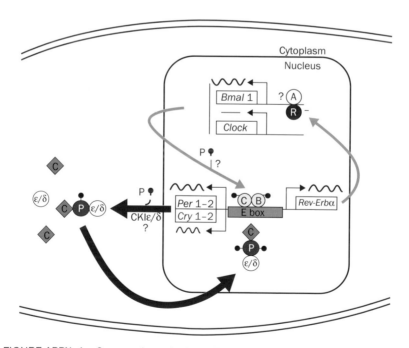

FIGURE APPX–1.   Genes and proteins in the SCN clock. Period genes and cryptochrome genes are activated by a dimer Clock and Bmal1 through the Ebox enhancer. As they accumulate, the period and cryptochrome proteins return to the nucleus to inhibit this transcription. (Reprinted from Reppert & Weaver, 2002, with kind permission of MacMillan Publishers.)

diurnal shedding of the discs in the photoreceptors, and release of dopamine and melatonin in the retina. This rhythm is not controlled by the SCN (Ruan, Allen, Yamazaki, & McMahon, 2008; Storch et al., 2007).

The clock in the SCN is entrained by input from the retina. This is direct via the retinohypothalamic tract (RHT) and also indirect through the intergeniculate leaflet within the lateral geniculate nucleus, via the geniculohypothalamic tract. Interestingly, this entrainment continues in the absence of the rod and cone photoreceptors (Freedman et al., 1999). This persistent photic influence on the SCN is mediated by a special class of ganglion cells, about 1%–2% of the total, called ipRGCs, that are capable of independent phototransduction (Berson, Dunn, & Takao, 2002). This sensitivity arises from their unique photopigment, melanopsin. Rods and, to a smaller extent, cones also excite these ganglion cells and contribute to the circadian entrainment. However, all photic influence on the clock seems to pass through the ipRGCs: ablating them abolishes entrainment altogether (Altimus et al., 2009; Guler, 2008). These ganglion cells give very sustained and sluggish responses with a long latency, and they have large receptive fields. The cells in the SCN have similar responses, and the intensity range of the response is narrow, from daylight to 100 times that, appropriately for their function (Groos & Mason, 1980). Both these points may be modified when the rod and cone input is active.

One of the targets of the SCN is the pineal gland, which produces melatonin (Moore & Klein, 1974). Melatonin rises in the evening and declines in the morning (Illnerova, 1991). Thus, melatonin is a component in several sleep medicines and jet lag pills. Melatonin in turn affects the SCN in another feedback loop. Other targets of the SCN are various regions of the hypothalamus nearby, which affect feeding, drinking, and sex (Rosenwasser, 2009). Thus, changes in the photoperiod from 16 hours light and 8 hours dark to 8 hours light and 16 hours dark affect sexual activity and the clock genes in the SCN (Tournier, Birkenstock, Pevet, & Vuillez, 2009).

Different animals have different sexual cycles, from short ones in rodents to annual ones in sheep. This is of particular interest to sheep breeders, who move their animals from the northern hemisphere to the southern hemisphere, for example from England to Australia. Such animals must change their breeding cycle by 6 months if they wish to continue to conceive in the fall and deliver in the spring. Changes in melatonin levels, as the day length shortens in the fall and lengthens again in the spring, control this cycle by acting on the pituitary (Dupre et al., 2008; Karsch et al., 1991).

Pupillary Light Reflex

The pupillary light reflex is also abolished by ablation of the ganglion cells containing melanopsin (Guler et al., 2008). This occurs through projections of these cells to the olivary pretectal nucleus (OPN) in the pretectum (Hattar et al., 2002).

Experiments in a variety of animals, including humans, show that there are different components to the pupillary light reflex, depending on the level of illumination (Gamlin et al., 2007; Lucas et al., 2003). In dim light this is due to rods, in moderate light levels to melanopsin as well as rods and cones, and at bright light levels to cones. When melanopsin is involved, it leads to a slow component to the reflex, because melanopsin is an invertebrate photopigment (Mure et al., 2009; Young & Kimura, 2008) and also because there is a different action spectrum (Lucas, Douglas, & Foster, 2001).

Human Disorders

The importance of circadian rhythms controlled by the SCN is emphasized by the variety of disorders that occur in disruptions of circadian rhythms (Moore, 1991). First, of course, is jet lag and "graveyard" work shifts. These lead to a feeling of sleepiness, fatigue, periods of inattentiveness during the waking period, and partial insomnia during the sleep period. Some individuals also tend to go to sleep early, like rodents with cycles less than 24 hours, and some go to sleep late, like rodents with cycles greater than 24 hours. Others have irregular sleep periods, like rodents that do not entrain to a 24-hour period. Moreover, retinally blind subjects who are missing the ipRGCs have free running circadian rhythms, leading to a mismatch between their clocks and the rest of society, which is a major complaint of the blind population.

Another problem is seasonal affective disorder (SAD). Individuals with SAD exhibit sadness, anxiety, irritability, and decreased energy in the winter. Exposure of such individuals to a bright light during the daytime can improve the symptoms.

Finally, older people tend to go to sleep earlier than younger ones, awaken earlier, and nap during the daytime. Whether this is related to a change in their SCN clock is not known.

References

Altimus, C. M., Guler, A. D., Villa, K. L., McNeill, D. S., Legates, T. A., & Hattar, S. (2008). Rods-cones and melanopsin detect light and dark to modulate sleep independent of image formation. *Proceedings of the National Academy of Sciences USA, 105,* 19998–20003.

Berson, D. M., Dunn, F. A., & Takao, M. (2002). Phototransduction by retinal ganglion cells that set the circadian clock. *Science, 295,* 1070–1073.

Dupre, S. M., Burt, D. W., Talbot, R., Downing, A., Mouzaki, D., Waddington, D., Malpaux, B., Davis, J. R., Lincoln, G. A., Loudon, A. S. (2008). Identification of melatonin-regulated genes in the ovine pituitary pars tuberalis, a target site for seasonal hormone control. *Endocrinology, 149,* 5527–5539.

Freedman, M. S., Lucas, R. J., Soni, B., von Schantz, M., Munoz, M., David-Gray, Z., & Foster, R. (1999). Regulation of mammalian circadian behavior by non-rod, non-cone, ocular photoreceptors. *Science, 284*, 502–504.

Gamlin, P. D., McDougal, D. H., Pokorny, J., Smith, V. C., Yau, K. W., & Dacey, D. M. (2007). Human and macaque pupil responses driven by melanopsin-containing retinal ganglion cells. *Vision Research, 47*, 946–954.

Groos, G. A., & Mason, R. (1980). The visual properties of rat and cat suprachiasmatic neurons. *Journal of Comparative Physiology, 135*, 349–356.

Guler, A. D., Ecker, J. L., Lall, G. S., Haq, S., Altimus, C. M, Liao, H. W., Barnard, A. R., Cahill, H., Badea, T. C., Zhao, H., Hankins, M. W., Berson, D. M., Lucas, R. J., Yau, K. W., Hattar, S. (2008). Melanopsin cells are the principal conduits for rod-cone input to non-image-forming vision. *Nature, 453*, 102–105.

Hattar, S., Liao, H. W., Takao, M., Berson, D. M., & Yau, K. W. (2002). Melanopsin-containing retinal ganglion cells: architecture, projections, and intrinsic photosensitivity. *Science, 295*, 1065–1070.

Illnerova, H. (1991). The suprachismatic nucleus and rhythmic melatonin production. In D. C. Klein, R. Y. Moore, & S. M. Reppert (Eds.), *Suprachiasmatic nucleus* (pp. 197–216). New York: Oxford University Press.

Karsch, F. J., Woodfill, C. J. I., Malpaux, B., Robinson, J. E., & Wayne, N. E. (1991). Melatonin and mammalian photoperiodism: Synchronization of annual reproductive cycles. In D. C. Klein, R. Y. Moore, & S. M. Reppert (Eds.), *Suprachiasmatic nucleus* (pp. 217–232). New York: Oxford University Press.

Lucas, R. J., Douglas, R. H., & Foster, R. G. (2001). Characterization of an ocular photopigment capable of driving pupillary constriction in mice. *Nature Neuroscience, 4*, 621–626.

Lucas, R. J., Hattar, S., Takao, M., Berson, D. M., Foster, R. G., Yau, K. W. (2003). Diminished pupillary light reflex at high irradiances in melanopsin-knockout mice. *Science, 299*, 245–247.

Moore, R. Y. (1991). Disorders of circadian function and the human circadian timing system. In D. C. Klein, R. Y. Moore, & S. M. Reppert (Eds.), *Suprachiasmatic nucleus* (pp. 429–442). New York: Oxford University Press.

Moore, R. Y., & Klein, D. C. (1974). Visual pathways and the central neural control of a circadian rhythm in pineal serotonin N-acetyltransferase activity. *Brain Research, 71*, 17–33.

Mure, L. S., Cornut, P. L., Rieux, C., Drouyer, E., Denis, P., Gronfier, C., & Cooper, H. M. (2009). Melanopsin bistability: A fly's eye technology in the human retina. *PLoS One, 4*, e5991.

Nishide, S. Y., Honma, S., Nakajima, Y., Ikeda, M., Baba, K., Ohmiya, Y., & Honma, K. (2006). New reporter system for Per1 and Bmal1 expressions revealed self-sustained circadian rhythms in peripheral tissues. *Genes Cells, 11*, 1173–1182.

Ralph, M. R., Foster, R. G., Davis, F. C., & Menaker, M. (1990). Transplanted suprachiasmatic nucleus determines circadian period. *Science, 247*, 975–978.

Reppert, S. M., & Weaver, D. R. (2002). Coordination of circadian timing in mammals. *Nature, 418*, 935–941.

Richter, G. P. (1967). Sleep and activity: Their relation to the 24-hour clock. *Research Publication of the Association for Research in Nervous and Mental Disorders, 45*, 8–29.

Rosenwasser, A. M. (2009). Functional neuroanatomy of sleep and circadian rhythms. *Brain Research Review, 61*, 281–306.

Ruan, G. X., Allen, G. C., Yamazaki, S., & McMahon, D. G. (2008). An autonomous circadian clock in the inner mouse retina regulated by dopamine and GABA. *PLoS Biology, 6*, e249.

Stephan, F. K., & Zucker, I. (1972). Circadian rhythms in drinking behavior and locomotor activity of rats are eliminated by hypothalamic lesions. *Proceedings of the National Academy Science USA, 69*, 1583–1586.

Storch, K. F., Paz, C., Signorovitch, J., Raviola, E., Pawlyk, B., Li, T., & Weitz, C. J. (2007). Intrinsic circadian clock of the Mammalian retina: Importance for retinal processing of visual information. *Cell, 130*, 730–741.

Tournier, B. B., Birkenstock, J., Pevet, P., & Vuillez, P. (2009). Gene expression in the suprachiasmatic nuclei and the photoperiodic time integration. *Neuroscience, 160*, 240–247.

Young, R. S., & Kimura, E. (2008). Pupillary correlates of light-evoked melanopsin activity in humans. *Vision Research, 48*, 862–871.

GLOSSARY

Accommodation Change in thickness of lens to bring objects into focus.

Achromatopsia Lack of color vision due to a lesion in the visual cortex.

Acuity Measurement of the smallest object that can be seen, using a grating (grating acuity), or letters on a chart (Snellen acuity).

Amacrine cells Cells in the inner layers of the retina with lateral connections.

Amblyopia Poor vision due to changes in the central visual system as a result of optical or motor defects as a child.

Amnesia Lack of memory.

Area centralis An area in the center of the retina where the photoreceptors are packed tightly together and acuity is highest.

Bottom up Effects due to projections from lower parts of the visual system.

Caudal Toward the tail; used to refer to anatomical areas that are located on this side.

Cones Photoreceptors shaped like cones that are active at moderate and high levels of illumination.

Convergence Movement of the eyes toward each other, to look at objects close by.

Depolarization Change in the membrane potential of a cell that makes the cell fire faster.

Dichromatic Color vision that involves two classes of photoreceptor absorbing light from different parts of the spectrum.

Diplopia Double vision, where the images of an object fall on different parts of the retina and two objects are seen.

Disparity The extent to which the images in the left and right eyes fall on corresponding, or noncorresponding parts of the two retinas.

FEF Abbreviation for frontal eye fields—areas in the frontal cortex that deal with eye movements.

fMRI Abbreviation for functional magnetic resonance imaging. A technique that shows which parts of the brain are excited by a task designed to bring out a particular function.

Fovea An area forming a pit in the center of the area centralis where the ganglion cells and other cells of the retina are moved sideways away from the photoreceptors to give a clearer image on the photoreceptors.

Frontal cortex The part of the cortex at the front, dealing with movement and higher functions.

Ganglion cell Cells that carry the output of the retina to lateral geniculate, superior colliculus, pretectum, and suprachiasmatic nucleus.

Gyrus An area in the folds of the cerebral cortex that is on the surface.

Horizontal cell Cells in the outer layers of the retina with lateral connections.

Horopter The surface in space comprising locations where objects all fall on corresponding parts of the two retinas.

Hyperpolarization Change in the membrane potential of a cell that makes the cell fire more slowly.

LGN Abbreviation for lateral geniculate nucleus. The primary nucleus on the route from retina to visual cortex.

LIP Abbreviation for lateral intraparietal area. An area between the sensory areas in visual cortex, and the motor areas in frontal cortex, involved in attention and deciding where to move the eyes.

Mesopic Vision at moderate levels of illumination where both rods and cones are active.

Motion parallax When the head moves sideways, objects move sideways in relation to each other. This can be used to tell which objects are in front and which are behind.

MST Abbreviation for medial superior temporal area (actually more in parietal cortex than temporal cortex) having to do with movement of the world around us.

MT Abbreviation for medial temporal area, having to do with movement of objects in relation to each other.

Nystagmus A backward and forward movement of the eyes, usually consisting of a slow movement in one direction, alternating with a fast movement in the reverse direction. It may be caused by rotation of the head (vestibular nystagmus) or rotation of the image around the head (optokinetic nystagmus).

Occipital The part of the cerebral cortex at the back, where visual input is analyzed.

Ocular following Following of an object with the eyes, usually used to describe the following when the whole scene is moving (rotating, expanding, contracting, etc.) as the head moves through space.

Optic flow Motion seen when the whole scene is moving (rotating, expanding, contracting, etc.)

Panum's fusional area Small disparities are tolerated. They do not lead to diplopia and are used to determine depth by stereopsis. Panum's fusional area is the limit of this toleration.

Parietal The part of the cerebral cortex on top of the head, between occipital cortex and frontal cortex. This is where input from the various senses is combined, and attention is important.

PET Abbreviation for positron emission tomography. An early technique to look at the activity of various areas in the brain. Now largely superseded by fMRI.

Photopic Vision at high levels of illumination where only cones are active.

Prosopagnosia Poor ability to recognize faces, due to a lesion near occipital, parietal, and temporal cortices.

Random dot stereogram A pattern of dots that is the same for the two eyes, except for some areas where the pattern is displaced laterally to give disparity and stereopsis.

Receptive field The area that affects the firing of a cell in the visual system. The classical receptive field is the area that has a direct effect on this firing. Outside this there may be an area that modifies the response to a stimulus in the classical receptive field, but it does not have an effect on firing when there is no stimulus in the classical receptive field.

Rods Photoreceptors shaped like rods that are active at moderate and low levels of illumination.

Rostral Away from the tail; the opposite of caudal. Like caudal, it is used to describe where an anatomical area is in relation to other anatomical areas.

Scotopic Vision at low levels of illumination where only rods are active.

SEF Abbreviation for supplementary eye fields. An area in frontal cortex that affects the frontal eye fields.

Stereopsis The prime cue to depth perception, coming from disparity of the images on the two retinas.

Strabismus Where the two eyes point in different directions due to some ocular or motor problem.

Striate cortex Primary visual cortex, which can be distinguished without magnification because of a stripe of myelin in layer IV.

Sulcus Where the cerebral cortex is not on the surface because of a fold inward.

Temporal cortex Lower part of the cortex, dealing with higher visual functions and memory.

Top down Effects from a higher visual area fed back to a lower visual area.

Transcription factors Factors that control the expression of genes.

Trichromacy Color vision that depends on three classes of photoreceptor that absorb in different parts of the spectrum.

V1 Primary visual cortex (the striate area in occipital cortex).

V2 Secondary visual cortex, receiving input from V1.

V3 Tertiary visual cortex, receiving input from V2.

V4 Visual cortex that deals with color and form.

V5 (MT) Visual cortex that deals with motion.

Vernier acuity Limit of ability to detect whether there is a lateral break in a line. Vernier acuity is an order of magnitude better than acuity for a grating or letters.

AUTHOR INDEX

SUBJECT INDEX